CONFRONTATION IN PSYCHOTHERAPY

COMMENTARY

"This is an unusual and useful book. Seventeen skilled and imaginative psychotherapists have focused on a single, often ignored therapeutic technique, and in a series of essays and clinical presentations define, refine and illustrate the uses and abuses of confrontation. One comes away from their discussions, amazed at the variety of maneuvers to which the term applies, instructed in their use, and inspired to add them, with appropriate and forewarned cautiousness, to one's armamentarium. The image of the psychotherapist as nothing but a friendly ear is challenged by these writings. Indeed, they face the traditional psychotherapist with a healthy confrontation with his perhaps overdone and monotonous passivity."

John Nemiah, M.D.

"The book is devoted to consideration of a specific therapeutic technique. Nevertheless, the authors always deal with it within the context of a broad therapeutic concept and not, as happens too frequently, as if this technique were the new panacea. The theoretical material is related to a wealth of clinical material and the style always highly readable."

Mortimer M. Meyer, Ph.D.

CONFRONTATION IN PSYCHOTHERAPY

edited by
Gerald Adler, M.D.
and
Paul G. Myerson, M.D.

NEW YORK • JASON ARONSON • LONDON

New Printing 1983

ISBN: 0-87668-670-6

Library of Congress Catalog Number : 84-450-65

Manufactured in the United States of America.

Table of Contents

Introduction

This book is a collection of essays written by a group of experienced psychotherapists striving to put into words aspects of the process of confrontation that they have considered to be significant. Though some of the authors have attempted to approach the topic from a broad and some from an in-depth perspective, none would claim to have arrived at an ultimate conceptualization of the issue. Furthermore, the contributions are too disparate in approach and, in fact, sometimes too contradictory in their formulation for the editors to be able to present an integrated overview that will be satisfactory to the various authors. Nor will the editors be able to offer readers who will have still different purviews of this complex subject anything like a final statement about the process of confrontation in the psychotherapeutic situation. Yet it is our belief that enough dialogue has taken place among the contributors, enough questions have been raised, enough answers groped for to make this presentation worthwhile.

Several of the authors—Adler, Boris, Havens, Mann, Murray, Myerson, and Zinberg—participated in the 1970 Tufts University School of Medicine Fifth Annual Sym-

9

posium on Psychotherapy, titled "Confrontation in Psychotherapy." Undoubtedly, the choice of topic was to some
extent influenced by the social and political overtones of the
period that penetrated into our consulting rooms, although
the effort was made to confine the discussion to the psychotherapeutic scene. More immediately pertinent to the choice
was our conviction that there was considerable disagreement,
at least among Boston psychotherapists, about the value of
confrontation as a psychotherapeutic technique. It was our
hope that the Symposium might at least clarify where we
agreed and disagreed on this issue. The Symposium brought
out the fact that there was less disagreement among the
panelists about when they use confrontation than about what
they mean by it. This observation led us to ask the other
contributors to this volume for their thoughts about the
process of confrontation, leaving quite open and unstructured
the choice of approach they might make to it.

A number of our contributors have delineated a confrontation as a forceful way to intervene; *e.g.*, the therapist
who confronts will make his remarks in a forceful rather than
in a gentle fashion in order to make sure his patient hears
what he has to say. The problem with this statement is, of
course, that what is intended to be a forceful or, for that
matter, a gentle way of stating something may be perceived
in quite a different manner by the patient. A gentle bit of
humor in the right context with the right patient might
confront him with something he has resisted. Or, as Weisman
states, quietly asking a woman her age at the appropriate
moment can be a major confrontation.

Moreover, the term *force* itself is a forceful one, and its
very use tends to polarize those who write about it. It is very
easy for some one arguing for the use of forceful confrontation to contrast it with a state of helpless passivity on the
part of the therapist; and for some one else who favors less
forceful approaches—*e.g.*, the consistent use of clarifications
and interpretations directed to the level of the patient's
potential insight—to view confrontations as hazardous and

even brutal assaults. Myerson attempted to counteract this tendency to polemicize the discussion by suggesting that the therapist at various times in the course of treating a patient is faced with a series of options, some of which involved the use of more force than others and that basically a confrontation was a comparative rather than an absolute way of describing the quality of the therapist's intervention. Corwin has tried to objectify what is meant by the force implied in a confrontation by reference to the therapist's aim in making this kind of an intervention. The therapist, when he confronts, has in mind getting the patient's attention, producing a reaction in him, and demanding that he change. Stocking and Corwin emphasize the difference in the therapist's attitude that is involved in making an interpretation with that in making a confrontation. When he interprets, the therapist shares a hypothesis with his patient; whereas when he confronts, he will present a unilateral view of what he considers to be reality. Attempting to engage the patient in the sharing of a hypothesis, even when it is a hypothesis about some distressing aspect of himself, appears to be a less forceful procedure than unequivocally stressing the validity of an aspect of inner or outer reality.

What does the therapist attempt to point out in confronting the patient? Many of the authors would agree with Weisman, who states that a confrontation is aimed at unmasking denial. Edith Jacobson's contributions have clarified that denial can take many forms. Among our authors, Sifneos, for example, describes a form of brief psychotherapy where the therapist is quite active in confronting the patients with feelings of which they were unaware; e.g., love for a parent who had been presented to the therapist only in hostile terms. Boris' technique was directed towards quickly bringing transference affects and fantasies to the patient's attention that ordinarily would be interpreted only after a long-standing alliance has been established. Havens emphasizes the importance of the therapist's willingness to confront the patient with the really malevolent actions and attitudes of his parents. Levin's confrontations are aimed at pointing out to his patients their self-centered and narcissistic attitudes and patterns of behavior. Weisman states that he confronts his narcissistic patients with their conviction of being unfairly treated, which he sees as a sign of protected vulnerability. He contrasts this with guilt and shame, which he considers to be symptoms. Stocking's confrontation of his child patient was his insistence that the patient acknowledge his act of stealing, which was apparently both a character trait and acting out, in the context of the treatment.

Some of the authors have described confronting procedures that were aimed at limiting or disrupting regressive reactions in the treatment process. Murray, very early in the therapy he presented, confronted his patient with his regressive paranoid perception of him, which threatened to sabotage the therapeutic work. Friedman, in the treatment of the late adolescents with whom he was working, also early emphasized to them their wish to be dependent and forcefully urged them to take meaningful steps that would help them in the future. Corwin very actively confronted his patients who had established a prolonged regressive "narcissistic alliance" with the fact that the treatment had stagnated; he made their more meaningful involvement the condition for his continuing with them. Shapiro refused to gratify his patient's regressive wish for direct signs that he would take care of her and insisted that she accept the deprivation. Buie and Adler confronted a borderline patient with the hazardous nature of his acting out. Welpton's empathic confrontation was aimed at his patient's reluctance to invest herself in the therapeutic process.

Thus the aspect of inner or outer reality unmasked by the procedure of confrontation is quite variable, including hidden affects, transference fantasies, memories of the past, attitudes, patterns of behavior, the significance of actions, the effect behavior has upon others, distorted perception of the therapist, regressive needs and wishes that might be gratified in the treatment, a reluctance to become involved in the therapeutic relationship, and undoubtedly others. The therapist directs the patient's attention in a forceful manner towards one or another of these unrecognized aspects of himself or the outside world. The therapist tries, in line with Corwin's formulation, to be forceful enough that his patient will now pay attention to what he had previously not been aware of, will have a reaction to it, and presumably will change in one fashion or another in response to his new, if painful, awareness.

However, looking at confrontation primarily from the vantage point of unmasking denial omits some very important considerations; *e.g.*, the meaning of the confrontation to the patient, its relationship to the patient's personality, and the therapist's basic attitudes toward the autonomy of patients. As we described earlier, Murray insisted to his patient that his view of the therapist was paranoid, distorted, and should be changed. At the same time he defined himself as some one who was willing to be very involved with the patient if he corrected the distortion. In the example cited by Myerson, Franz Alexander confronted the patient with a piece of reality he had not recognized; namely, that his regressive, unappreciative, demanding behavior did affect other people, including himself. But Alexander was simultaneously and very forefully indicating to the patient the terms under which he would like him enough to work with him. The therapist accomplished his aim; *i.e.*, he effected a change in the way the patient related to him not so much by unmasking the patient's denial of the effects of his behavior on others but by bringing him face to face with what the therapist would or would not accept from him.

It is clear then that if we are to understand how a confrontation works and why it sometimes is or is not effective, we need to know more about the broader nature of the transaction that occurs when the therapist confronts his patient. Many of the contributors explicitly or implicitly delineated the conditions they felt were necessary for a confrontation to be effective. Buie and Adler, Mann, Murray, Myerson, Sifneos, and Weisman were all explicit in indicating that the therapist had to communicate his caring, concern, and even love as he made his confrontation. What they have in mind apparently is that the therapist somehow communicates to the patient his genuine interest in him and his desire to be helpful as he unmasks painful aspects that the patient had not wanted to recognize or do anything about. The problem again in evaluating such statements resides in the fact that what the patient hears may be quite different from what the therapist intends. The therapist may be in the position of the parent who tells himself he is spanking his child for his own good and then is very surprised to discover his child's rage at him.

The character structure of the patient is clearly important in assessing his response to a confrontation. Among the contributors, Arvidson, Myerson, and Corwin are particularly concerned with the meaning of a confrontation to a patient who, for example, will respond characterologically as if it were a sadistic attack which can be masochistically gratifying. In these and other situations the confrontation may reinforce what the therapist wishes the patient to give up through the patient's compliance.

Many of the authors are sensitive to the dangers of the patient's compliance, identification with the aggressor, or identification with the victim as a consequence of a confrontation. Mann feels that a confrontation can be the use of rewards and punishments, diminishing the patient's choices and sense of autonomy. Arvidson describes a therapeutic "style" of confrontation that tells the patient what he feels and what he is like, thereby decreasing his personal authority and fostering magical attitudes of fusion with the therapist. Welpton distinguishes between angry confrontations, in which the therapist wants to change something in the patient that he cannot stand, and empathic confrontations, which occur when the therapist accepts the patient for what he is. Shapiro emphasizes the need to encourage the patient's independent modes of interacting rather than to foster dependency in making a confrontation. He feels the former attitude was crucial to his patient's ability to accept his confrontation. Corwin illustrates that a confrontation can be a limit-setting device that successfully ends a stalemate, but at the same time can be part of a patient's compliance— unless it is ultimately analyzed when no longer needed by the patient. Boris calls all confrontation that is directed to the ego's relationship to the external world "social confrontation" and feels that compliance and identification with the aggressor are inevitable. He describes a technique that allows the transference anxieties to gravitate rapidly to the surface, where they can be interpreted, as one that skirts this problem.

Yet several of the writers, Havens, Levin, Myerson, and Weisman, have proposed that the indications of the therapist's anger or negative countertransference may, in the proper place, communicate to the patient that the therapist is deeply involved in what he is trying to point out to the patient, that he is not only caring and concerned about the patient, but he means business—an attitude that may enhance the patient's sense of security and belief that the therapist knows what is good for him. Undoubtedly of value to the practicing therapist who is on the firing line in the therapeutic encounter and is trying to decide how to proceed is delineating the process of confrontation in terms of the aspect of inner or outer reality confronted or of the necessary conditions for the confrontation to be either successful or counterproductive. Yet the questions raised and the answers available in this order of conceptualization do not get at the core of the complex transactions that are taking place between patient and therapist. To do this, we believe, it is necessary to examine the process of confrontation in the *context* in which the question of whether to confront or not is raised by the therapist. This has not always been made explicit by the authors although the many clinical instances permit us to attempt to examine the several contexts in which the issue of confronting is pertinent.

Many of the authors discuss the need to confront in the context of the vicissitudes of the therapeutic alliance. The breakdown of the therapeutic alliance through regression or acting out is seen as a major reason for confrontation. It may occur early in treatment, as with Murray's confrontation of his patient's sudden regressive paranoid flight from painful issues; or it may be a "heroic confrontation," as described by Corwin, utilized after careful analytic, interpretive work had had no effect on stalemated acting out and regressed patients. In Corwin's cases, it is done to save a chronic treatment situation that is about to fail. As Stocking has clarified, when the therapeutic alliance is good, the therapist is in a position to share a hypothesis; *i.e.*, an interpretation. But where the alliance has not been well established or has receded, the therapist may decide to confront; *i.e.*, state something not as a hypothesis, but unilaterally as if he were sure of its validity. What effect the confrontation will have on the alliance is another question, but there are undoubtedly occasions where forcibly calling the patient's attention to regressive behavior improves the alliance—it helps him to be able to share a hypothesis rather than increases his compliance.

Thus confrontations are sometimes made either when the therapist feels that this is the only way to improve the alliance or when he feels that he has to show the patient something in spite of the absence of an alliance. Buie and Adler describe a confrontation where the therapist vigorously pointed out to his patient that he could destroy himself—clearly a procedure that was felt necessary in the context of massive acting out. That the patient might have been acting out in order to get attention from the therapist or that the act of confrontation might have given the patient the sense the therapist really cared was secondary to the immediate context of the therapist's concern for his patient's welfare.

Among other contributors, Welpton's empathic confrontation occurred in the context of his awareness that his patient was reluctant to become involved with him. His purpose was to help his patient overcome her reluctance to invest feelings in him and eventually to work with him in examining these feelings. In a certain sense his confrontation had the ultimate goal of establishing the therapeutic alliance. Boris, although he stated that his approach was aimed at establishing an alliance with his patient's id rather than with her ego, was clearly trying to involve his disturbed patient in the therapeutic work on her own terms.

For some authors—*e.g.*, Levin and Sifneos—a confrontation is made in the context of a good alliance to point out something a patient (or couple) is avoiding. The clinical situations and patients they describe, however, make it clear that they are working with patients with a solid capacity to maintain a good alliance and the ability to be confronted by a skilled therapist without losing that alliance.

At the other extreme, some patients appear to require confrontation so that the therapist can make contact with them and initiate a tentative alliance. As Zinberg graphically describes, a confrontation may be a crucial technique in siuations where there is a major class difference between therapist and patient. The confrontation becomes the means of helping; *e.g.*, an addict recognizes that both he and the therapist are individuals and not part of systems that are attempting to change or resist change.

The personality of the therapist is repeatedly discussed as an important factor in the success or failure of a confrontation. Shapiro stresses the therapist's basic character structure in relating to specific impulses and conflicts of a specific patient. He contrasts the personalities of two therapists in treating the same patient, illustrating the comfort of the second with the patient's anality. The second therapist, as part of that comfort, could also confront the patient with her regressive wishes in the transference and set limits on their gratification. Havens describes the personality, or person, of the therapist as important in cutting through a patient's resistance. He argues that it is often the quality of that personality that is the confrontation rather than the words of the therapist. Myerson and Levin discuss the capacity of the therapist to use his irritation as an indication of the patient's transference and imply that certain qualities of the therapist's personality facilitate acquiring such a skill. Levin stresses that a therapist must feel comfortable with a patient's anger since a successful confrontation almost inevitably results in the patient's becoming angry. Adler and Buie feel that the therapist's capacity to tolerate his own sadistic, destructive feelings in response to the hate of his patient is crucial, especially in more disturbed patients. They describe the capacity of a therapist to care in spite of his fury and to use his own angry feelings as a signal of the content of his patient's concerns as well as of the potential dangers of his own fury.

Countertransference issues also are stressed by some of the authors. Weisman describes four varieties of counter-tranference. One of them, antagonistic countertransference, can lead to overt or more subtle attacks or to devaluation of the patient that add an increased burden to the tendency of patients to perceive a reproach in every confrontation. Adler and Buie discuss the destructive use of confrontation as an expression of the therapist's fury and envy. They feel that there are serious risks present when therapists confront borderline or psychotic patients with their "narcissistic entitlement" when the patient is using it to cling to life. They feel that these therapists are confusing this higher level of narcissism with the more desperate "entitlement to survive" and undermine this latter entitlement in their angry confrontations. Related, but at the opposite pole, Sifneos delineates the countertransference problems of therapists who can only be gentle and permissive rather than confronting when appropriate. He sees such therapists as struggling with fantasies of their own omnipotence and superiority over a patient. Myerson clarifies that the therapist's irritation with the patient's resistance is not wholly countertransference in its literal sense but may also include his annoyance that his patient is not accepting his aims for the treatment.

This volume, then, offers no ready prescription for when or when not to confront. It describes the varieties of confrontation, its meanings to patients and therapists, its indications, and above all, its dangers. The contributors all use confrontation in their therapeutic work, but vary in their comfort in its use. They all share a concern about confrontation that gives the reader a variety of approaches to an important issue in contemporary psychotherapy.

Gerald Adler, M.D.
Paul G. Myerson, M.D.

The Meanings of Confrontation

PAUL G. MYERSON, M.D.

In the interest of finding a focus for discussing a topic that has so many ramifications as the concept of confrontation, I decided, at least to start with, to choose an empirical approach, hoping that the nature of the phenomenon rather than *a priori* ideas might help me select a meaningful aspect of this subject. In preparation for this paper, therefore, I asked a number of colleagues to describe clinical vignettes in which they felt they had "confronted" a patient during some phase of psychotherapy. Several of the examples that were reported referred to the therapist's interventions at the onset of treatment where a patient was reluctant to remain in therapy or to become involved with the therapist. In these instances the therapist actively indicated to the patient the hazards of not staying and not becoming involved. For example, in one of the more extreme examples, the therapist stated that he would hate to see the patient in ten years if he did not commit himself fully to the therapy. In other instances, the therapist "confronted" the patient with his unwillingness to recognize one or another distressing aspect of a person close to the patient. One thera-

23

pist insisted that his patient face the fact that his mother had in fact rejected him.

The majority of the examples reported appeared to fall into two categories of psychotherapeutic interventions. In these, the therapist either actively pointed out to the patient how his behavior affected other people, including the therapist *or* the therapist persisted in demonstrating to the patient a feeling or urge that he was reluctant to acknowledge.

What all of the examples appeared to have in common was the element of forcefulness in the therapist's attitude and behavior. The therapist apparently at these times felt the therapeutic situation called for forceful, persistent, insistent interventions and carried them out in this fashion. *Forcefulness, persistence,* and *insistence* are relative terms that inherently suggest contrasting attitudes and modes of behavior; *e.g.,* gentleness, tentativeness, persuasiveness. In a general sense the notion of a *confronting* intervention suggests a contrast with an approach that aims at *enhancing* the patient's capacity to observe one or another aspect of himself that he has been reluctant to recognize.

The use of a comparative term such as *criteria* to decide whether or not the therapist's approach is confronting obviously presents difficulties. What one therapist considers to be gentle persuasion may be viewed by another as forceful persistence. One therapist may "confront" his patient's regressive behavior in an abrasive, direct manner, while another may "confront" the same behavior with patience and persistence. Moreover, what on the surface appears to be a gentle enhancing approach may be responded to by the patient as if it were a demand placed upon him. Therapists or observers of the therapeutic process have no absolute indices to decide whether one approach is more or less forceful or persistent than another, particularly in view of the fact that in any given context the patient's perception or meaning he ascribes to the therapist's intervention is so often an unpredictable but decisive factor.

Nonetheless, the use of comparative terms in discussing

the concept of confrontation is relevant, for it corresponds, I believe, to the *state of the therapist's mind at the time* when he decides to confront his patient and likewise in many instances when he decides to employ a more enhancing approach. One of my colleagues, in reporting how he confronted his patient, emphasized that he had "seized the initiative to show his patient something he was avoiding" in contrast to "leading him gently to some insight or letting him develop at his own pace," the latter seeming to meet the criteria of an enhancing approach. Quite apart from how observers might rate it on scales that contrasted forcefulness and gentleness or confrontation and enhancement, he himself felt that he was confronted with a choice—should he "seize the initiative" or should he lead "him gently to some insight" or let "him develop at his own pace." Let us concede, especially because a clinical vignette can only be a stop-action view of events that are isolated from the overall context of the unfolding therapeutic process, that this particular therapist's decision to seize the initiative was based largely on well-thought-out therapeutic principles and that it was a highly appropriate way of intervening. Yet, based on introspection into my own therapeutic experiences and on observations of therapists I have supervised, I believe that if we do examine the context in which we decide to confront or not to confront, we will frequently find that our decision is influenced in part by nonrational factors, in effect by our countertransferences. This is not to say that our decision at such instances, whether we decide to confront or not to confront, may not be appropriate or useful for our patient, though it may not be. What I am pointing out is that we will better understand the process of confrontation and of many apparently nonconfronting approaches if we examine the context in which we as the therapists decide to confront or not to confront.

This mode of examination, in fact, corresponds to what we do in the therapeutic situation when we are functioning most therapeutically. We not only ask ourselves what kind of changes we want to effect in our patient and/or what kind of relationship we want to establish with our patient so we can effect these changes, but we also ask ourselves why we are choosing at this particular time to effect these changes and/or establish this kind of relationship. This is particularly the case when the therapeutic situation gets heated up— when we sense that we and our patients are interacting in an intense manner. It is at such times, I am suggesting, that we decide, consciously or preconsciously, whether or not to confront.

It is generally true that attempts to conceptualize the psychotherapeutic process start from the vantage point of the therapist's intention to effect changes in the patient or patient-therapist relationship and are discussed in terms of the reasons why he is choosing to intervene. For example, in recent years there has been much discussion and writing about the therapeutic alliance, the therapist as a real person, the therapist presenting himself as a mother of separation, the therapist as someone holding out for the patient the possibility of change, etc. The focus of these presentations is on how the therapist can best present himself to the patient so that their relationship is most useful in the therapeutic process and ultimately in effecting changes in the patient. The emphasis is on the rationale for the therapist's mode of presenting himself or his manner of intervening and not on the context in which he decides to present himself or to intervene in one or another ways.

This is equally true of Edward Bibring's (1954) systematic and thoughtful way of delineating the psychotherapeutic process. Bibring's formulations start from the vantage point of an emotionally uninvolved therapist who, on the basis of his knowledge of how psychotherapy works and of his clear notion about what he wants to accomplish, decides which is the appropriate intervention to produce the desired changes in his patient. The intervention is the stimulus and the change in the patient is the response. This frame of reference allows us to examine and give partial answers to such fundamental questions as what methods we have of modifying the patient's behavior, how our various efforts work, and what happens to the patient as the result of our efforts. However, this frame of reference puts us in the somewhat unreal position of the detached, basically uninvolved therapist rather than in that of the position of actual therapist trying to work with his resistant patient. Thus his approach is not applicable if we are considering how far and in what ways our emotional reactions to our patients and their emotional reactions to our reactions actually influence, interfere with, and sometimes promote the therapeutic process.

Bibring asked how the various principles work. For example, Bibring indicated that manipulation, one of his principles, accomplishes this effect when the therapist can mobilize or activate what he designated as an "ego system" in the patient. For example, the therapist, presumably in a calm and detached manner, manipulates an uncooperative patient to become more cooperative by telling him that he doubts if he will be a good patient. In short, he challenges him. According to Bibring's formulation, the patient's potentiality for being challenged is the ego system, which has been mobilized or activated by the intervention of the knowledgeable and detached therapist. Yet an uncooperative patient, for whatever reason he may be uncooperative, generally produces a heated-up therapeutic situation. How really calm and detached is the therapist who challenges his uncooperative patient? What is the patient really reacting to if a somewhat annoyed or, even for that matter, a "cool" therapist tells him he doubts if he will ever be a good patient? Is it his potentiality for being challenged that is activated? Or do we come closer to the nature of the therapeutic process if we consider how he reacts to the therapist himself, who tells him he doubts if he will ever be a good patient—is his reaction one of fear, anger, or admiration?

And don't we have to consider, if we are trying to understand the patient's reaction, how the therapist himself was feeling when he manipulated his patient?

Bibring also delineated the criteria that distinguish clarification from interpretation, two of his other therapeutic principles. He found these criteria primarily in the response of the patient. He indicated that an interpretation leads a patient to resist what has been pointed out to him because it touches the patient's unconscious conflicts. He contrasts this with a clarification, which the patient accepts with some degree of pleasure because the new knowledge evokes in him a sense of mastery rather than a sense of danger. A clarification does not threaten the patient; and if it is relevant, it is accepted. An interpretation does threaten and, if it is relevant, will increase the patient's resistance. A detached therapist decides to interpret, to point out something he thinks will evoke connections with his patient's unconscious conflicts; he will then have some indication that his intervention is effective if his patient stops talking, gets angry, comes late the next time, etc., but later on appears to know something new about himself. This way of conceptualizing tells us a great deal, but it depicts events in terms of a stimulus-response sequence. The therapist decides to interpret: the stimulus; and the patient partially accepts, partially rejects the interpretation: the response. But what really happens is much more complex. Not only is the therapist's decision to interpret based on a number of factors, some unconscious; but even more significantly, the patient reacts not merely to the interpretation but also to the therapist who is interpreting rather than doing something else, such as approving of him or being supportive in one way or another. The patient's coming late next time may be due as much to his annoyance that the therapist chose to interpret and the way he interpreted as to his perturbation at the latent content of the interpretation.

Bibring's principles, as I have indicated, are delineated from the vantage point of the therapist's intention to effect one or another type of change in his patient. As such they are of value in helping the therapist himself or the observer of the therapeutic scene plan for or follow the sequence of events, even if one does not consider the effects the therapist's less conscious motive may have upon his decision about how and when to intervene with his patient. The concept of confrontation I am delineating appears even more directly related to the therapist's state of mind than do Bibring's principles. The decision to confront or not to confront occurs in the context of a tense therapeutic situation. It is, therefore, essential for understanding this process to consider the possibility that the decision can be influenced by the therapist's countertransference.

As I have suggested, the decision of whether or not to confront is best examined in the context of the overall therapeutic process. For example, a therapist decides to interpret some aspect of the transference with the intention that this will inhibit his patient's regressive or uncooperative behavior and further the treatment. The therapist intends that his patient will realize he is struggling with angry feelings towards the therapist and will consequently try to be more cooperative. However, the therapist may find after he has made his interpretation that he encounters further resistance. It is in this context that the therapist becomes involved with the issue of how forceful he should be, and this concern often stems as much from his irritated reaction to his patient's resistance as from an objective evaluation of the factors relevant to the question of forcefulness.

When the therapy reaches this point the therapist cannot escape, to some extent at least, the sense of being in a struggle with his patient. His decisions of how forceful or how enhancing he should be in making his remarks are inevitably influenced by his countertransference and his counteridentification with the patient. His decision about his forcefulness will, to some extent, be influenced by his need to overpower his patient's resistance. He will either justify the force he uses or be influenced by his fear of hurting his patient and, therefore, advocate a nonconfronting, enhancing technique. He will put himself in the place of his patient; and depending on how much he welcomes or resists being confronted himself, he will tend to act in a forceful or a less forceful way. The more the therapist knows about his own impulses and his fears of his impulses when he makes his decision about how confronting he should be, the less likely his decision to confront will be influenced by his counter-transference. Nevertheless, however meticulously we try to think out what we are doing, once we are in the real, emotionally charged situation where we are trying to modify another human being's behavior and are confronted our-selves with our patient's reluctance to change, we cannot avoid being somewhat influenced by the way we have resolved our own problems about forcing, being forced, hurting, and being hurt. Moreover, our patient will be influenced in one way or another, not just by our conscious intentions, but by the way we react to the way he reacts to us, by our irritated concern at his resistance or by our apparent patience in the face of this resistance filtered through his correct and not so correct perceptions of our motives for behaving the way we do.

I have chosen a fairly well known clinical vignette to illustrate the relevant factors that one might consider in trying to understand the nature of the process of confronta-tion. In this instance the therapist felt it was essential to modify aspects of his patient's uncooperative behavior that interfered with his capacity to make use of the treatment— that, in effect, served as an impediment to a therapeutic alliance. The therapist attempted, through his confrontation, to alter a behavior pattern in his patient rather than to interpret aspects of his unconscious conflicts.

The vignette I will discuss is one described many years ago by Franz Alexander (1950), which he used to highlight his concept of a corrective emotional experience. His patient was a young man who had been overindulged by his father and who started an analysis because of difficulties in his interpersonal relationships. From the start of his therapy, this man was complaining and demanding. He dressed in a disheveled manner, was frequently dirty, whined a great deal, and reacted to Alexander's clarifying remarks with complaints that he was being criticized and was not being helped. His behavior on the couch paralleled the way he related to many people outside of the analytic situation.

In the analytic situation his behavior and attitudes precluded the establshment of a working relationship. After a period of nonproductive work, Alexander confronted him with the maladaptive character of his behavior and its effects on other people, including himself. The actual confrontation occurred after the patient had reacted to a clarifying remark by protesting that no one liked him and no one tried to help him. Alexander stated that it was no wonder no one liked him if he behaved in such an unpleasant manner when people tried to help him. This confrontation had a striking effect on the patient. He stopped complaining and became much more cooperative. He subsequently was able to listen to what Alexander was trying to point out to him. They established a therapeutic alliance, and the patient profited from the subsequent period of analysis.

Alexander's approach fits the criteria of a confrontation as I described it earlier. He was involved in an intense way with a patient who was reluctant to change his behavior, and Alexander had the option of choosing between more and less forceful methods of effecting a change in his patient. He chose a quite forceful method to modify the patient's behavior in the treatment situation. Alexander himself delineated his intervention as a corrective emotional experience. He apparently felt that he intervened with the intent of presenting himself to his patient in a manner that corrected certain misconceptions the patient had about the way his own behavior affected other people. He believed that the patient had not known that his regressive behavior antagonized other individuals. It was not until he recognized this disturbing fact through his analyst's response to his behavior that he could enter into a meaningful cooperative relationship with the analyst and presumably with other individuals outside of the analytic situation.

Alexander's intervention might also be considered as a manipulation. From Bibring's frame of reference, this type of intervention might be made with the intent of activating a potential ego system in the patient—the therapist might have intended through his remarks to challenge the patient, having correctly judged that the patient could respond to a challenge. However, this way of viewing the effects of the intervention appears even less complete than Alexander's manner of conceptualizing the sequence of events. I find it hard to escape the conclusions that the average therapist in Alexander's position, who might tell a patient that it is no wonder no one likes him, is at least somewhat irritated at his patient's regressive behavior and that the patient is at least somewhat affected by the therapist's irritation. Thus I am presuming that Alexander's decision to be confronting was made in the context of his increasing annoyance at his patient's reluctance to be cooperative and his resistance to change and that the effectiveness of his confrontation bears a relationship to the way his irritation was perceived by the patient.

We have no way of knowing, of course, whether Alexander consciously considered other options for coping with his patient's lack of cooperation. Therapists in Alexander's position will, to varying degrees, be aware of their own irritation and will, to varying degrees, take it into consideration as they decide how forcibly "to confront" their patients' regressive and defensive behavior, which is the source of their irritation. Thus there will be therapists who become quite irritated in similar therapeutic situations, who are relatively unaware of it, and who "decide" to be confronting. Other therapists, equally irritated and equally unaware of their irritation, will "decide" upon other options. Under these circumstances the other options may turn out to be as much a way of not dealing with the patient's resistance as of serving to effect the changes the therapist has in mind. Therapists who are more aware of their irritation and use it as a signal to help them understand what is happening in the therapeutic situation are generally in a better position to choose between various therapeutic options and to intervene in a well-considered way, whether or not this way involves forcibly and persistently facing the patient with his resistant behavior.

What are some of the options open to the therapist who is in touch with his own irritation and takes it into consideration in his decision how to intervene? He might, of course, decide to be confronting and express himself quite similarly to the way Alexander intervened in this episode. On the other hand he might decide upon interventions that, in his mind, would be relatively less forceful and confronting. For example, he might consider the patient's regressive behavior to be essentially a transference defense; that is, a way of avoiding experiencing the dangers of closeness to the analyst, the dangers of yearning for love without hope of the love's being returned and of experiencing intense rage at not being gratified. Bearing this formulation in mind, the analyst might have tried to give the patient another type of corrective emotional experience but in a more gradual and less drastic manner. That is, he might, through patient and gentle attempts to clarify aspects of his behavior, try to show him that the analysis was not a place where he would flounder from want of help or be left to rage because of frustration but was a place where in fact he could discover something about himself. Or another analyst might have tried to demonstrate to him that his demandingness and complaints were a reaction to certain disappointments he was experiencing in the analytic situation; the analyst would try to tune in with the events that evoked his sense of disappointment and carefully and tactfully indicate the connection of these with his demandingness. Both of these alternative approaches appear to be more enhancing than confronting.

It is easier to explain why an approach fails than to ascertain the reason why it works. If, for example, we confront a demanding patient in a similar manner to Alexander's and the patient hears only the "no wonder I don't like you" and stops treatment, we can conclude that we inflicted a narcissistic blow: the patient was too narcissistically vulnerable for the kind of confrontation we made to him. If another demanding patient responds by hearing only the "I don't like you because you are so unpleasant" and becomes a good patient in the sense that he stops his demands but does not subsequently listen to what we are saying, we can conclude that we frightened him into adopting a compliant attitude: the patient was too afraid of abandonment to be other than compliant when confronted in this manner. If still another patient's enjoyment in having us treat him roughly leads to a transient cessation of complaints but is followed by frequent efforts to provoke us into being forceful once again, we would feel that the patient's masochism interfered with our therapeutic attempt.

Similarly, one might compile a list of reasons why a patient fails to respond favorably to one of the more enhancing approaches I have just delineated. There are, for example, many patients who can respond only to a much more active demonstration of the therapist's involvement with them than is possible if he decides to offer clarifications to indicate he is trying to be helpful or if he decides to point out the connection between regressive behavior and disappointment in the therapist.

As I have stated, it is more difficult to account for the success of any one approach than to understand why it fails. Alexander apparently was successful in achieving his goal with a confronting approach. One cannot tell, of course, whether a less confronting technique might also have achieved essentially the same goal. But let us assume that Alexander had, through his clinical intuition and his knowledge of psychodynamics, found the keystone for promoting a favorable change in his patient. Under this assumption, only a confronting technique of the nature Alexander employed could be successful in the sense of involving the patient in a cooperative way in his treatment. Sometimes, after trying a variety of approaches, a therapist evolves a method of reaching a patient. If this was the case, what was the specific factor or factors in Alexander's approach that were responsible for its effectiveness? Also what were the corresponding specific aspects of his patient's personality that allowed him to respond favorably to this approach?

Alexander's intervention indicated, at the very least, that he was directly interested in the patient, that he wanted him to grow up; and more immediately, he conveyed his concern about the patient's demanding behavior, stating that this type of behavior alienated people. This might have been what his patient needed to hear at this particular time. Alexander felt the patient was behaving like a young child who is demanding and complaining but who is ashamed of his behavior and wants someone to show interest, to tell him that his childishness is inappropriate, to imply that he is capable of acting in a more grown-up way, and to indicate how he can be more grown-up. Alexander intervened in a way that convinced his potentially responsive patient that he was deeply interested in him. This patient, like many others, may have both needed and been capable of responding favorably to the analyst's very direct, concrete type of involvement, which indicated to him that, while regressive behavior was not acceptable, the analyst had confidence that he could behave in a more cooperative fashion. There is a directness and genuineness to this kind of interchange that is not satisfactorily delineated by the concepts of manipulation or corrective emotional experience. Other individuals, of course, may not be reached by this type of intervention and may perhaps respond unfavorably to its intensive aspects.

Many therapists treating this patient would be more than "involved with" and "concerned about" him. They would be irritated with him. In addition, the more the therapist is aware of his irritation, the more likely he will be able, if he decides to be confronting, to intervene without communicating his irritation in a manner that is distressing to the patient. But is communication of the therapist's irritation sometimes the essential factor that leads the patient to shift from a regressive to a cooperative relationship even when the therapist himself is not truly in touch with his own irritation? Is the therapist's irritation itself, in the context of his overall concern and involvement even when he is unaware of his annoyance, the crucial quality that reaches some patients and affects them favorably? Is it the therapist's irritation that convinces these patients that he is real, truly involved, and interested in his welfare? It may be that therapists without much awareness of their irritation who also have an overall concern and care are more effective in reaching some patients in this kind of therapeutic impasse than therapists who pay too close attention to their countertransference. Too close attention to inner reactions may sometimes limit the directness of their confrontations and give their patients the sense that they are not being genuine.

Obviously the way the patient perceives or the meaning he ascribes to what the therapist is attempting to convey to him is the decisive factor in whether the therapist's response is appropriate. The question raised by this case vignette is how best to delineate the nature of the character structure of individuals who respond appropriately to intervention of the type made by Alexander; *i.e.*, who shift from a regressive demanding mode of interacting to a cooperative relationship without becoming unduly compliant or masochistic. This is a difficult question to answer in the light of our present knowledge about character structure. What is the best way of describing the elements of the personality structure that allow someone, when confronted by a therapist's irritated concern, to stop his demands and complaints without developing dependent and unresolved transference that interferes with his becoming open about his feelings and listening to what the therapist has to say? Bibring's principle of manipulation, whereby a potential ego system is mobilized, and Alexander's concept of a corrective emotional experience, whereby a distorted notion of a relationship can be corrected by the way the therapist presents himself, try to get at this process, although these concepts are not addressed to the question of which individuals the process is effective with. Moreover, the way these concepts are delineated does not consider what I believe to be crucial; *i.e.*, how the affective tone of the therapist affects the patient.

There are many other issues already alluded to that are raised by this case vignette. Which patients will respond inappropriately to this approach? How do they perceive and what meaning do they ascribe to the affective tone associated with the therapist's intervention? What is the nature of their character structure? To what kinds of interventions do they best respond, and what is there about the therapist's attitude and affective tone when he intervenes that is most appropriate for these patients? These are difficult questions. But they have to be asked, and we should try to answer them. Till we do, I submit that the therapist's best instrument is his awareness of the nature of his countertransference when he is faced with a resistant patient and chooses a confronting or nonconfronting approach.

Bibliography

Alexander, F. (1950), Analysis of the therapeutic factors in psychoanalytic treatment. In *The Scope of Psychoanalysis*. New York: Basic Books, Inc. 1961, pp. 261–275.
Bibring, E. (1954), Psychoanalysis and the dynamic psychotherapies. *J. Amer. Psychoanal. Assn.*, 2: 745–770.

Confrontation as a
Mode of Teaching

JAMES MANN, M.D.

It is wholly impossible to engage in psychotherapy or in psychoanalysis without necessarily confronting the patient once, twice, or many times. Confrontation cannot be avoided; nor should it be avoided. The issue, rather, is to accept confrontation as an integral aspect of psychotherapy and to raise critical questions as to the effect that confrontation is intended to produce following on our understanding of the nature of confrontation as a process. Some answers to these questions may then lead to a clearer appreciation of how best to confront a patient.

As is true in all psychological issues, the subject of confrontation is multifaceted. There are many vantage points from which one may study confrontation. It may be worthwhile, however, to seek out among the many avenues to confrontation some central focus or issue that may be pertinent regardless of the particular theoretical or clinical approach one may take. With such a central issue in hand one may then extend, think through, and test out the various rich ideas and approaches to the meaning and clinical use of confrontation.

I would like to consider the central issue as consisting

of the statement that, whatever else it may be, confrontation is predominantly a device for teaching. Whatever the mode of confrontation and whether it be in individual psychotherapy, psychoanalysis, group psychotherapy, or encounter-sensitivity groups, the aim of the confrontation is to teach something to the recipient of the confrontation. At stake in this discussion is not whether the substance of a confrontation is correct but rather whether our mode of teaching is more or less effective.

A discussion of confrontation from this point of view illuminates the three basic underpinnings of any kind of teaching: one, teaching by explanation in order to enhance understanding; two, teaching by employing a system of rewards and punishments, which presumably will reinforce desired behaviors; and three, teaching by offering oneself as a model with the expectation that the student (or patient) will take the best qualities of the model and will internalize those qualities and the lessons that go with them so that they are experienced as a syntonic part of oneself.

All these modes of teaching are present in the various meanings of confrontation. In some a single mode is easily distinguishable and in others one may observe a mix of two or even of all three. We must ask, therefore, whether the purposes of confrontation are best served by explanation, by rewards and punishments, by offering oneself as a model, or by what kind of mix of two or of three of these. It may be equally important to determine whether all confrontations include all three of these basic tenets of teaching and whether the decisive factor is the extent to which one or another dominates.

Generally, we tend to think of confrontation in psychotherapy as being a means of bringing up for the patient's consideration certain attitudes, character traits, and life styles that, by virtue of the preceding work of psychotherapy have now become conscious or preconscious. There is also a type of confrontation that addresses itself to that which is unconscious, distorted, and expressed primarily in the seemingly mysterious symbolic communications of the patient. The second instance refers, of course, to the psychotic patient in psychotherapy. I believe that this is a vastly different situation and carries significantly different meaning as compared to the more usual use and meaning of confrontation.

Confrontation may foster a therapeutic alliance in any case at some given moment, but that is not the same thing as saying that confrontation and therapeutic alliance are necessarily related one to the other. In the more neurotic type of patient, his inner life remains unknown to him for the most part. A variety of ego defenses and adaptive moves as well as symptoms serves to keep out of his conscious mind the conflicting wishes and fantasies that would make life even more unbearable were they to be undefended. A very different state of mind exists in the psychotic patient. His inner life, unfortunately, is not secret, and the defenses against knowing it are few and vulnerable. His adaptive moves and his symptoms barely serve to maintain survival. To the psychotic patient, his inner life is a ghastly cesspool of horrible secrets of which he is all too much aware. Confrontation that reads through the distorted, symbolic communications of the severely disturbed patient is not, strictly speaking, a mode of teaching. It is not explaining anything; it is only, in an exquisitely subtle manner, rewarding or punishing; and it is not offering oneself as a model. Rather it is a means of letting the patient know that the therapist knows; a means of telling the patient that one knows what the patient is suffering. It is a means of letting the patient know that the therapist knows too that the patient did not know how to communicate to others and could barely tolerate knowing himself. In this sharing and in the relief for the patient in finding someone at last who also knows and yet continues to attend, a therapeutic alliance is established that rests on the most profound meaning of empathy. This kind of alliance becomes the prelude to the more difficult work that will follow in reconstructing what has happened to the patient. In a lighter vein, the situation is not unlike that of two evil-appearing men meeting in the dark forest and discovering that they are both psychiatrists or psychologists.

Gentle, caring concern of the therapist for the patient may well be the most important element in a proper, effective confrontation. Such an attitude in the therapist is important not only because all people need to know that someone cares and is tender in his caring but also because such behavior in the therapist carries with it a genuine message that the therapist is equally devoted to the maintenance of the patient's autonomy—his unique individuality. It communicates to the patient his privilege to choose the direction that he would like to move in rather than communicating a directive to which the patient feels impelled to yield. Implicit in a confrontation that is affectively shaped with gentle, caring concern is a mode of teaching that enhances understanding and offers a model for identification rather than teaching by suggesting reward or punishment according to whether the patient does or does not do as we might wish him to do.

It is apropos that we be sensitive to the fact that certain styles in the treatment of psychiatric patients are directly influenced by the historical tides that are current. At this time in history, confrontation is the order of the day in widespread areas of our lives. Instant demands are often made for instant action. Encounter groups, marathon groups, and so-called sensitivity groups are in good measure responses to demands for instant change. It is no accident that the primary so-called therapeutic method in these groups is confrontation, in which the reward is acceptance and the punishment rejection by the group. In our individual work, too, we should remain aware of the extent to which we may be responding to the demands of patients for instant change in a profession in which instant change is impossible.

From this point of view, the particular emphasis on

gentle, caring concern and respect for the individuality of the patient as central should not be underestimated as a most positively weighted teaching method at a time when all of us are tempted to exercise control wherever we can. After all, we are very much limited in how much control we may exercise in the conduct of our own lives.

Another aspect of confrontation arises in the comparison between the therapeutic methods of the psychoanalyst as compared to the psychotherapist. In this connection, certain myths continue to thrive. These are at least two-fold: first, that the analyst is, for the most part, extremely passive, spends too much time saying nothing, does not intervene actively, and does not use himself in the treatment process; second, that the analyst pays little attention to the *reality* of the patient's past and current life experience. Both these myths perpetuate an image of the psychoanalyst at work in an ivory tower. The further implication is that confrontation is clearly outside the province of the psychoanalyst insofar as he has separated himself both from the real life of the patient as well as from any kind of activist position in respect to his therapeutic relationship with the patient.

Again, in this active historical period, active consideration of the patient's reality and active intervention by the use of the self in the treatment process too often come to mean that it is the job of the therapist to determine what the reality is *for the patient*. It follows then that he is to tell the patient how he should conduct his life. Is it not a better teaching method with more effective reverberations in the patient if the therapist limits himself toward helping the patient discover which new choices or alternatives previously obscured or unknown to him because of his neurotic distortions are now open to him? Is it not for the patient to make the choice as to the direction he will take? He may choose to continue as he always has or he may choose a new direction. Whichever he does choose must be of his own doing and responsibility. The patient's privilege of maintaining his own individuality must be secure even if it means making no change at all and even if we do not ourselves like the kind of change he chooses to make. The freedom to change and the wish to change will flow from the relationship with a therapist who explains so that the patient better understands and who, in his confrontations, offers a model of gentle, caring concern. We need not concern ourselves with the concept of 100 percent neutrality in the therapist since such a state simply cannot exist in any kind of sustained relationship, therapeutic or otherwise.

It is not an unusual experience to find that our well considered, affectively appropriate explanations are met by a "so what" from the patient. This type of response is too often accepted as an invitation to the therapist for action, to do something about it and not just talk. There is enormous temptation as well as culturally sanctioned inclinations for the therapist to respond with action. The danger lies in the fact that it becomes too easy to read into this an appeal to force as the missing ingredient in psychotherapy, let alone psychoanalysis, today. Too much emphasis may be unwittingly placed upon teaching by a system of rewards and punishments. This may readily lead to the misuse of such a system so that the eventual result becomes control of the patient and identification of the patient with the aggressor model. Unknowingly, we may find ourselves adherents to a variant of the Skinnerian model. Such a state hardly leads to the kind of inner freedom to choose that speaks for mental health; rather it directs the patient toward social adjustment, and the nature of the social adjustment is dictated by the therapist according to his lights. The cry of certain groups today that psychiatry and psychoanalysis are means of brainwashing young people may, as is usually true in delusions, have its small core of truth. Characteristic of the contradictions that exist in these very same groups is the fact that it is these same groups that seem to seek most the instant change suggested by the various kinds of encounter groups in operation. Basic to this is the wish for magical solutions to problems, and it behooves us to be careful ourselves that we fall prey neither to their demands nor to our own wishes to exercise some magic.

There is much to say for the voice of reason tempered and softened with compassion and even with passion. How can we combine objectivity and passion at the same time? Since no one therapist of any persuasion has the one correct answer, each of us seeks to find his own way. Nevertheless, in any discussion of confrontation in psychotherapy or in psychoanalysis, the weight lies heavily in favor of a concept in which gentle, caring concern becomes our guide. Such concern does not mean passivity, nor does it mean avoiding confrontation; but it does mean that we leave the way open for our patients to *learn* to make their own choices, as much as is possible in the light of their own wishes rather than ours. All varieties of psychotherapy and of psychoanalysis are processes of *reeducation*, of *reteaching*. The issue then is whether we choose to teach by explanation, to enhance understanding coupled with offering ourselves as a model, or whether we choose to teach mostly by a system of rewards and punishments centering on a core of coercion. The more we experience increasing pressure and coercion in our everyday environment, the more must we guard against taking it out on the patient under the guise of treatment.

Of course, every patient brings to the treatment situation attitudes about and reactions to rewards and punishments. Only the use of some kind of mechanical speaking device could avoid the communication by the therapist of some degree of approval or of disapproval. Each of us does have the moral and ethical and human judgments by which we live and in which we express our sense as individuals. After all, gentle, caring concern is itself a reward.

The problem becomes one of deciding on which of the three aspects of teaching shall the therapist *attempt* to place greatest emphasis. Each of the three is complex; each plays upon the past history of the patient, and each is so related to the other as to be impossible of total separation. Explanation and gentle, caring concern as a method of confrontation, in good times and in bad, will lead to identification with a model that, more than anything else, will allow the patient freedom of choice. Such a result speaks for the highest order of both teaching and learning. This result is the proper goal of confrontation.

The Purpose of

Confrontation

JOHN M. MURRAY, M.D.

On speaking with colleagues about confrontation in psychotherapy, I have a distinct impression that there is an underlying agreement among many therapists on this issue. I think that deep inside, many feel that confrontation is a highly effective instrument when properly used but that it must be used wisely and not at all in a haphazard manner. The conditions for its proper use are very specific and will be defined later.

First, I would like to deal with the underlying elements of the treatment situation that make the use of confrontation desirable and at times mandatory. The basic element in all manifestations of psychopathology is a simple, clearly definable fact. Man is a creature of two worlds—one the pregenital world outlined in Freud's conception of the early months and years of life, with its special system of logic, interpretive function, and emotional relations. These are the years when reactions are dominated by the patterns of reflex limbic lobe response (to use the neurological model), dominated by characteristics beautifully set forth by Freud in his description and definition of the responses and attitudes of the pregenital era. The second and later-appearing world is the world of cortical control, the world of reality, dominated by cause and effect. The patterns of this world of ego control begin to dominate at the time when the formal educational process is introduced into the life of the developing child. It is with this in mind, I believe, that Boris (Chapter Nine) describes the ego as "Janus shaped," with one face looking toward the external, real, or social world and the other toward inner feelings and fantasies. I agree with Boris that confrontation can be effectively utilized in dealing with situations that arise from either of the two sources, from the external world or the inner one.

In my view the primary purpose of the confrontation under these circumstances is to unite the two different functioning worlds in a common meeting ground, as Freud defined when he described the purpose of psychoanalysis by saying that where id was, there shall ego be. To paraphrase this statement in terms of a neurological model, where the limbic lobe (primitive paleocortex) reflex response obtains, there shall the cortex take over and dominate. It is the failure of these two worlds to get together in effective functioning that is the basic cause of the phenomena of psychopathology. The conflict between the two is the determining factor. And I believe confrontation is an important element in the technique of resolving the conflicts between the two worlds.

Confrontation implies use of force (Myerson, Chapter One), but is force appropriate? Freud specifies that in repression a force is always and continuously at work—a force that must be overcome if repression is to be dissolved. The same is true in avoidance, an early phase of repression. In the course of our analytic work, over and over we encounter avoidance and repression that require force to alter the pattern. As a matter of fact, each interpretation has an element of force.

Freud's work clearly demonstrates that a libidinal position once assumed is given up with the greatest reluctance. To overcome this great reluctance, at times force—

direct force—is appropriate; but it must be expressed with love, with understanding, with sympathy and not from a vis-à-vis position such as exists when the patient conceives of the analyst as a being similar to a hostile introject.

To enlarge this conception of the importance of the patient's attitudes, let me turn to the most valuable work of Wilhelm Reich (1933) on character analysis and the role of psychoanalysis in the problems of so-called character neurosis. The cardinal question is: Is this an appropriate sphere of psychoanalytic involvement and endeavor, or should we limit our endeavors entirely to libidinal conflicts and to the trauma associated with childhood sexuality? Should we not broaden our endeavors to include the comprehensive analysis of the characterological defects that arise from the defensive, regressive return to pregenitally oriented patterns of reaction set up to protect the child from the pain of these experiences? These patterns of reaction are permanently established and returned to in the forms of their neuroses and reproduced in the transference. The impetus for this regression takes place in reaction to the frustration of the Oedipal situation. The patient as a child experiences frustrations; he receives these in a traumatic way; he develops anxiety, fear, and phobias; he experiences loneliness. And as a reaction to these traumas, he regresses back to the earlier emotional patterns of his pregenital experiences that now become a working part of his way of life. If you reject the need for the analysis of these characterological defenses, I believe you will rule out nine out of ten cases that consult you for your help. In my practice, at least nine out of ten patients have defensive attitudes based on regression to pregenital elements in their character structure that must undergo alteration before the potentials of maturity are able to be utilized. This involves the expressions of their love life as well as of their character. And so I believe the attitudes involved in this sick way of life must be analyzed and altered. Franz Alexander (1953) expressed agreement with this point of view:

... obviously the great variety of patients makes necessary variations in approach. . . . The fact that most psychoanalysts used precisely the same, so-called classical procedure for all their patients has been due to various circumstances. For many years the general practice among psychoanalytic therapists was to accept those cases for therapy which appeared suitable for the classical procedure and to advise the others not to undergo psychoanalytic treatment. In other words, the patients were selected to fit the tool.

Moreover, psychoanalytic treatment is the primary source of psychoanalytic knowledge and the original procedure is best suited for research. Since in the early phases of psychoanalysis the primary concern was quite naturally that of increasing basic knowledge, the classical procedure was rather universally used. Some of us have come to the conviction, however, that the time is now ripe to utilize the accumulated theoretical knowledge in different ways, so that not only those patients who appear suitable for the original technique, but the whole psychoneurotic population as well, could benefit from our present knowledge. This extension of psychoanalytic help to a great variety of patients is another important new trend in our field. (pp. 282–283)

In extending psychoanalytic help to patients of this kind and in order to accomplish this effectively, more or less force needs to be applied (with love!) to change the pattern. A regressed patient wallowing in his symptomatic behavior is acting out part of his character neurosis and illustrates a most important element in the "greatest reluctance" to give up the pattern. We have to apply a greater or lesser degree of force if the patient is to accept reality and to experience the limitations imposed by his illness and to be willing to live within the limits of the social mores, as opposed to the world of his childish fantasies of omnipotence and narcissistic entitlement. These two worlds are opposed to each other and frequently a confrontation has to occur if change is to be possible.

Myerson (Chapter One) describes a confrontation by Alexander of a patient who regressed in the analytic situation to a whining, complaining position. In spite of Alexander's clarifying and interpreting statements, he complained that he was being criticized and was not being helped. After a long period of this behavior, Alexander finally confronted him that it was no wonder that no one liked him if he behaved in such an unpleasant manner when people tried to help him.

First I wish to make certain basic assumptions about the clinical aspects of the case and the resultant problem that Alexander faced. I assume he was well aware that his patient was suffering from a definite character disorder of a considerable degree of depth. This is the number one facet of the clinical problem, and he knew from Wilhelm Reich that one had only a vague chance of altering symptoms due to instinctual conflicts until some effective analysis of the character defenses and structure was accomplished.

My second assumption, which I make from years of experience in contacts with problems of this kind, is the belief that in this patient's developmental history he resolved his Oedipal conflicts by regression to earlier pregenital attitudes and made these regressive pregenital attitudes a very important part of his basic character structure and his attitude toward the world around him. And thirdly I assume that his character structure was based on what I have so often described—Murray's triad (Murray, 1964): first, regression to narcissistically determined great expectations to have life on his own terms; second, massive rage reactions following the inevitable failure of the narcissistic expectations; and third, projections and other pregenitally determined character patterns to justify, validate, and continue the rage reactions and underlying hostility.

If my assumptions fit the clinical facts of this patient, one day he has to face them as facts—reality demands it— and give up looking at all people as hostile introjects. I believe Alexander was correct in what he did—to delay would have been to have the patient identify his analyst with his regressive defensive patterns and to continue the regressive, nonproductive pattern.

A case illustrating these issues concerns a twenty-three-year-old undergraduate who throughout his life had presented behavior of a deeply narcissistic and aggressive character, rather devoid of the attributes of friendliness and desire for mature social relationships. All his social relations were based on regressive rivalry reactions and deep feelings of hostility to all his associates, including his family, his peers, and his teachers.

Following graduation from college, he went to another university in an advanced study program. In this new situation, he immediately began to get into trouble. The only reaction he had to his colleagues was one of very hostile rivalry. He began to develop anxiety reactions and became phobic to various situations that arose in his educational program. He began to react with feelings of depression as these regressive reactions continued to intensify. They increased to the point where the anxiety and depression were so great that he had to withdraw from the university.

During his earlier years, he had been continuously in analytically oriented treatment programs with three different, highly competent analysts. These endeavors were ineffectual and resulted in no improvement or change or development of insight into the nature of his maladaptation. He had an impervious system of projections and rationalizations to justify his hostility, and this remained unaltered in the treatment situations.

He consulted another well known analyst who was dubious about the outcome of further treatment and suggested there was a high probability of a psychotic reaction that would require hospitalization. This angered and frightened the patient but did increase his realistic relation to his life's problem. When he approached me about taking him into treatment, the rigidity of his defensive patterns had lessened; and he had some healthy trepidation about his future. Very early in his first interview with me I pointed out to him the intensity of the rage that I felt was behind all his relations with people and things. This was surely an abrupt confrontation. But he responded in a positive way and agreed as to the correctness of my interpretations. This was a marked turnabout from his attitude and his relations with his previous therapists. It was also the beginning of his acceptance of the intensity of his rage and aggression and his willingness to question the propriety of these feelings and to evaluate them realistically. On his third interview he stated that he had many problems in his sexual life that he had deliberately withheld from his three previous therapeutic experiences. He said he was now willing to talk about his sexual reactions. At the next hour he spoke frankly about sex. He spoke about his compulsive masturbation, of his exciting fantasies about older, aggressive women as sexual objects, and of his intense rivalry fantasies with other boys and his hatred of them for successes he did not enjoy.

He left this hour with the determination to continue speaking of his sex life at the next interview. On the next occasion, however, he avoided dealing with sexual topics and reported a dream that took place in a New England country town with a central green and two white churches on the green. In the dream he dealt with an older man, an untrustworthy, scurrilous, red-faced alcoholic, of whom he was very suspicious. He was aware of the connection of this character with his analyst and saw the dream as a warning that the analyst was probably not worthy of the trust given him in speaking frankly for the first time about his sexual life. On the following day he came to his hour in a towering rage and began an attack on his university, saying it was dominated by a narrow group of socially oriented prep school graduates and Jewish boys like him were excluded and discriminated against. He then lapsed into an attack on the whole American scene as being a narrow-minded WASP culture that he hated.

At this point I determined he was at the important crossroads of a return to his previous paranoid attitude or of holding onto the alternative positive relationship he had established with me. I decided that an abrupt confrontation with this fact was in order if the treatment situation was not to deteriorate into a psychotic-like acting out experience akin to his three previous treatment situations.

I confronted him with the fact that his basic rage was against me, a response to the fears engendered by his approaching facing his sexual attitudes and anxieties. I stated that his raging at the American scene was just a cover for his rage at me who was identified as an exponent of the culture, being a WASP myself. I went on to say that I had many friends and colleagues who were Jewish, most of them highly intellectual; but I did not know of one who did not basically feel that the American way of life as formulated by the WASP founding fathers was the culture in which they wished to live, in spite of some minor disagreements with the way it was carried out. No other country would be as agreeable to them.

The reaction to this confrontation was most dramatic. The paranoid reaction was practically completely dissolved. A most effective therapeutic alliance was immediately established wherein he identified with me and went to work vigorously on the analytic task at hand—to understand the vicissitudes of childhood upon which his sickness was based. There was no return again to the paranoid defense device or even to set up differences between us which precluded a meeting ground. I would call the response almost miraculous, so far as overcoming the paranoid defensive attitude was concerned. Of course we had a long hard journey down the analytic road of understanding his neurosis, but the confrontation resulted in a resolution of the critical defense reaction, which at that time was an immediate threat to the treatment situation and which, if not overcome, would have resulted in a long acting-out period of his paranoid defenses. I recognize the fact that his previous therapeutic failures had placed him in a receptive frame of mind to respond positively to my procedures and that I was working with a distinct advantage over my predecessors. But the confrontation itself turned out to be a very appropriate procedure and truly effective in its response. The patient later stated he had real affection for his university and looked back with fondness to his years there. He also saw that his criticisms were largely projections and that his attitude was primarily responsible for the shortcomings of his undergraduate days.

And now let us examine the nature of this wallowing in neurotic patterns of a pregenitally determined nature. Freud (1916) has given us a magnificent picture of this phenomenon in his paper "The Exception." In brief his thesis is as follows: to live in culture one accepts restraints as one pays taxes. Primitive aggression and its direct manifestations are taboo and are accepted as such by non-neurotic people. But as Freud says, some regard themselves as exceptions to this and lead their lives expressing defiance to this taboo to a greater or lesser degree. Freud's example of Shakespeare's Richard III and his quote of Richard's soliloquy, plus his interpretation of its meaning are given in preference to clinically determined supporting case history material. As you know, Richard was born a cripple and Shakespeare accords him this soliloquy:

> But I, that am not shaped for sportive tricks,
> Nor made to court an amorous looking-glass;
> I that am rudely stamp'd, and want love's majesty
> To strut before a wanton ambling nymph;
> I, that am curtail'd of this fair proportion,
> Cheated of feature by dissembling Nature,
> Deform'd, unfinished, sent before my time
> Into this breathing world, scarce half made up,
> And that so lamely and unfashionable,
> That dogs bark at me as I halt by them;
> And therefore, since I cannot prove a lover,
> To entertain these fair well-spoken days,

I am determined to prove a villain,
And hate the idle pleasures of these days.

(I, i, 14–31)

The soliloquy then signifies: nature has done me a grievous wrong in denying me that beauty of form that wins human love. Life owes me reparation for this, and I will see that I get it. I have a right to be an exception, to overstep those bounds by which others let themselves be circumscribed. I may do wrong myself, since wrong has been done to me.

And now we feel that we ourselves could be like Richard, nay, that we are already a little like him. Richard is an enormously magnified representation of something we can all discover in ourselves. We all think we have reason to reproach nature and our destiny for congenital and infantile disadvantages; we all demand reparation for early wounds to our narcissism, our self-love. And so Richard emerged a lust murderer as part of his way of life and justified this attitude by the fact that he was a cripple.

So many neurotics like Richard III emerge from their Oedipal experiences with a rejection of their loving qualities and adopt a regressive return to their pregenital hostile and aggressive attitudes and allow this orientation to become the essential element of their character structure, based upon the triad I described earlier. Hence the intense tendency to wallow in the transference situation and repetitively act out these patterns. I believe that force is required to overcome and change the pattern—and again force *with love*. To delay confrontation too long is, I believe, to risk allowing the analysis to become becalmed, ineffective, unproductive, and to encourage wallowing in transference acting out.

All of these remarks are predicated on my earlier comments that nine out of ten neurotic illnesses we encounter today have elements of a defective character structure based upon a regression to pregenital dispositions. As stated, some analysts feel these cases are not suitable for classical analytic endeavors. My feeling is that we have to face the clinical problems as we encounter them and do our best as therapists to overcome all aspects of the illness.

To develop my convictions further I wish to make brief reference to the Dora case. Freud (1905) used the Dora case as an illustration of the unconscious fantasies at work behind somatic symptoms and the meaning the symptoms have in terms of unconscious fantasies. Dreams were revealing of her tabooed sexual and incestuous fantasies and were expressive of the wishes that were closely related to her symptoms. Her resistances to change and negative transference were great, and she abandoned treatment before any definitive therapeutic response occurred. In detailing her life history and fantasy life, Freud makes it amply clear that Dora had undergone a definite regression to pregenital attitudes and had a deep seated hostile attachment to three women: to her mother, to Frau K, wife of her fantasied Oedipal substitute lover, and to her governess. This paranoid homosexual attachment of a deeply hostile nature is all too apparent in Freud's case history of Dora. The intensity of her primitive rage is likewise clearly shown.

Felix Deutsch (1957) published a paper following Dora's death stating he had seen Dora as a patient after Freud and outlined her subsequent life history. She turned out to be a very sick, almost psychotic, paranoid personality, whose main object in life was to be as mean as she possibly could both to her husband and her only son. This life history was quite predictable from the material Freud wrote in her case history. And so we see two layers or levels of illness in Dora: first, superficial hysterical or somatically determined illness expressing her unconscious erotic fantasies and the conflicts which ensued from them; and second, a deeper more malignant core of a paranoid nature, stemming from her regressive pregenital hostility toward the women in her life. This was a deep-seated regressive character illness. Attention is directed to the interconnection of the two basic elements of Dora's neurotic composition—her libidinal conflicts and her character neurosis.

The all important question now comes up: can psycho-analysis relieve Dora's libidinal conflicts and straighten out her love life without an alteration in her neurotic character structure? Reich indicates the answer is no, and I would agree. I do not believe one can analyze and transform such regressive character structure without confrontation, without experiencing her acting out and wallowing in the transference situation. Her pregenital orientation must undergo analytic transformation and this demands a greater or lesser degree of confrontation repeatedly. Dora's insight into the symbolic meaning of her symptoms would not have provided a permanent and effective way of expressing her love needs without some alteration in her character structure. And as Freud says, this libidinal position would be given up with the greatest reluctance. This is why some force is required.

And now what are the essential goals we aim at in the psychotherapy of an illness like this? The first goal is the alteration of the pregenital character traits. In attempting to clarify what is necessary to accomplish this I would like to call attention to what takes place when the growing child normally transforms his primitive impulses into feelings of value to him in a family and social setting. Again I refer to Freud's (1916) paper on "The Exception":

> . . . the doctor in his educative work makes use of one of the components of love. In this work of after-education, he is probably doing no more than repeat the process which made education of any kind possible in the first instance. Side by side with the exigencies of life, love is the great educator; and it is by the love of those nearest him that the incomplete human being is induced to respect the decrees of necessity and to spare himself the punishment that follows any infringement of them. (p. 312)

In viewing the function of love as an educator one frequently encounters the role of confrontation. It is an important ingredient of love in action. One's love for an "incomplete human being," be it a child or an overgrown and emotionally underdeveloped child, prompts one to confront him with his areas of immaturity. Love exhorts the child to abandon the delusional hope of getting life on his own terms and replacing this with the dictates of the reality principle.

One of the great joys of reading Freud is to so frequently encounter a gem, a jewel of a comment sort of hidden in the substance of his main theme. This jewel is so apt, so pertinent, so revealing. The above quotation from "The Exception" is surely one of these gems. In it, I believe, is contained the whole basic essence of what we are striving to accomplish in our analytic work with the character neuroses. The basic developmental failure and defect in these patients' growth was in the fact that they never really left behind the special world of omnipotence and narcissistic entitlement to embrace the world of true object relations and to develop the joys of loving objects in the outside world of non-self. If analytic work and activity can belatedly achieve this objective, then analysis can be a greater or lesser success. If it fails to accomplish this, analysis will have a very limited meaning, both in the area of character and adaptation and in relation to neurotic libidinal conflicts.

A neurosis is like a diamond—it is comprised of many facets, all of which must be dealt with in the analytic situation. What I have described refers to but one facet of the neurosis, but it is a most important one. And in my approach I have stressed that if we can foster and develop the ability to love, to achieve genitality, then the ego can assume its proper role in adaptive functioning and replace the primitive reflex patterns that comprise the neurotic reactions. Anna Freud (1936) states that this task goes beyond the field of strict analysis and is part of the task of the business of education. She states:

When the ego has taken its defensive measures against an affect for the purpose of avoiding "pain" something more besides analysis is required to annul them, if the result is to be permanent. The child must learn to tolerate larger and larger quantities of "pain" without immediately having recourse to his defence-mechanisms. It must, however, be admitted that theoretically it is the business of education rather than of analysis to teach him this lesson. (p.69)

The results of our analytic endeavors in illnesses of this kind hinge on one factor—how malleable is the process in the character structure. Will the patient accept the return of the pain that prompted the original regression and turn to new patterns? Will the patient respond to our efforts for change, or is he so rigid and inflexible that alteration is not possible? Our therapeutic efforts are directed to reestablishing the education process, to developing the potential for growth into maturity, against which the pathological character structure is rigidly opposed. I believe a majority of patients will respond to a greater or lesser degree in a positive way, though certainly there are those who will not give up their narcissistically determined entitlement and prerogatives. But I believe our attempts to give the patient a new choice in his way of life are worthwhile and often effective. Therefore, the described analytic approach to the problem of character neuroses is a justifiable expedient.

Bibliography

Alexander, F. (1953), Current views on psychotherapy. In *The Scope of Psychoanalysis*. New York: Basic Books, Inc., 1961, pp. 276–289.

Deutsch, F. (1957), A footnote to Freud's fragment of an analysis of a case of hysteria. *Psychoanal. Quart.*, 2: 159–167.

Freud, A. (1936), *The Ego and the Mechanisms of Defence*. London: Hogarth Press, 1937.

Freud, S. (1905), Fragment of an analysis of a case of hysteria. *Standard Edition*, 7: 7–122. London: Hogarth Press, 1953.

——— (1916), Some character-types met with in psychoanalytic work. *Standard Edition*, 14: 311–333. London: Hogarth Press, 1957.

Murray, J. M. (1964), Narcissism and the ego ideal. *J. Amer. Psychoanal. Assoc.* 12: 477–511.

Reich, W. (1933), *Character Analysis*. New York: Orgone Institute Press, 1949.

Therapeutic Confrontation from Routine to Heroic

HOWARD A. CORWIN, M.D.

Confrontation as a therapeutic maneuver has been employed for many years in various forms of psychotherapy and psychoanalysis. Recent usefulness of confrontation in socio-political situations has created an environment in which psychotherapists must carefully reconsider the utilization of confrontation in the practice of psychotherapy. Without thoughtful consideration of the appropriate place of confrontation, it can lead to detrimental or even wild technique. Here we will examine the use of confrontation in classical psychoanalysis and psychotherapy and bring this into a current perspective. Confrontation as a technique, its relation to interpretation as well as to the state of the therapeutic alliance, its utilization as a parameter, and its employment at a state of impasse will be examined. Confrontation as considered in this paper includes a spectrum of activities whose polar positions are defined in terms of their routine versus their extraordinary aspects. The term heroic confrontation is introduced to define a therapeutic tool that has long been utilized but rarely highlighted in the analytic literature.

There are three noteworthy features from the area of

socio-political confrontation that have something in common with analytic confrontation. The first is that the confrontation is effective in calling attention to an issue. The attention appears to call forth a second feature, reaction, with the promise of some change being effected. There is thirdly an emphasis on rapidity of change. The overall atmosphere of socio-political confrontation is one of frustration, which is partly responsible for its effectiveness.

The success of the socio-political confrontation has been appealing primarily because of the rapidity with which it effects change. Direct equation of a technique applicable to structures in society with individual treatment is unwarranted by a careful examination of the process of therapy or analysis. Techniques that promise rapid movement are appealing in areas where we have become accustomed to rather slow change, finding that resistances are tenacious and the acquisition of meaningful unconscious insight is a difficult process. Confrontation is viewed by many as primarily an active technique, and active techniques that promote more rapid change have been previously reviewed from a theoretical standpoint.

Bibring (1954) described the process of therapy and outlined four therapeutic principles (procedures and processes) and five therapeutic techniques. The procedures are "(a) the production of material; (b) the utilization of the produced material, . . . ; (c) the assimilation by the patient of the results of such utilization; and (d) the processes of reorientation and readjustment" (p.746). The therapeutic techniques are those of suggestion, abreaction, manipulation, clarification, and interpretation. He observed that alterations in the classic technique relied heavily on manipulations "in combination with or in place of insight" (p.768), and he felt a theory of experiential manipulation was an urgent task for those seeking shorter therapies.

In his discussion Bibring noted that alterations of classical technique in general were best at rapid production and some type of utilization of the material; however, assimilation and processes of reorientation and readjustment were slower to take place. Manipulations were increasingly viewed as curative processes by their proponents through a process of experiential retraining or utilization of some latent ego system.

Bibring did not discuss confrontation as a basic technique. He viewed confrontation as taking place in the process of reorientation and readjustment; namely, *"confronting* the ego with the 'repressed' . . . with the task of reorientation and readjustment of finding new solutions to the partly reactivated infantile and later conflicts" (p.765; italics mine). Apparently he considered confrontations as no more than a routine aspect of the classical analytic process and not a major technical tool.

The use of a technique of confrontation applicable to individual psychotherapy that utilizes attention, reaction, and change can be seen to work through several therapeutic principles. Focusing attention is an ordinary activity that goes on in every form of therapy. It is essentially an attempt to get the observing ego to focus on some situation, problem, or conflict and bring it within the analytic purview. The manipulative use of confrontation to focus on a failure to have developed a good observing ego and on the resultant inability to form a good therapeutic or working alliance may become parametric. Bibring's review left us prior to full development of the concept of the therapeutic alliance and just following Eissler's (1953) introduction of the concept of the use of parameters in psychoanalysis. Bibring viewed manipulations[1] as frequently used therapeutic techniques in analysis, but he felt that ultimately classical technique employed use of insight through clarification or interpretation. Implicit in this is that the manipulative use of a confrontation would eventually require working through and its

---

[1] Manipulation as used by Bibring is a sophisticated maneuver making use of unconscious patterns and ego systems triggered by comments by the analyst.

reduction as a parameter. Techniques that were not analytic would not require this final step and would be content to find some curative principle within the confrontation manipulation itself.

Almost two decades have passed since this classic paper, which adumbrated the trends that we currently must examine. From a classical point of view, we must consider that the use of some forms of confrontation has always been a routine aspect of analysis, no different from what we clinically talk of as "helping the patient to see," "pointing out," or "calling it to his attention."

Devereux (1951) has considered confrontation to be a routine aspect of analysis. "In simplest terms, confrontation is a device whereby the patient's attention is directed to the bare factual content of his actions or statements or to a coincidence which he has perceived, but has not, or professes not to have, registered" (p.19). He views the most fundamental difference between a confrontation and an interpretation as the fact that the former is usually a starting point for the bringing up of new problems or associations whereas the latter is a means of bringing to a head and resolving some hitherto insoluble problem. Confrontation, he says, is "an analytic device only in so far as it leads to the production, or to the mulling over, of some new material, *which is, eventually, interpreted* in terms of the logic of the unconscious" (p.20). In his view confrontation does not demand unusual appropriateness in timing but may be made whenever the analyst has noticed something that the patient has not. For Devereux it is "a rather superficial manipulation of cathexes, *i.e.*, of attention" (p.20). It presages future interpretations and "facilitates transition to new material" (p.20).

Greenson (1967) has shown the routine usage of confrontation in the everyday work of the analyst. He uses the term variously but suggests that it is a part of routine analysis of the resistance. "Demonstrating the resistance may be a simple or even unnecessary step if the resistance is obvious to the patient. If this is not the case, if the patient is unaware of the resistance, then it is essential to *confront* the patient with the fact that a resistance is present before we attempt anything further" (p.104; italics mine). He advises caution against premature confrontation. For Greenson, appropriate confrontation leads systematically to the clarification, interpretation, and working through of the resistance.

In this aspect of both Greenson and Devereux there is the tendency to accentuate the routineness and the lower order of relevance in use of confrontation as compared with interpretation. However, this is just one pole of the use of confrontation. There is another, which in its background, employment, and intention is at the opposite end from the routine, which is distinguished in being considered something heroic, that which is perhaps a memorable part of the analyst's day. It necessitates understanding of the countertransference prior to its delivery in order to make sure that it is not being delivered solely out of countertransference irritation and frustration.

This procedure, which may also be illustrated in the examples cited elsewhere in this book, is what I designate as the dramatic or heroic confrontation. This has very specific characteristics and is employed at varying phases of analysis or therapy. A heroic confrontation may be defined as an emotionally charged, parametric, manipulative, technical tool demanded by the development of an actual or potential situation of impasse and designed ultimately to remobilize a workable therapeutic alliance. Myerson (Chapter One) focused on such an illustration in quoting Alexander, who said to the patient that it was no wonder no one liked him if he behaved in such an unpleasant manner when people tried to help him. This focused on the fact that the patient would have to consider his behavior within the transference and in real life essentially ego dystonic if they were to proceed effectively. He worked towards Bibring's manipulation, in that he activated an "ego system" within the patient that led him to a more cooperative position. In modern terms, he essentially activated a system that enhanced development of the therapeutic alliance. I am mindful of Myerson's excellent discussion of the possibilities that existed that might have been employed by Alexander. However, it is a dramatic moment and has confronted the patient with several alternatives even as it has been stated. It has given the patient an instant awareness that it is he who is doing something that makes himself offensive to others. It informs him that he has a responsibility for his behavior and that he, in the analyst's opinion, can take a more constructive approach to what it is that he is doing. It defines for him an *alternate pathway* that is implicit in the analyst's having made this type of confrontation.

Murray (Chapter Three) also illustrates masterfully what is involved in the heroic confrontation. He takes up a situation with a patient that could readily alter the course of the analysis. Initially, a previous confrontation was made by the interim consultant prior to seeing Murray. The consultant had told the patient that he was a therapeutic risk and that he might become sicker or have to be hospitalized if further therapy was undertaken. When Murray in the first few hours of analysis was able to see the paranoid position evolving, he made his confrontation in which he dramatically gave a message to the patient that emotionally was as follows: "Your premises are really wrong. Out of your anger you can become paranoid with me if you wish, but you can also accept that I can accept you and you can accept me and that either we can learn to get along with each other or you can essentially have the other fellow's predictions come true for you." This was a dramatic confrontation with many meanings, clearly avoiding the development of a too early, too intense psychotic transference with paranoid ideation predominating and permitting the development of an alliance within which they could consider how to get the patient to participate in a successful analysis. Again, an experienced therapist had reacted with an intuitive feeling that nothing else might work, and this was the introduction to setting up a situation within which an analysis might proceed.

A third example might be that of Greenson's (1967) analysis of a candidate who was in a prolonged resistance with a pseudo-therapeutic alliance and not doing analytic work. The patient was making a mockery of analysis, refused to take his affects seriously, and enabled nothing to develop in the analysis. He used persistent reasonableness as a means of avoiding or belittling his deeper feelings and would not permit the tracing of historical origins of the mode of behavior. He was reenacting a nonconformist in the analysis and led Greenson to a feeling that the patient could not work consistently with the material. Greenson said,

I finally told the patient that we had to face the fact that we were getting nowhere and we ought to consider some alternative besides continuing psychoanalysis with me. The patient was silent for a few moments and said frankly he was disappointed. He sighed and then went on to make a free association-like remark. I stopped him and asked what in the world he was doing. He replied that he guessed I sounded somewhat annoyed. I assured him it was no guess. Then slowly he looked at me and asked if he could sit up. I nodded and he did. He was quite shaken, sober, pale, and in obvious distress. (p.202)

Subsequently this led to an analysis that permitted this type of behavior to be analyzed as a resistance to the development of the transference neurosis. "Only when . . . he was about to lose the transference object did his rigidly reasonable behavior become ego alien and accessible to therapy. . . . Then he became able to distinguish between genuine reasonableness and the teasing, spiteful reasonableness of his character neurosis and the analysis began to move" (p.203).

These three examples, Alexander, Murray, and Greenson, are what I would prefer to see in terms of the non-routine but dramatic and heroic form of interaction that may occur in some analyses. All three were dramatic interventions, which thereafter permitted analysis to proceed along usual technical modes and in accordance with more classical features. Each enhanced the therapeutic alliance. They were special, forceful, attention getting, reaction producing, and change demanding confrontations. They did not deal with intrapsychic, classical structural conflict, but dealt more with the patient's character and extra-analytic situations.

We can now consider times at which a heroic confrontation is necessary in classical therapies. One such situation may occur when the patient develops a narcissistic alliance[1] that defies development of a therapeutic alliance. The concept of narcissistic alliance is not generally understood and will be developed here. Often the conscious reasons for entering analysis have to do with character change or symptom relief, and the patient is willing to enter into a therapeutic alliance in which he undergoes that which is necessary for his cure. Unconsciously, some patients, those with more narcissistic predispositions and defenses, may hope that through the analytic procedure they will, in fact, make some alliance in which the therapist or analyst will help them to attain an unrealistic position. Sometimes this is entirely a narcissistic wish-fulfillment system and may be clinically manifest in terms of fulfillment of an instinctual desire or ego ideal aspiration. It may promise extraordinary reward of a sexual nature or intellectual giantism, and it may include omnipotent or grandiose fantasies. It is at variance with what is appropriate and realistic. What it promises, or what these patients promise themselves, is that the limitations of their character and symptomatology may be overcome in magical ways through the relationship with their omnipotent analyst-parents. Though unrealistic, it may be an operative

---

[1] I am indebted to Dr. Robert Mehlman for the origin of the term narcissistic alliance and numerous discussions with him on the evolution of this concept and its clinical relevance.

force and is one of the elements that motivates these patients to enter a therapeutic procedure. While present to some degree in all patients this sometimes masks the lack of development of a workable therapeutic alliance; and sometimes a therapeutic alliance is not present at all, but the narcissistic alliance is highly operative. A patient who is under the influence of this narcissistic alliance has the expectation that his analyst will help him to realize his goals. Here the analyst actually has the technical task of developing and channeling the healthy narcissism and converting the pathological narcissism into the development of a therapeutic alliance.

An excellent example of this type of narcissistic alliance is illustrated by the following case. The patient in diagnostic was convincing in that he wanted to alter himself and not his environment. He said that he wanted to improve his relationships with women and develop more mutually acceptable relationships. On this basis he was considered an acceptable analysand. Shortly after starting analysis he began to reveal that he had no intention of really changing himself, that what he wanted in fact was to attain omnipotence and a union that would permit him to gain all his ends without regard to what it might mean or how unrealistic it was. As such, he entered analysis having decided that participation in analysis was an alliance based on the promise of his realizing all the gratifications that he felt he had been denied by his past. The therapeutic alliance was not in evidence—he did not want to work or observe but merely wanted a total experience of gratification. The alliance was conceived of in terms of a narcissistic wish fulfillment, rather than a realistic working alliance based on the need for analytic work with eventually a development of a greater capacity for mutual object relations and more deeply, an awareness of the inability to gain total control over the frightening and threatening world of his childhood. It should be understood that a realistic working alliance is a gradual development in analysis. It develops by the substitution of therapeutic attitudes through the medium of the transference, which itself is narcissistically founded, and, gradually, through analytic work into a therapeutic alliance. When the patient is under the influence of a narcissistic alliance, as all patients are to some extent initially, it must be gradually transformed into a working alliance as the analysis itself is structured. The narcissistic alliance operates as the glue between therapist and patient yet may also operate as a resistance. The patient may not be prepared to undergo the rigors of a frustrating transference neurosis and may be basically unwilling to bear pain in the analysis and thereby work on the mastery of painful affects. When the narcissistic alliance is used as a resistance, the patient wants the gift to be bestowed magically upon him rather than working to overcome his limitations and develop through affect mastery. To such a patient all attempts to analyze will be seen as hostile attempts to deprive him of his narcissistic wishes and their realization. Only with the development of an alliance of more ordinary proportions can an analysis proceed. Confrontation with such a patient includes recognition that he is not working in the analysis until he can conceive of doing analytic work, that there is no magical result in the analysis, and that he has the choice either to work on enabling himself to participate or to terminate the experience. This may be brought to his attention as an early issue; namely, whether analysis is possible or desirable, or whether he is holding to a status quo of narcissistic alliance because he cannot undergo the development of a working alliance, which itself implies a major alteration of his wish-fulfillment system and willingness to engage in the deep and demanding process. He gets his choice as to whether he really is in it for a therapy or whether he should not be in analysis but should be undergoing a different procedure preparatory to or substituting for the analytic process. Preparatory to any confrontation it is desirable that the analyst deal with the patient's initial attitude in terms of its resistance potential, its defensiveness, and the fears of the early stages of therapy and in terms of the fundamental aspects of why the patient is so afraid to put himself in any other position than the omnipotent one. The confrontation comes only when the routine analysis of the situation has been exhausted and still no movement to real analytic or therapeutic involvement is discernible. Again, this is analogous to Greenson's confrontation.

This type of confrontation might be made as a more or less routine analytic procedure for the patient, if he is willing to hear it in such a way; or on the other hand, it might be considered a major threat to him. The confrontation may, through its analysis, facilitate an attitude that will enable the analysis to proceed; or it may just clarify enough to allow the patient to leave without his getting into a situation that might portend too much loss of control, too much regression, or too great a possibility of disappointment, with concomitant release of unbearable affects.

From these observations it is apparent that the use of the heroic confrontations may occur at any time during the therapy or the analysis. The therapist might be faced with the possibility of having to deviate from what he would classically like to do depending on the actual or potential development of an impasse situation. The purpose is invariably to facilitate or make the therapy or analysis possible. The therapist attempts to work from the standpoint of routine confrontation as much as possible. The patient himself sometimes is the one who determines whether a confrontation will be merely routine and ordinary or dramatic and heroic. He does this by hearing what the analyst says from the standpoint of a good therapeutic alliance or a poor one. In a poor alliance, no alliance, or a narcissistic alliance, what is said may invariably be heard on some level as critical, rejecting, punitive, authoritative, but not as merely good analysis trying to bring something of importance into an analytic purview. The key to understanding the nature of confrontation and that pole it leans toward appears to be at the level of the development of the real or working alliance. When that is good, most elements will at least be admitted for analysis, be they symptoms, behavior, acting out within or without the transference, or the more silent aspects of character resistance. It is always to be hoped that the patient can accept the therapist's confrontations as routine and necessary help in setting up that which has to be analyzed, rather than perceive attack in the confrontation.

Impasse can occur, as demonstrated above, immediately or after many years of therapy. If the fundamental tenets of the analysis or therapy are not taken up early, the entire analysis may be under misguided notions; and therefore, great expectations may proliferate that could lead to massive stalemating within the analysis. Such a situation should be faced sooner rather than later. It is possible, however, that only after several years and after analysis of many more superficial layers will a deeply regressive impasse develop in which the alliance is so broken down that the patient is more devoted to hurting the analyst (or the analysis) or the transference figure (parent) than to continuing to analyze productively. It is at such a point that it is often necessary to confront, but at this time heroically and in an effort essentially to save the therapeutic situation. It should be noted that much negative direction and negative transference do not portend the development of impasse. There are many times in analysis that are temporarily difficult but fall short of impasse and that are critical in giving the patient the idea that he and the analyst can work through a particularly difficult situation together. It is in such circumstances that the therapist avoids heroic confrontation rather than precipitate anything beyond the scope of the ordinary.

The ways in which confrontation differs from interpretation must be considered. In the interpretation the patient is offered a hypothesis, one that he has the opportunity to verify, elaborate, contradict, but above all, investigate. This occurs after a reasonable clarification of other levels of behavior or thought processes. Ideally, the interpretations are hypothetical, not charged as such, but observational, unemotionally delivered. They are given in the context of awareness that the analyst and patient together are joining with an observing ego to deal with the experiencing part of the analysand in order to uncover some unconscious material. Both are in agreement that an experiential regression is going on involving part of the ego and the instincts. At the same time, a split-off aspect of the observing ego, which will work together with the analyst on the interpretation, is reserved for the therapeutic alliance. This is analogous to the analyst and patient flowing along a river in the same direction;[1] the common cause is agreed upon; mutual trust is established; and even if there is disagreement, they are willing to work out their differences. They can participate in negative transference reactions, can analyze them, and can maintain respect while they work through the negative responses. Such is the classical therapeutic situation, one in which all confrontations will be seen as routine and parameters are by and large unnecessary

What is to be emphasized is that the atmosphere for such work is constructive even if the material itself is painful. Confrontations given in such a context may also serve as interpretations, depending on the definition of interpretation.

In heroic confrontation, the atmosphere is different. To further the river analogy, it is as if the current were going against the therapist. In the ideal case he has made the routine confrontations, clarifications, and interpretations; he has considered the different levels of the resistance and has followed the rules of classical analysis carefully, has interpreted from superficial to deep, has worked on resistances of superego, ego defenses, secondary gains, etc.; he has made adequate reconstructions and has pointed to the anxieties of different levels. Though he has done this, he nevertheless sees his alliance eroded away, his patient beginning to oppose him no matter what he says. It is in this situation that he has analyzed the countertransference and struggled to under-

---

[1] I am indebted to Dr. Jeffrey Nason for development of the river analogy.

stand the patient's position. He has done all that he might reasonably be expected to do, all that is in fact, analytic. At this point, having worked also with his routine analysis of the negative therapeutic reaction, he then recognizes that he has to do something that in effect is extra-analytic, or parametric. It is at such a point that planned heroic confrontations are made.

What then is the purpose at this point? It is as if the analyst were saying, "We no longer are going the same way in this analysis or therapy." The therapist is going upstream against the patient's resistance, against the current; they are not going together. The analysis can make no further headway because the flood of resistance is such that nothing that is said is useful and is only responded to negatively. The tide has turned against the analyst and his procedures. Patient and therapist may have been caught for a while in an eddy, but then it becomes clear how forceful the mainstream of resistance is. The analyst feels that he can proceed along the usual lines, but all he says will be washed downstream. He must, therefore, do something beyond his usual procedure.

At the moment that he does it, the analyst takes a position that is never implied in an interpretation. In common with some forms of interpretation, he says something with surprise and shock value that may be dramatic and may touch the patient's narcissism. Beyond this, and exclusive to heroic confrontation, he says something that implies action, either his own (the analyst's) or the patient's. What he says may be heard in many ways: some as positive and loving, but others as a warning, a prohibition, a threat, or a punishment. It must inevitably arouse an anxiety on some level within the patient. The deepest dread is that of abandonment, though unconsciously other patients will have castration or superego anxieties aroused. The real strength of such a confrontation on its deepest level is that it often implies that unless the patient is able to hear it, to rise above his current difficulties and the regressive state within which he is living in his analysis, he will inevitably go downstream with a tide running out and the analyst will not be able to stop him. Going downstream is really succumbing to the illness and to analytic or therapeutic abandonment. The heroic confrontation here reestablishes a healthy narcissistic alliance that may be utilized in recreating a therapeutic alliance.

This is, to my way of understanding, why a heroic confrontation is a distinct entity that differs from an interpretation. An interpretation, well timed, well worked, leads to further insight. It does not imply that a working through will take place or that an assimilation will necessarily result. It may provoke more resistances, but it is given in an atmosphere in which there is a reasonable expectation that patient and therapist will continue to work on its hypothetical importance.

The heroic confrontation, however, says essentially either the patient must do something—i.e., *change* in some way within the analysis—or he and the analyst will have to stop the analytic work, which has become nonproductive. When such a statement is made, it is an *emergency situation*, acute or chronic. The analyst knows it, the patient is either vaguely or distinctly aware of it. But both know the moment it is uttered that it may have a prophetic significance for the patient. In short, it implies that a psychic reaction must lead towards reestablishment of a working alliance.

In short then, the interpretation puts less burden on the patient than the heroic confrontation. The heroic confrontation is the emergency measure, not the routine measure; it is the dramatic, not the common procedure.

Why it is effective then, is an important question. Preceding discussions of confrontation have emphasized that it may eliminate the development of expected transference (even if these were to be paranoid or psychotic) or that it involves a terror, either of abandonment, castration, or punishment in some way. There is little doubt that the immediate mechanism of such a confrontation is that the patient is forced to accept and make the change for the time being. Not to accept the confrontation will leave him the choice of the *or*, which is that analysis or therapy will not go on or cannot be successful. That means to the patient that he has to live with himself in his old sick ways, the ways that originally motivated his coming to the therapist. For most, this is not adequate and will mobilize ego systems to work productively again with the therapist.

It is in this period following this shock that the patient may undergo his most agonizing periods in analysis. Often terrified, having an anxiety of various dimensions but basically related to a dread of abandonment, he may be willing to mobilize all his forces to continue the analysis. He may do it simply out of his fear—an identification with the aggressor is perhaps the most common way. But this does for him something he considers vital, if not yet productive; namely, it preserves the relationship with the therapist. It makes him reevaluate his position and may begin to help him mobilize a more workable alliance with the analyst, if he is capable of doing so. It may ward off his deepest terror if he is willing to make the indicated changes that the confrontation requires. Even if he employs the mechanism of identification with the aggressor temporarily, at another level he may get the message that the analyst has cared enough to interact in a vital way with him, in a manner that indicated that the love [1] of the therapist was available—but that it was conditional. This love, actual or transference, is one of the elements that must be perceived at some level by the patient, even if the more superficial mechanism is that of the identification with the aggressor. Here we are again reminded of Eissler's warning that the use of parameters might substitute obedience for structural change and that they must be capable of being reduced to zero.

---

[1] Perception of the loss of the therapist is part of the narcissistic alliance. This may be a positive and useful force and may "touch" the patient enough to let him see the necessity of transforming his narcissistic alliance into a useful rather than resistance form. The therapeutic alliance is the evolutionary form superimposed on the narcissistic alliance and has conditional elements involved.

If no element of love is discernible by the patient, then the confrontation can be taken as a proof by the patient that in the end the analyst will be just as cruel, rejecting, demanding, punitive, or unnecessarily harsh as the negative side of the parent in transference. For some patients, the analyst's heroic confrontation may finalize their case against the analyst. It is in such circumstances that the analyst should avoid the confrontation until the patient himself makes the confrontation, brings to light the state of impasse, and essentially confronts himself with the possibility of the bleak outlook unless he makes some changes. We are therefore presented with the consideration of when not to confront. Such a situation is spoken of by Balint (1968) in the cases where he feels that a therapeutic regression is taking place that is in the area of the basic fault and where words are relatively meaningless. Such situations must be lived through as supportively and non-threateningly as possible. There are special situations and their recognition is essential if destructive heroic confrontations are to be avoided.

I shall now illustrate two cases in which heroic confrontation as a critical intervention appeared to be a constructive measure. Both were at a situation of impasse: the first due to chronic discharge through acting out, and the second through the development of a negative transference of unworkable proportions. Both interventions came after long preparatory periods with painstaking and careful work carried out in accordance with classical methods.

Case I

The patient was a 36-year-old married man who entered analysis for work and marital difficulties. His narcissistic and exhibitionistic character traits took the form of aggressive outbursts that immediately embarrassed him and thwarted his work interests and attainments. Every aggressive foray that he felt compelled to enact ended in his masochistically arranged-for punishments from superiors. Narcissistically oriented sexual exploitations were also frequent.

The early analytic work was marked by external or analytic frustrations invariably provoking these episodes. Routine clarification of this behavior, the specific forms that it took, its relation to frustrations in the analysis, and attempts to make up some blows to self-esteem were investigated. Some vague outlines of the infantile neurosis were dealt with intellectually, but affects were so discharged that analysis began to appear stalemated. A repetitive cycle of discharge through acting out with guilty return for forgiveness and marked contrition was apparent.

Of interest was that despite the repetitive cycle of acting out, the patient wished for the analyst to provide some acceptable superego controls and a model of mature identification as part of his ego ideal.

Following a year of acting-out behavior that did not abate, the analyst avoided prohibition but confronted the patient analytically with the fact that the analysis could not proceed if all the feelings were being discharged into the rationalized acting out. It was indicated that his acting out made a mockery of the analysis, the analyst, and the patient himself.

The patient was surprised and upset, felt that he was being given the choice of continuing as a sick person or getting better through the analytic procedure. What became clear was that the sick actions were those that were an identification with a manipulative, primitive, sadistic, rationalizing, con-man father. On the other hand he had the analyst, who was at once the ego ideal and the good superego model. He really had no choice. His reponse was dramatic. He stopped his overt acting out and began to contain it within the analysis. He was fearful of losing the analysis more than he yearned for the opportunities to reenact. Then all that had been pale in the previous descriptions of the infantile neurosis and trauma became alive within the analysis. The specific details of the infantile neurosis that led to the marked acting out are beyond the scope of this paper.

The confrontation, therefore, was parametric and manipulative. It was a Hobson's choice for the patient, in view of the fact that the patient was certain to continue with his old behaviors, jeopardize marriage and career, and put himself in a permanently punitive position. When he stopped this he had great struggles with his control but basically did it partly out of tremendous anxiety, partly out of a need to identify with an aggressor who could really put him out, and partly out of a need for development of some internalization of the ego ideal and superego aspects of the analyst.

The analysis and the patient's life then began to proceed. A distinctly less narcissistic usage of people began to provide some reality reward as his work and marriage flourished. A good alliance developed, and within it he worked on negative transference feelings but with containment of acting out. When he began to consider termination, the analyst reminded him of the unfinished business; the actual (heroic) confrontation itself had not been dealt with fully, and he still felt that he was on good "behavior" out of anxiety and terror. At this point, the patient viewed the analyst as too petty, too perfectionistic. But simultaneously, the acting out began, was initially concealed and then brought out. This then was the opportunity to work with the patient on the meaning of the current behavior in terms of a loss of the analyst. That he had to alter his position from identification with the aggressor to integration of all the modified superego and ego ideal identifications was apparent and was the work of a prolonged termination. As the deep hostility for the aggressor was worked through, he began to feel that he was doing what he did for himself and not simply to satisfy his analyst.

This is to be seen as significant in terms of Eissler's caution on reducing the parameter to zero in order to complete the analysis. The confrontation in this case was used at a point where acting out interfered with any productive work of assimilation. It provided a period of anxiety and then motivation to work in the classical manner. Then there was some sense of mastery, some growth, and some resolution of the initial traumatic issues that were woven into the neurosis. Finally a stage was necessary in which the patient no longer had to accept the confrontation, but could incorporate a mature identification and could develop into what he himself would desire, rather than merely being under the domination or control of the analyst.

Case II

The patient was a 30-year-old man who was referred to earlier in the section on reducing the pathological elements of a narcissistic alliance and allowing development of a therapeutic alliance. The patient was at this time in his fourth year of analysis, having shown little movement. His initial year, following the earlier confrontation, had been slow-moving and characterized by performance, conformity, and suppression of hostilities. Then as the analysis deepened, it dealt with early traumatic situations. A sibling was born when he was two, at which time he lost his world of fantasied omnipotence. Having recovered from this, a year later he had faced the birth of another sibling coincident with his own actual life-threatening illness, a further severe trauma, from which he had recovered intellectually but never emotionally. His intellectual brilliance was manifest again, but never his former sense of omnipotence, as he had in fact retrospectively idealized his previous situation. In latency and on through adolescence and into adult life, he nurtured the illusion of magical restoration of his previous powers through possession of a dream woman, whom he could take over, become like, and share in her magical powers. The essence of the fantasy was that through it he would regain all he had lost at the time of his narcissistic injury. He held this illusion through-out the analysis and eschewed work on it. The transference gradually got beneath his brilliant and clever defensive intellectualization and led to a position wherein the intense bitterness and hatred toward the negligent mother came out. After an earlier isolation of affect at his mother's coldness, he began to develop a real bitterness that led to breaking all contact with her. He shifted his hatred onto the analyst and began to luxuriate in fantasies that attempted to prove to the analyst how poor the analyst was and just as terrible, inadequate, incompetent, and unloving as the real mother. This went on for the better part of a year. It gradually became clear that the patient was again at an impasse. This time the impasse was such that he was gratifying his hatreds, becoming less able to do anything outside the analysis, and only demanding the analyst's help in order to make the analyst feel helpless, thereby proving the analyst's stupidity, incompetence, and indifference. All of these attacks had previously been leveled at the mother.

Ultimately the analyst made a heroic confrontation in which he stated, "I agree that we are at an impasse. The impasse is one in which you are not analyzing but just luxuriating in the hatred and destruction of me. I am willing to go on if there is motivation for further analytic work, but this cannot simply become the gratification of your hatred at such great expense to your real life."

The patient was furious. He said that the analyst was "kicking him out," that it was true that the analyst was no better than his parent had been. He went on to note that this was another abandonment, leaving him helpless, and proved his principal theme that the patient was helpless, that he had a bad and abandoning analyst, and that it justified his permanent position of doing nothing and his hopelessness, helplessness, and depression.

He evoked within the analyst the feeling of "I am bad, and I have done such harm to this patient that it can never be undone." The analyst had, however, many previous times dealt with this and could point out how the patient was using an old tactic, one that was labeled "guilty analyst," a technique that he employed to avoid actually examining his positions in order to avoid responsibility, analyzing, and as part of his projective system of blaming parents, world, and analyst. The analyst then stated that the destructive use of the guilty analyst position by the patient was intended to force the analyst to retract the confrontation and essentially continue to set up the bad analyst position that was the real impasse.

The analyst therefore stuck to his position and pointed out that he was entirely willing to work with the patient, who wanted to work through this position, but would not be willing to go on if the patient over a period of several months did not get back to analyzing. The patient then underwent some remarkable work. He realized that all previous situations had in fact been those he took out of terror. He certainly felt terrorized by this confrontation—to be without analyst was indeed an abandonment; he could do so little on his own. However, he began to find a more positive side of the relationship, began to have dreams in which he questioned himself regarding his responsibility for misuse of the relationship with the analyst. He began to consider that he would have to give up the fantasied dream girl and with it an approach to life. He underwent with this a different degree of depression, one that could now be felt as a real depression that was not used merely for manipulative purposes. He had real confusion at having to give up a fantasy that was restitutive for many years. Here the analyst's support, now no longer confrontational, began to have meaning for the patient, who moved into areas of feeling within the analysis that had not previously been touched upon and that dealt with the much defended against, positive side of the relationship.

This confrontation had again been used at a point of impasse, here later in the course of the analytic work. What had been going on was that the analyst was becoming more of an object of the anger that was less and less within a therapeutic alliance and more and more distorted. When the analyst confronted the patient, it was to avoid stagnation and dissolution of the analysis. The analyst had dealt with the negative countertransference feelings which were acknowledged at appropriate times in the analysis. Because this preliminary work had been done, the analyst was prepared to deal with the patient's resistance as he used the "guilty analyst" ploy. Ultimately, the situation showed considerable improvement as the work once again began to proceed following the confrontation. At this stage of the analysis the confrontation was useful, though ultimately the analysis was interrupted prematurely.

The above cases are illustrative of the heroic type of confrontation. In the first case the analysis approached impasse through the excessive acting out of the patient. The acting out of the patient was not prohibited, but the question of proceeding with analysis with such massive acting out had to be confronted. In the second case, the confrontation was made in face of the patient's luxuriating in what promised to become a stalemated negative transference. Both were memorable. Both occasioned dramatic responses. The analyst was in neither case angered at the point of confrontation, but sought to make these moves as manipulations to get some kind of productive work and alliance going again. The analyst paid the price of the patient's undergoing a temporary parametrically induced identification with the aggressor, and only much later could the analyst really deal with this initial confrontation. Both of these confrontations were effective because the fear of losing the analyst was greater than the tenacity of the particular form of the resistance. There are, without doubt, many other levels of confrontation, but this is basically what is implied in confrontations that are heroic.

There is a further type of confrontation that is heroic but is one that is made by the patient. This was first drawn to my attention by Dr. Ralph Kahana; shortly after a patient presented an excellent example.

The patient was a 25-year-old obsessional character in the second year of analysis. What had come out repeatedly was his fear of entrapment of any sort. Descriptions of sadistic treatment by a consciously perceived tyrannical father abounded in his work. Over the issue of vacation, which had been carefully scheduled prior to start of the analysis, the patient underwent a strongly regressive moment. He chose to schedule different vacations from the analyst. This alteration was due to certain events that seemingly justified a change in his schedule but progressed from taking off a day, to a week, and then to a month. As the analyst commented on this progression and its deleterious effect on analysis, the patient got frightened. Suddenly there loomed the image of his father and unconscious fears blossomed forth. He wanted to break off the analysis. "Did he have to be there?" he wanted to know. The analyst pointed out the realities of the treatment situation—that it imposed some restriction on both patient and analyst. However, the patient then said in his confrontation, "Do I have to be here on those days. I am confronting you. If you are that rigid, then we cannot work together any longer." It was clear that the patient in work and deed was presenting with heightened emotional meaning a major feature of his obsessional character structure. He could not tolerate anything being beyond his control. Momentarily he could have no trust and no belief in the analyst. The confrontation came as a question of the analyst's flexibility so that he could be differentiated from the father, from whom he could expect only sadistic treatment that could be meted out through the father's rigidity. The analyst accepted the patient's confrontation, letting him know that he was responsible for the hours but did not have to come. The analyst then went on to point out the terror that being under someone's control caused him and took the opportunity to clarify the tremendous need for control that existed in the patient.

This confrontation, though accepted at the time by the analyst, was itself indicative of the need ultimately to analyze the patient's need to control the environment, which was manifested in the rigidity so characteristic of his personality. Here the analyst accepted a confrontation made by the patient with the idea that at a later time it too would be analyzed in depth and that it actually would be a central issue of the analysis of the transference. The confrontation and the parameter it introduced were a direct result of the patient's heroic confrontation.

The price of heroic confrontation is one that is never fully paid until the waning period of the therapy or analysis. It is then, in termination, that the analyst can see whether the parameter employed was really worthwhile. The patient can ultimately help resolve the parameter by permitting its analysis. Ultimately he must work through to the point where he can accept the threat implicit in the confrontation as necessary at a time in the analysis when he could not resolve his resistances in any other way. Essentially a parameter, the heroic confrontation is used in situations of impasse when the dynamic situation is adequately grasped by analyst and patient, at least intellectually. The transference has been clarified and interpreted. The anxieties of other positions have been interpreted. The patient continues to prefer the resistance position and this necessitates considering discontinuation of therapy. The patient may begin to play out a deleterious game in the analysis that is antitherapeutic or may even threaten to exceed reality bounds. Such a situation calls for the heroics of a heroic confrontation. It may then save the patient from deteriorating into a sadomasochistic and destructive game, moving into a psychosis, or moving into other forms of stalemate.

It should finally be stated that the confrontational manipulation itself should hopefully coincide with a good opportunity of having a positive effect. At the point of impasse, it is important that the analyst combine his soundest knowledge, his keenest foresight, his greatest empathy, and maximum intuition in a move that can hopefully resolve the impasse, save the therapy, and give the patient the opportunity to free himself from further neurotic suffering.

It should be noted that the confrontation here is viewed

as being done not electively but by the demands of the particular case after adequate assessment of all variables involved. It is heroic in that it is a measure reserved for situations that require other than the ordinary treatment; thus the term is borrowed from the field of medical heroics.

Bibliography

Balint, M. (1968), *The Basic Fault. Therapeutic Aspects of Regression*. London: Tavistock Publications.

Bibring, E. (1954), Psychoanalysis and the dynamic psychotherapies. *J. Amer. Psychoanal. Assn.*, 2: 745–770.

Devereux, G. (1951), Some criteria for the timing of confrontations and interpretations. *Int. J. Psychoanal.*, 32: 19–24.

Eissler, K. (1953), The effect of the structure of the ego on psychoanalytic technique. *J. Amer. Psychoanal. Assn.*, 1: 104–143.

Greenson, R. (1967), *The Technique and Practice of Psychoanalysis*. New York: International Universities Press.

Murray, J. M. (this volume), The purpose of confrontation.

Myerson, P. G. (this volume), The meanings of confrontation.

Confrontation, Countertransference and Context

AVERY D. WEISMAN, M.D.

The turning point of psychoanalysis came at that moment when Freud told his hypnotized patients to open their eyes. He stopped squeezing the skull for traumatic memories, as if the head were a pus pocket of noxious events. Instead, he invited the patient to participate in a mutual quest that would end when both understood how the past influenced the here-and-now.

Psychoanalysis was at first an exercise in resurrection of what had happened (catharsis), then, what must have happened (reconstruction) and, after that, what might have happened (fantasy and psychic reality). Patients were urged to recall the unrecallable, to relinquish burdensome memories they had not known about. Above all, they were asked to gaze into the darkness of the mind and find clarity. To do so, they were encouraged to abnegate surrounding reality, including their own critical faculties.

True, it was something like a conjurer and his assistant, working with the properties of mental functions and with the ceremonials of medicine. Nevertheless, in many studies, Freud laid down principles of psychopathology that we use today to understand the value of confrontation.

These principles declared that mental life has a common basis in a dynamic psychology, that we withdraw from painful stimuli but seek satisfaction. In any case, we move toward an equilibrium of impulse and quiescence. Words, thoughts, and actions are parts of a single process; each stands in the place of the other at times, so that unimpeded utterances must sooner or later restore what has been forgotten by retracing old pathways. Self-illumination has a healing effect, Freud thought; and by regaining awareness of faulty experiences, by finding the time and place of the original trouble, the mind's aberrations could be cured.

From the perspective of so many decades and generations these principles seem naive, indeed. The psychoanalyst was not like a surgeon who extirpates a source of infection, and yet must remain aseptic himself. When Freud's patients opened their eyes, what did they see? He, too, had to join them in a moment of confrontation. They could see that historical facts are not the same as psychic reality and that psychic reality has a way of rewriting the past. Mere uncovering of past events was doomed to fail; moreover, patients were apt to oppose efforts on their behalf. They could look without seeing and could also refuse to acknowledge what was too revealing. Denial and repression thus formed the basis for later theories of defenses.

Psychoanalysis depends upon a concept called the "dynamic unconscious." But constant preoccupation with what is unconscious and forgotten may blunt our appreciation of an active and dynamic consciousness, which can perceive and select, act upon and assess its own experience.

In early days, psychoanalysts tended to slight consciousness as if it were merely a smudge on the pages recording unconscious events. Consciousness was an obstacle or, at best, a pathway from the land down to the sea. The analyst's job was to submerge himself as quickly as possible into the depths.

No one can analyze or be analyzed entirely from the position of what is unconscious. Critical faculties cannot be arbitrarily suspended; people cannot say, "I am not aware of what I am aware of." We are conscious and often conscious of having a purpose. Consciousness is not limited to whatever we passively perceive; it is an active response to demands that reality makes upon us. Perception itself is activity incarnate. We respond and are responsive as well. We reach out with our minds and are grasped in return by entire worlds of objects, people, things, symbols, and so forth. Similarly, we may be threatened and shrink back, preferring to deny, to mitigate, displace, and qualify our fears into extinction.

For similar reasons of active consciousness and reciprocal responsiveness to confrontations, analysts cannot be so disengaged from what they are doing that their responses can be separated entirely from the thrust of what patients report. The analyst is not an educated scavenger searching his patient with a mental Geiger counter, nor are patients paragons of passivity who lie obediently and un-critically, awaiting moments of illumination or an epiphany. Indeed, if this were so, it would be a sign of stagnation, not one of expectancy.

Consciousness is dynamic enough, if we insist upon drawing too sharp a distinction between what is self-evident and what is latent and emergent. Memories may be the building blocks of therapy, but remembering is not a thera-peutic act in itself. It is only in the here-and-now that we find a place to stand. And it is from where we stand that we can open our eyes, confront, and be confronted with how we contribute to each other's reality.

Everything else seems to be fragments dissected away from the tissue of contemporary experience. The mystique is gone; contemporary doctors, by which I mean doctors who deal with the contemporaneous, instead of with the remote past or the immediate moment of behavior, strive to uncover the problematic, to define the ambiguous, and to assess potentiality for change.

We do not know if anyone is ever cured by psychotherapy or what the factors are that facilitate benefit. We do know, however, that communication makes a difference to people and that confrontation is a significant, even decisive, element in that professional format of communication called psychotherapy.

The aims of this chapter are four-fold: (1) to define *confrontation* as it is used in psychotherapy, (2) to show how *countertransference* slants the nature of confrontation, (3) to emphasize anew the significance of the emotional *context* in which the encounter between doctor and patient takes place, and (4) to underscore the significance of the doctor as an *instrument of assessment*.

In what follows, I use common terms like *therapy*, *doctor*, and *patient* simply because I am accustomed to the medical model and synonyms are too cumbersome. Nevertheless, I am persuaded that medical models and their idioms do not adequately encompass that process called psychotherapy. People consult psychiatrists because of personal vulnerability, not because of mental illness. Insofar as people can be influenced by psychological means, undertaken with an informed consent, we can scarcely confine ourselves to the special world of couch and chair. The analytic viewpoint, however, is typical of one such strategic pursuit of the way people think and feel about key life events.

CONFRONTATION

The language of confrontation is active or passive; the object may be the patient or the doctor; confrontation can be directed toward something else, or the doctor can be confronted.

The term, confrontation, has become a cliché in our times. In modern parlance, it has come to mean the very opposite of true communication; it signifies a moment of high antagonism when we face our adversary. This is, of course, not what I mean here. In psychotherapy, the purpose of confrontation is very simple: to separate what a man is from what he seems to be, states himself to be, or would have us believe he is.

We are not concerned with how this man got the way he is nor with theories about how he might have become something else. We do not really know how people get to be the way they are. The doctrinal determinism that analysts sometimes espouse covers our soft data and manifest indeterminism. Fortunately, etiology is not the purpose of therapy. Were psychological topics wholly deterministic, we would not be so concerned about confrontation. Instead, we would merely rationalize our hopelessness and forget about the creative potential residing in the future, sometimes in the form of surprises, good or bad, that reality holds in store.

Although there may be much communication between two people, there is not true confrontation without a strategic effort to unmask denial. This does not imply that confrontation crudely and relentlessly attacks a point of protection. But it does mean that verbally or non-verbally, directly or indirectly the target of confrontation is a point of protected vulnerability. There is a difference among the content, or "what," of confrontation, the implementation, or "how," and the timing, or "when." It is equally important to know who confronts whom, as well as his purpose in doing so.

If my definition of confrontation as the "tactics of undenial" seems too simple, it is because confrontation can be implemented in various ways and can have subsidiary purposes as well. We can elicit or impart information that seems quite impersonal and objective; yet, in doing so, the patient is confronted with something he might have taken great pains to deny. For example, to ask certain women how old they are may be tactless; but, in a suitable context, the correct answer may undercut a source of denial and self-deception. Confrontation can evoke emotion or can direct behavior—subsidiary purposes that in themselves may not be recognized as part of undenial. Doctors are not opposed to offering comfort and support, nor does good medicine necessarily taste bitter. But the opposite of true confrontation is a strategy for comforting, assuaging, and reassuring. Perforce, confrontation is an effort to penetrate a screen of denial, aversion, or deception.

In general, communication in psychotherapy is a report of things not directly observed or presented in evidence. These may be events that happened to the patient or ideas pertinent to the patient that the therapist communicates. Confrontation, however, has a *direction* that most forms of communication do not have. In most cases, the direction is toward significant vulnerability and heightened defensiveness.

General problems of when to confront and the reasons for confronting cannot be dealt with categorically. The clinical condition known as narcissism may be used here as an expedient example.

Narcissism is necessary for a healthy self-regard, but the "clinical condition" may create more problems than it solves for certain patients. In these instances, someone may be sheltered by his narcissism, but at the cost of constant vigilance against assaults on self-regard. He may be protected in his everyday transactions, but in psychotherapy be extremely sensitive to confrontations. He may fluctuate between overweening arrogance, braggadocio, or self-righteousness and unnecessary self-abasement, self-pity, and sense of shame. During psychotherapy, he protects himself againt anticipated punishment and criticism by cultivating the therapist's good will and approval. When this seems unrealistic, he may seize the initiative and blame himself before the therapist does. Or he may accompany his statements with benign disparagement, as if to neutralize criticism in advance and to extract some reassuring word from the doctor.

It is futile to reassure such patients about the doctor's forebearance and understanding. Life-long obeisance to (and resentment of) higher authority, combined with chronic conviction of being unworthy (and unjustly treated), is not relieved by being told how wise, unprejudiced, and compassionate the judge happens to be. Refusal to pass judgment is not a method for assuaging guilt. Although the therapeutic task is very difficult, unwarranted guilt can be relieved only by switching standards of judgment and by reversing the nature of the unspoken guilt. Punishment has at best only a temporary effect and provides no additional understanding and protection.

Superfluous guilt and . arbitrary abasement usually correspond to some "psychic crime" or "surplus reality." But, reasonable as this theory is, the precise offense, real or fantasied, seldom can be identified and, by suitable tactics, dispensed with once and for all. Such "crimes" as can be identified are not very horrendous; and because the therapist has not been injured, he cannot forgive, even if it were in his power and interest to do so.

Many male patients believe that it is unmanly to admit fear or to acknowledge dependency or to yearn for unconditional love, especially when dealing with a male therapist. It is part of the narcissistic image and system of defenses to call upon certain stereotyped relationships and styles of communication. That illness is a part of being alive, not a moral judgment, and that a sense of unnatural pride may conceal a precarious trust are utterly unacceptable to people with the "clinical condition" of narcissism. As a result, such patients accumulate an endless list of accusations and reasons for counteraccusations: "You are angry at me for being late, for being early, for smiling, for being glum, for being lazy, for being ambitious, for being inhibited, for acting out. . . ." For the purposes of discussion, these antithetical *mea culpa* are paradoxical efforts to maintain a high level of self-respect and to deny an unnaturally high demand upon the therapist.

No one denies in a vacuum. Denial is part of a social process that relieves a potential threat by replacing it with a more acceptable version of reality. In psychotherapy, the denial is intended to bring about an acceptable relationship with the doctor, on whom the patient depends. In highly narcissistic patients, dependency is at once a demand and a threat, not very far removed from a fear of submission and of being victimized.

Narcissistic patients are difficult primarily because their demands constitute a *confrontation* for the doctor. He is confronted with a persistent, intractable challenge to his competence, compassion, objectivity, moral impeccability, and professional calm.

If there is any valid general statement about when to confront, it is probably when the doctor feels confronted and, simultaneously, calls upon his patient to relinquish his denial, thereby reestablishing or solidifying their relationship. In the example of a narcissistic patient, the doctor confronts the patient with his attitudes toward the therapy. He does not challenge the validity of self-rebuke; instead, he points out the patient's seeming anger because the doctor is invulnerable in the patient's eyes, in addition to the patient's wish for an unconditional, responsive expression of love. Anything that falls short of this unconditional vote of confidence is construed as punishment or deception. When anger has been excluded or denied, the result is an inappropriate and ambivalent idealization; the therapist has become the arbiter of guilt and the responsible source of unconditional love.

With this brief and somewhat inconclusive example, I emphasize that the target of confrontation in psychotherapy is not the predominant symptom, but is whatever seems to be a *sign* of protected vulnerability. Guilt and shame, and self-rebuke alternating with arrogance are symptoms; the sign is conviction of being treated harshly. Signs are usually interpreted as "defenses," which, in this case, are projection and rationalization.

In contrast to the courtroom where a crime is in evidence but the sentence has not been pronounced, the patient who suffers from the "clinical condition of narcissism" comes in with the sentence but not the explicit crime. He probes for approval and disapproval with differential protests and confessions. In this way, he hopes to discover what the doctor considers deplorable or praiseworthy. It is only when the patient acquires a modicum of trust that confrontation begins to take effect. Without trust, confrontations are as futile as a telephone that rings when there is no one to answer.

It is quite easy for a doctor to ask patients for trust. Most therapists assume that they are always trustworthy. Hence, because guilt and shame are opposites of trust and confidence, the doctor who is not spontaneously trusted is confronted with an attack upon his own self-regard; and many feel guilt and shame. When this occurs, it is time for the doctor to examine and assess his own "clinical condition" so that he can at least trust the patient who does not immediately trust him.

The essential ingredient in trusting is that the therapist cares. He can be wrong, but he cannot be indifferent or disrepectful. When Alexander (1950) spoke sharply and correctively to the disagreeable young man, he might have antagonized the patient without producing the constructive changes he reported. But nothing succeeds like success, and the case would not have been reported if the confrontation had failed. Even so, I cannot believe that this was a one-shot confrontation and that it came from the blue, like one of Jove's thunderbolts. Testimonials always smack of the miraculous; i.e., a wonder of nature that follows a bold intervention and yet by its very spontaneity seemingly contradicts laws of nature. Testimonials may come from grateful patients and proud therapists, and both may be equally dubious. In Alexander's reported case, we do not know about the underlying stratum of trust that provided a fertile matrix for the confrontation. We are told only of the mistrust.

Confrontations should be studied apart from their therapeutic effect. Too much emphasis upon cure or transformation of character leads to a disparagement of how and when we confront as we do. Our discussion would be shortsighted, indeed, were we to overlook the therapist's investment in being right or in reporting successes. While there are comparatively few doctors who claim medicine-show cures, many psychotherapists tend to explain away their refractory cases by translating their patients' characters into confrontations that blame the patients for being as they are.

Part of the overemphasis upon "treatment" comes from a skewed version of the transaction between doctor and patient. Confrontation, as has already been pointed out, is but one aspect of communication; it is not necessarily tied to a medical model of disease, cure, and causality. Indeed, it makes more sense to regard "treatment" as a special form of confrontation, within the broad scheme of communication tactics (Watzlawick, Beavin, and Jackson, 1967). Unidirectional treatment is based upon an image of a doctor imparting something to a patient. Confrontation, however, is a reciprocal process in which the doctor is called upon to correct his own interventions.

Even though some people willingly surrender their autonomy, trust does not flourish when one person is overpowered by another. We cannot agree to trust wholeheartedly; we can agree only to a common field of acceptance, with each person accepting the significant participation of the other. It is around this axis that confrontations operate, and the process of revelation and undenial begins.

Confrontations deal primarily with reality, not with what is true. As a result, we can effectively confront with an incorrect assessment! What is more important is the immediate context of experience that is shared. It is this that enables the doctor to recognize that denial, reaction formation, and negation are effective vehicles of self-revelation. After all, scientific reliability is based upon a common agreement, and validity consists of a search for justification of our beliefs.

COUNTERTRANSFERENCE

When we try to expose an area of denial, to challenge a

belief, or to influence the direction of behavior, we confront. But what determines how we influence the direction, selection, and assessment of what we do? Even though we examine ourselves for bias, preconception, value judgments, and our own existential position within a common field of reality, it is inevitable that correction is not always possible and that our private reality shapes, colors, and gives substance to our perceptions, performance, and pronouncements within psychotherapy.

Transference is recognized to be a regular part of any therapeutic encounter. Therapists are much more reluctant to talk about countertransference. However, as with patients, doctors often reveal themselves through their efforts to deny and to preserve detachment. The graven image of an impersonal therapist is often a mask covering a fear of causing harm or of disclosing the effect of the patient's confrontations.

Transference may be defined as a claim that a patient makes upon the reality of his doctor. Although transference is, theoretically, not identical with what is called "transference neurosis," the transference that we usually pay attention to is the one in which the claim is thought to be unjustified but the patient insists that the doctor cooperate by making his own reality available. Consequently, doctors view this aspect of transference as pathological. When their own counterresponses are revealed, however, it is seldom thought to be constructive, but only to be pathological. The image of the unresponsive therapist is so closely treasured that a legitimate response is almost unthinkable. Countertransference, therefore, is often thought to be a kind of secular sin.

I do not deny that some forms of transference and countertransference are "pathological," but only because the claims and counterclaims obstruct the other person's sense of separateness and right to freedom. Unless the psychobiological medium that we call therapy is merely intended to consolidate illusions, countertransference should be recognized for what it is—the *directional determinant of confrontation.*

Confrontation is a strategy in which the aim is to separate the reality of one person from his neurotic expectations of himself and others. Transference and counter-transference tend to become mirrored images of each other. If neither is assessed accurately, one is confused with the other. Both may take over therapy, so that mutual expectations and reality claims become too enormous. These expectations and claims, we must add, may produce excessive frustration or undue gratification. But so much has been written about transference that I can confidently leave it aside and offer a more systematic, albeit brief, account of countertransference.

The attitudes that convey countertransference arise from the same internal sources that contribute to other kinds of attitude, feeling, disposition, and behavior. These sources are conveniently called *primary, secondary,* and *tertiary processes.* Primary processes refer to that collection of undifferentiated appetites and aversions, wishes and fears, attractions and repulsions that preempt our attention, draw us onward, or push us away from various kinds of relationships. Primary processes lend *direction* to what we do, or think, or say. Secondary processes designate the habitual, preferential pathways that enable us to carry out or to refrain from unqualified participation in various relationships. These pathways lend style and shape to our idiosyncrasies; they standardize our responses and limit our options. Secondary processes provide the means of *selection* for perceptions and performances.

The third source of countertransference attitudes is seldom made explicit. Tertiary processes are the values, standards, directives, prohibitions, and imperatives that determine how and when we pass judgment upon what is good or bad, right or wrong, true or false, successful or unsuccessful. Collectively, tertiary processes provide the *assessment* of whether or not what we do is worth doing.

I have not resorted to more conventional terminology, such as id, ego, and superego, nor made use of reifications, such as ego functions, coping mechanisms, and defensive formations. I have omitted them not only because these terms suggest that we know more than we do but also because I am primarily concerned with the field of communication and the forces of countertransference. Countertransference, like transference, is a truncated form of action, transmogrified into speech. Its thrust is determined by memories, expectations, perceptions, fantasies, experiences, and whatever other elements of satisfactory, unfulfilled, and surplus realities can flow into the crucible of what we do. In the case of countertransference, what we do, or say, is a claim upon that portion of another person's life that impinges upon our own.

The substance of countertransference shapes itself according to the field of interaction, real and potential. Conversely, countertransference may mold the field itself, enabling observers to infer kinds of countertransference and transference that are different from the types of interaction that prevail. Let me illustrate with brief descriptions of *complementary, antagonistic, parallel,* and *tangential countertransference.*

Complementary countertransference may occur when the special strengths of the therapist seem designed to fit the problems of the patient. For example, certain tempestuous, impulsive patients are helped by a somewhat steadfast, organized doctor who understands and identifies the critical situations that trouble them, although he is not influenced by these forces. Such a doctor may be a rock of dependability for moody, erratic patients. Analogously, certain rigid, conscience-ridden patients may derive much benefit from being treated by a colorful, open, and emotional doctor who does not hesitate to express his face judgments without endlessly debating and weighing alternatives.

Complementary countertransference may, therefore, fulfill the doctor's personality requirements and simultaneously enhance the background of mutual trust that therapy requires. It does not always work out well, however. For example, it is not unusual to find a patient who reports that he has been in psychotherapy or analysis for well over ten years. Typically, the interaction starts in college after the patient undergoes a depression, disappointment, failure, or loss of some key relationship. With the doctor's help, he is able to continue in school, graduate, and, sometimes, even marry, when the doctor indicates that this step is warranted. Then, for some reason, therapy is interrupted, often when circumstances require a move to another city. The patient wants to resume therapy even before he is settled in the new community, and the first doctor often selects his successor. Nature abhors a vacuum, and some professional patients abhor life without a therapeutic relationship. While we can call this "unresolved transference," what about "unresolved countertransference"? The next therapist finds that the patient has certain "unresolved" expectations that only his first doctor can fulfill. Because no two relationships are quite identical and no two countertransferences are the same, the patient may begin to treat himself, according to his latent identifications with the former therapist. The second doctor is tacitly excluded; the patient becomes his first doctor's double, or stand-in.

Antagonistic countertransference is easy to recognize when a therapist is openly critical, as a result of antagonism or exasperation. But there are less conspicuous forms of antagonism that even the therapist fails to detect. The therapist may be disrespectful, self-righteous, belittling, or indifferent to the patient or to the patient's reigning standards, way of life, or scale of success. Every confrontation transmits a reproach or devaluation. In response, the patient is apt to become overly submissive and so quietly resentful that one day he walks out. There are many moral dilemmas in psychiatry, and therapists are far from paragons. Antagonisms are to be expected, because, after all, we care only about things we care about, and some people are simply incompatible. Moreover, false forebearance, gritting one's teeth, and intractable boredom usually produce a hopeless standoff, seldom a significant confrontation.

As a rule, antagonistic countertransference can be better understood, even if resolution is not always possible. In the first place, anger, jealousy, and so forth need not doom therapy, but instead can be an entering wedge for a more complete clarification of the interaction as a whole. We do not send angry patients away, why are there not similar options for therapists? In the second place, the insidious quality of antagonistic countertransference shows up in the direction and selection of confrontations. Should an observant therapist start to question himself, he could well begin with the state of trust between himself and his patient and then begin to identify the ways in which his patient has implicitly confronted him. If antagonism can be honestly confronted, the countertransference may be converted into a more productive, adversary approach, one that challenges shibboleths but does not require argumentation. To challenge without rancor may be a fresh approach, but the therapist should be prepared for fresh and explicit counterchallenges.

Parallel countertransference refers to a situation in which therapist and patient share the same problem, almost to the same degree. Could I look at the world through your eyes, and were you to see things as I must do, we might exchange viewpoints; and then never again would I see the world in the same way, nor would you be the same person you were before.

What if doctor and patient, by having the same problem, can look at each other only through mutually blinded eyes? It is wholly possible, even common, that two human beings share a mutual failing, point of vulnerability, or conflict. Few therapists could work effectively, or ineffectively, for that matter, without a strong sense of empathy. However, parallel countertransference is most difficult when the two participants seem to share common defenses and denials.

Then there is scarcely any true confrontation, other than gentle conversation that excuses and supports their mutual well-being.

We can sometimes find therapists who identify with a repudiated aspect of their patient and, as a result, become antagonistic toward the defensive operations that the patient uses. This is probably not an instance of parallel counter-transference, because it is feasible that identification with someone else's ambivalent or repudiated attitudes might create rather interesting confrontations!

Parallels between doctor and patient are, understandably, very difficult to detect. Mutual denials never cancel each other out. Consequently, characteristic examples of parallel countertransference are very elusive. Let me cite only one example. When doctor and patient are both people who are accustomed to doing things for themselves and by themselves, an impasse of extremes may ensue. Either the doctor restrains himself unnaturally from offering confrontations, lest he unduly influence the patient, or he resents efforts of the patient to confront him with his inactivity. Needless to say, both alternatives may coexist. In response, the patient who prefers to do things his own way finds that his doctor objects when he makes mistakes, as if he should know better, and that the doctor's confrontations tend to deflate and devaluate.

Tangential countertransference may be suspected when everything that the doctor says or understands seems grossly inept, irrelevant, peripheral, or out of focus. There is no "meeting of minds." Mutual expectations and available attitudes offer too few points of contact for a genuine exchange and confrontation, even though therapy may continue. Tangential countertransference often occurs when doctor and patient come from dissimilar subcultures and backgrounds. Is it possible, for example, for a white, middle-class therapist to understand the demands, disappointments, and demoralization that a black youth encounters while growing up in a ghetto? Conversely, does the therapist's awareness of his alien attitude and limited experience lead him to over-emphasize sociological deprivations and to overlook highly personal issues that he could recognize, trust, and offer confrontations about?

It is sometimes easier to put oneself in the place of a psychotic than to understand a person from another culture or country. Psychiatric training has, at least, equipped us to find our way around and to ask directions in the realm of psychosis. In another culture, we may know similar words, but with dissimilar contexts and meanings. As a result, the verbal instruments of confrontation are not available; countertransference can make few claims upon the other one, unless it is that we bid him to make use of trust, without confrontations.

These comments may suggest that countertransferences always mean trouble and that confrontations based upon countertransference are bound to be egregious distortions. Not so. Because there are so many possible varieties of countertransference, confrontations may be productive or nonproductive in degrees, depending upon how readily and intelligently the therapist can correct his own responses. Moreover, countertransference is simply one indication of how the therapist looks at the here-and-now. His confrontations bear witness to a process of mutual recognition. Stereotyped countertransference means a stereotyped pattern of confrontation, and we all know what this means. Flexible and responsive therapists are not strangers to discordance, diffuseness, and uncertainty and, we hope, are not unfamiliar with concordance and a sense of closure in the course of confrontation.

CONTEXT

The therapeutic encounter is primarily contemporaneous, but it stretches beyond the moment, beyond hypothesis and technique, and beyond mere facts. Its open-endedness should not be confused with haphazardness. The contemporaneous is not necessarily extemperaneous. A skilled interviewer is a practiced professional, and a skillful professional has a variety of options when dealing with emerging situations.

Unfortunately, whenever we talk about context, communication, relationships, meanings, defenses, and so forth, our efforts sterilize the immediacy of the here-and-now, contemporaneous event. The flow, quality, and intensity of how one person defines himself with respect to another can seldom be characterized. Even the simplest transaction requires so much explanation, that, like a joke, its impact is destroyed. Nevertheless, it is the context that provides the meaning and the motivation for whatever happens. How we happen to say what we do when we do cannot be understood apart from the context in which it occurs.

Any scene acquires its meaning by relating it to the drama as a whole. Situations cannot be isolated from an implicit totality, however vaguely that whole is defined. And it is not altogether paradoxical to recognize that the totality cannot be grasped until we know something about individual moments.

It would not do for me to discuss the philosophy of contextualism at this point. Whitehead (1933), Mead (1956), Pepper (1948), Polanyi (1964), Moreno (1953), and Korzybski (1950) are only a few illustrious people who have enlightened us about this viewpoint. As if to illustrate the thesis, each man approached the subject in his own way, according to a still larger context and sphere of operations. Definitions are scarcely ever relevant or revealing, but let me characterize what I mean by context: it is a concatenation of whatever is contemporaneous to a specific instant. It is not strictly circumscribed by time, because other times and places can be brought to a confluence of the moment. Thus, a casual conversation may exemplify a context; a conference or a hospital record may be considered a context, and so can a fleeting memory or image that thrusts itself upon consciousness. Contexts are *ideographic instances*.

No therapist can be a complete outsider in his contacts

with patients, just as there is no contact between people without some version of communication. The context defines his participation in psychotherapy as both an *encounter* and an *evaluation*. He brings himself into the situation and is an instrument of assessment. In the previous section, I described different ways in which countertransference influences the encounter. The therapist, I urged, should be able to correct his private distortions. When he evaluates and assesses the therapeutic context and its content, he must also be able to select significant dimensions in the transaction. In brief, given an encounter, he looks for an available and significant interface with which he can make contact.

No therapist can or should be wholly objective unless he is sure that his capacity for denial and self-deception is limitless. There is always some self-correction and self-validation at work, so we can be objective only insofar as we recognize our habitual viewpoints and perseverations.

It is customary for psychiatrists to assume a position of solemn, antiseptic scientism when talking to their colleagues or writing for publication. In actuality, however, we do not painstakingly collect data and patiently wait for validating evidence for our hypotheses. For the most part, our work runs far ahead of our theories; the image of a careful laboratory experiment is most inappropriate. In the immediacy of the encounter, we deal with what seems real and relevant at the time, and we confront according to the same criteria. Naturally, we look for thematic realities that persist. But primarily we sense the intentionality and involvement (*i.e.*, direction) that characterize the context (*i.e.*, selection), and bind it together according to an inner validity (*i.e.*, assessment). I encounter, I evaluate, and so, too, does the other person.

The simultaneous assessment and evaluation inherent in the psychotherapeutic occasion discourage free-wheeling improvisation. Moreover, our purpose in confrontation is always to recognize and respect mutual fields of reality. Whatever we do, it is to undeny, to dissipate deception, and ultimately to increase the range of options that any person has for contending with what imposes unnecessary control over him. We do not merely think or talk. Descartes's familiar formula, "I think, therefore I am," is a very specialized viewpoint. We could not take psychodynamics very seriously if we did not believe that human interaction is directional, interrelated, and purposeful. The formula ought to be, "I am, therefore I think, act, feel, falter, encounter, assess, and do a great many other things, many of which I don't understand at all."

How can we draw a line around our encounters and understand the special context more effectively? Not too long ago, the psychotherapist wrote notes during sessions. This was ostensibly because he wanted a jog for his memory, but often enough it was because he wanted a barrier. Fortunately, this situation and the psychotherapist who exemplified it are almost extinct. He wanted to emulate a tape recorder and, of course, he failed. And if, today, a psychotherapist expects to emulate a computer, he will also fail. What he eliminates (and what is more critical than his fallible memory?) is a sense of personal involvement and intentionality that grasps the totality while struggling to assess details. None of us is exempt from our shortcomings, distortions, narcissistic disavowals, and denials. I have urged you to heed the directional component of countertransference, because our confrontations depend upon self-correction as well as upon our alertness in assessing the context as a whole and the individuality of the other person (Wolstein, 1959). With these precautions, I present the following guidelines as a summary:

1. Confrontation draws upon empathy, but empathy does not mean that we share an identity or an ideology.
2. Countertransference distortions are likely when we find ourselves angry, disappointed, exasperated, gratified, especially frustrated, jealous, or in some other way imposing our individual imperatives upon the confrontations.
3. Confrontations can be contaminated by fantasies of

being the magic healer, rescuer, shaman, sage, or parent, because this may not be the level of need and communication on which the other person is operating.

4. Confrontation consists of mutually self-corrective activities. It is not intended to be a directive or a prohibition. We seek forebearance, not compliance, firmness, not coercion. We cannot offer options, we can only help someone to use the options he has.

5. Efforts to understand too much are suspicious indications of countertransference ambition. We cannot respond to every demand and confront along a vast panorama. Denial cannot be eliminated completely, because strategic denial may be a requirement of living itself.

6. A tendency to overemphasize technique or, conversely, to discourage thoughtful reflection as "cerebral" are signs of countertransference distortions of the field.

7. Trust means only that we have a common field of acceptance. Although it is feasible to have a mutual alliance at the outset, trust is always conditional. The term *trust* is often a shibboleth in psychotherapy, but it can become a euphemism that conceals an impasse.

8. Words are not magic, nor must confrontations be followed by signs of conspicuous change. Confrontations are only special vehicles of communication that seek an opening at a point of contact with protected vulnerability.

9. On the whole, confrontations are only statements about the other person's existence, not hypotheses about his status as a scientific object. We respond to his separate reality and cannot, therefore, be too punctilious about the longitudinal truth of what we say.

10. We can generalize; we can be precise. But it is essential that we also be contemporaneous.

Bibliography

Alexander, F. (1950) Analysis of the therapeutic factors in psychoanalytic treatment. In *The Scope of Psychoanalysis*. New York: Basic Books, Inc., 1961, pp. 261–275.

Korzybski, A. (1950), *Manhood of Humanity*, Second Edition. Lakeville, Connecticut: International Non-Aristotelian Library Publishing Co., Institute of General Semantics.

Mead, G. H. (1956), *The Social Psychology of George Herbert Mead*, ed. A. Strauss. Chicago: University of Chicago Press.

Moreno, J. (1953), *Who Shall Survive? Foundation of Sociometry, Group Psychotherapy and Sociodrama*. Beacon, New York: Beacon House, Inc.

Pepper, S. (1948), *World Hypothesis: A Study in Evidence*. Berkeley and Los Angeles: University of California Press.

Polanyi, M. (1964), *Personal Knowledge: Towards a Post-Critical Philosophy*. Harper Torchbooks. New York and Evanston: Harper & Row.

Watzlawick, P., Beavin, J., and Jackson, D. (1967), *Pragmatics of Human Communication: A Study of Interactional Patterns, Pathologies, and Paradoxes*. New York: W. W. Norton & Co., Inc.

Whitehead, A. (1933), *Adventures of Ideas*. New York: The Macmillan Co.

Wolstein, B. (1959), *Counter-Transference*. New York, London: Grune & Stratton.

The Uses of

Confrontation

in the

Psychotherapy

of

Borderline Patients

DAN H. BUIE, JR., M.D. AND
GERALD ADLER, M.D.

$\mathbb{E}$xperience convinces us that confrontation is useful in treating all borderline patients. For certain ones, it is essential to their progress. But borderline patients are more vulnerable than neurotic patients to misuse of confrontation. Misuse can arise from faulty clinical understanding as well as the therapist's transference and countertransference problems.

DEFINITION OF CONFRONTATION

No single definition is widely accepted, and some disagreements on the subject are the result of covert differences in the way it is technically defined. Some problems also arise out of confusing the technical meaning of confrontation with some of the meanings given in standard dictionaries. "To stand facing . . . in challenge, defiance, opposition" is one such meaning (Webster's New World Dictionary, 1960). This confusion, also covert, leads to implications that by confronting, the therapist necessarily endangers his constructive working alliance with his patient. Another source of confusion arises from teaching and writing about confrontation through the use of clinical examples. These examples are complex. The specific confrontation is usually artfully integrated with other manuevers, such as clarification or interpretation; the affects and personal style of the therapist are also expressed. Separating out that which constitutes the confrontation can be quite difficult, and discussions about it can imperceptibly shade and shift into the pros and cons of the other elements, any of which may come to be mistaken for facets of confrontation.

In response to these problems we have attempted to work out a definition. We approach it through the teachings and writings of Semrad (1954, 1968, 1969),[1] Murray (1964, Chapter Three), and E. Bibring (1954). Semrad's work concerns psychotic and borderline patients. He emphasizes their reliance on certain defenses—denial, projection, and distortion—that he terms "the avoidance devices." These defenses operate to keep conscious and preconscious experience out of awareness. As such, they are to be differentiated from other defenses, such as repression, which serve to keep experiences not only out of awareness but also unconscious. To help patients become aware of avoided painful feelings, impulses, and experiences, Semrad uses a combination of support and pressure. The support makes distress more bearable, thus lessening the need for avoidance. The pressure against avoidance is then applied directly and actively, usually by a series of questions along with various counter-moves in response to the patient's evasions.

Murray writes about work with borderline and neurotic patients who exhibit considerable regression to the pregenital level. An infantile, narcissistic entitlement to life on their terms is often a major force behind resistance of these patients to clarifications, interpretations, and acceptance of the real world. Even after clarifications and interpretations have been thoroughly established, this kind of patient tries to maintain his pleasurable pregenital world by avoiding

---

[1] Also *cf.* E. J. Khantzian, J. S. Dalsimer, and E. V. Semrad (1969).

acknowledgment of what he now consciously knows. In the setting of support, Murray, like Semrad, applies pressure in various forms (surprise, humor, forceful manner, etc.) against these avoidances. Murray refers to this technique as confrontation. It seems to us appropriate to apply the same term to Semrad's technique.

In his classical paper, Bibring listed five groups of basic techniques used in all psychotherapies. His categorization continues to be very useful, but it was derived primarily from work with neurotic patients. As such, he described a technique, interpretation, for working with those defenses that keep material unconscious. But no method was included for working with defenses that simply prevent awareness of material that is already available in consciousness; i.e., is preconscious or conscious.[2] Because avoidance devices are used so prominently by psychotic, borderline, and pregenitally regressed neurotic patients and because confrontation, as employed by Semrad and Murray, is specifically designed to deal with these defenses, we believe that confrontation should be added to Bibring's categories of techniques.

Accordingly, we would define confrontation as follows: a technique designed to gain a patient's attention to inner experiences or perceptions of outer reality of which he is conscious or is about to be made conscious. Its specific purpose is to counter resistances to recognizing what is in fact available to awareness or about to be made available through clarification or interpretation. The purpose is not to induce or force change in the patient's attitudes, decisions, or conduct.[3]

---

[2] One of Bibring's techniques, clarification, does deal with material that is preconscious or conscious. He described it as a method for bringing into awareness or sharpening awareness of behavior patterns. However, he specified that *no resistance is encountered to acknowledging that which is clarified*. The patient accepts it readily.

[3] This definition resembles Myerson's (Chapter One); i.e., confrontation involves the use of force. It is, in fact, built upon it. The difference lies in being more explicit about the purposes for which the force is and is not to be employed.

Confrontation can be used in combination with other of the basic techniques. For example, when a patient can be expected to mobilize denial against a clarification that he otherwise is able to grasp, the therapist may combine the clarification with a confrontation. Instead of delivering the clarification as a simple statement, the therapist will try to capture the patient's attention at the same time, perhaps by using a loud voice, an explicative, or an unusual phrase.

This definition of confrontation involves differentiating it especially from two of the techniques listed by Bibring, suggestion and manipulation. Some clinical vignettes offered as examples of confrontation are in fact accurately described by Bibring's accounts of these two techniques. They amount to forcefully executed suggestion or manipulations. Limit-setting is one such maneuver. Often it is presented as a confrontation when it is well subsumed under the category of manipulation.

DESCRIPTION OF CONFRONTATION

There are, of course, very many methods used by patients for avoiding awareness of that which is consciously available. Suppression, denial, projection, and distortion are the ones classically described. Diversion through activity, superficial acknowledgment followed by changing the subject, rationalizing, and intellectualizing are a few more of the ways to avoid. Any complete discussion of the topic of avoidance would carry us beyond the scope of this paper. Anna Freud (1936), Jacobson (1957), G. Bibring et. al., (1961), Lewin (1950), Vaillant (1971), and Semrad (1968, 1969) are among the authors contributing to our understanding.

We should, however, make a few more comments describing the technique of confrontation. Occasionally the verbal content of a confrontation is itself sufficient to claim the patient's attention. More frequently the manner of delivery is the effective agent. Surprise, humor, and unusual choice of words, or an emphatic delivery might capture the patient's awareness. Or the therapist might choose to use a show of personal feelings, such as obvious person-to-person caring, sadness, frustration, or anger. Essentially, any departure from the usual tone or format can be used in the service of confrontation.

A caveat for the therapist has been issued by Murray (Chapter Three) and Myerson (Chapter One). It is specific for confrontations that involve the therapist's showing his feelings: his feelings must always in fact be experienced by the therapist as being in the patient's behalf. This is especially true of anger. Otherwise the therapist violates his part of the working alliance. Such violation constitutes a narcissistically based power play in the form of antitherapeutic suggestion or manipulation.

QUALITIES OF BORDERLINE PATIENTS

In order to describe the use of confrontation with borderline patients, we should specify more exactly the characteristics of these patients. Chase (1966), Little (1960), Kernberg (1966, 1967, 1968), Grinker, et al. (1968), Zetzel (1971), and Balint (1968) are among the authors and teachers who have clarified the qualities that make up the borderline aspect of a patient's personality. Briefly, these qualities are fear of abandonment, belief that closeness means destroying and being destroyed, self-esteem precariously oscillating between omnipotence and worthlessness, a concrete and severe superego, inadequate reality testing, and defenses that are brittle and deficient, as well as higher level neurotic structures that can crumble under stress. Although borderline patients have received much attention in the literature, we would like to comment in some detail on certain of their attributes in preparation for our discussion of confrontation.

The borderline patient's psychopathology is founded on one fundamental belief: that he is, or will be, abandoned. He believes it because internalization of basic mother-infant caring is incomplete. His fundamental feeling is terror of utter aloneness, a condition that feels like annihilation. Concomitant and derivative experiences are emptiness, hunger, and being cold, within and without.

Abandonment by the person needed to sustain life— mother or her surrogate—is not simply terrifying; it is enraging. His rage may be simply destructive, but more often it is experienced together with desperate efforts to obtain the needed person permanently. All this occurs in the mode of the infant at the oral level. He urgently, savagely, wants to kill that person, eat him, be eaten by him, or gain skin to skin contact to the extreme of merging through bodily absorption or through being absorbed. This oral raging acquisitiveness, mobilized in response to abandonment, brings in its wake further difficulties. Destroying his needed object mobilizes primitive guilt; it also threatens him again with helpless aloneness. He may attempt to save the object from his destructive urges by withdrawal. But that, too, threatens intolerable aloneness. Projection can be called upon to deal with his rage. But projecting it onto his object now makes the object a dreaded source of danger; self-protection is once again sought by distancing, and by with-drawal—again the state of aloneness is faced.

The borderline patient is self-centered and appears to feel entitled to life on his terms, whatever they may be. This orientation can be manifest to an extreme. Murray (1964, Chapter Three) has described narcissistic entitlement in excellent detail. It represents essentially an arrest in development with little modification of the infant's or child's feeling that he is entitled to have his way. Murray ascribes this arrest to two influences: one is overgratification, such that the child believes he has been promised that he will always be granted his wishes by the world; the other is deprivation, on the basis of which he insists the world owes him reparations in the form of granting indulgence of all his wishes. Narcissistic entitlement forms part of the borderline's self-image. He is a special person with special rights to have his way. Like the normal infant, severe frustration of his narcissistic entitlement shatters his self-esteem, and he feels himself to be powerless and unloved.

The borderline patient, then, fluctuates in his self-image and self-esteem between extremes of overvaluation and devaluation. We must add that his fall in self-esteem is accompanied by other reactions. The frustration that precipitates it is also experienced as an outrageous all-or-none deprivation. He may react by trying to force whatever he wants from his object. Or he may reject his object and, in doing so, threaten himself with aloneness and becoming all the more frightened.

We have listed these reactions to frustration of narcissistic entitlement because we would like to differentiate narcissistic entitlement from another phenomenon that on the surface appears to be identical but that actually arises from a different source and involves different stakes. We would call this other phenomenon *entitlement to survive.* When an infant's mother is not in touch with him, is emotionally unresponsive, or is destructive, his feeling state is one of aloneness. His inner world is empty. This state is experienced as a threat to his survival, and survival (for all but the most seriously damaged infants), is felt to be his entitlement. Threats to this entitlement are terrifying and vastly enraging. We have already, without using the term entitlement, described this experience as central to the borderline patient's illness. We have outlined his reaction of devouring rage as he attempts to regain his object, and we have enumerated the reasons he must take flight from the object.

Now we can compare the patient's response to challenges to narcissistic entitlement with his response to challenges to entitlement to survive. On the surface they appear similar or identical—both involve rage, grasping what they feel they deserve, rejecting the object, followed by aloneness and fear. Psychodynamically, they are very different. One is related to wish-fulfillment, the other to the supplying of a relationship necessary for survival. More succinctly, one is a wish, the other a need. One involves rejecting the object out of anger; the other involves rejecting in order to preserve life; *i.e.*, to avoid destroying and being destroyed. One involves fear of being powerless but still somebody, the other presents threat of extinction.

Threats to entitlement to survive exert a particular influence on self-image and self-esteem. The original pathogenic threats involved the patient's having been treated as if he were without meaningful existence and worthless or nothing. He experienced this with his primary objects, chiefly his mother. In part because of defensive efforts that reinvolved him in the same experiences, subsequent adult life reinforced this self-image. As a result, the self-esteem of a borderline patient is precarious. From whatever higher levels of development he has achieved, he has attained some degree of self-esteem; however, insofar as he is borderline, he has none.

For neurotic patients with pregenital fixations, the problem with self-esteem primarily relates to narcissistic entitlement. For borderline patients, narcissistic entitlement is the healthier level of their self-image and self-esteem. It may at least provide them with an overlay of megalomania. Without it, they face a highly painful belief that they are devoid of significance. Under these circumstances they find comparing themselves with others, especially a valued therapist, to be a devastating humiliation.

We have already described two of the borderline's methods of defense. One is projection of his oral destructiveness. By projecting, he achieves only the partial relief offered by externalizing; he still feels in danger, but now from without rather than from within. Related is projective identification that includes projection plus the need to control the object in order to avoid the projected danger (Kernberg, 1967). The other defense is mobilization of rage in the service of defending against expected abandonment or oral attack. This defense is very primitive, derived more from the id than from the ego. As such it constitutes an impulse that is nearly as frightening to the patient as the threats against which it defends.

Kernberg (1967) has elucidated the borderline patient's use of splitting his internal objects in an effort to deal with intense ambivalence. These patients also employ displacement and turning against the self. Repression and a variety of other defenses are likewise available to them. In our opinion, however, Semrad (1968) is correct in emphasizing the avoidance devices as their main line of defense. Specific methods of avoidance, as he lists them, are denial, distortion, and projection—they are put in operation against conscious content in an effort to keep it out of awareness. We would add yet another mode: avoidance by taking action.

Having already described the borderline's use of projection, we can turn to denial, distortion, and avoidance by taking action. Denial, as defined by Jacobson (1957) and G. L. Bibring, et al. (1961) may be employed lightly by the borderline; or it may be used massively, to the point where he is unaware of any feeling or impulse life. Much the same can be said of distortion, whereby the patient not only denies inner or outer reality but also substitutes a fantasy version to suit his defensive purposes. Denial and distortion carry two serious defects. One is that they are brittle. When threatened with facing what he avoids, the patient can intensify his denial or distortion. But he is likely to become desperate in doing so. And when the defense is cracked, it too readily can give way altogether. The other defect is that these defenses heavily obfuscate reality.

Avoidance can also be achieved by discharging impulses and feelings through the medium of action. The action may be a more or less neutral form of outlet, or it may express, at least in part, the nature of the feelings or impulses that the patient does not want to acknowledge. Since it always involves taking action more or less blindly, without understanding, this method of avoidance is hazardous. Through it, the patient allows himself action that is directly destructive or places him in danger. Avoidance through action is commonly used along with massive denial of feelings, so that the patient may be in the especially dangerous situation of discharging impulses like an automaton, feeling nothing at all, and even utterly devoid of awareness of the nature and consequences of his acts. This problem will be discussed further in a later section.

On the basis of this description, we can make three general statements about the borderline's defenses: (1) they are maintained at a sacrifice of being in touch with reality that is far greater than that involved with higher level defenses; (2) they tend to be inadequate to maintain equilibrium, to be brittle, and to be a source of distress themselves; and (3) they can place the patient in danger.

THE NEED FOR CONFRONTATION IN
TREATING BORDERLINE PATIENTS

Intensity and chaos characterize life insofar as it is experienced at the borderline level. Most borderlines occasionally experience their lives almost solely at that level, unmodified by more mature attainments. But usually their borderline problems are simply interwoven into the music of everyday life, sometimes in counterpoint and sometimes in blending with healthier themes and rhythms. At times they swell to dominate the composition; at other times they are heard only softly in the background.

Most therapy hours are, then, characterized by steady, undramatic work by therapist and patient. Is confrontation needed, or useful, during these hours? In our opinion, it is. The reason lies in the borderline's extensive use of avoidance defenses. An example follows.

The patient was a young social scientist who was progressing well professionally. His specialty allowed him to remain relatively distant from people. But his inability to form stable relationships and his sense of aloneness and hopelessness had brought him to the brink of suicide. He entered psychotherapy and very quickly was deeply involved in borderline issues. The belief that he would be, and indeed felt he was, abandoned by his therapist dominated the work of the first year. At the same time he gradually and intermittently became aware of intense longing for the therapist. As treatment proceeded, he recognized vague sexual feelings towards him that resembled those he felt as a child when he stood close to his mother, pressing his head into her abdomen. He also became aware of urges to rush or fall into his therapist's chest and was afraid because it felt to him that he might in fact destroy his therapist in this way, or perhaps be destroyed himself.

With these transference developments, he resumed an old practice of promiscuous, casual homosexual activities. He reported seeking to perform fellatio when under pressure of severe yearning to be with the therapist. In one treatment hour he described these feelings and activities as he had experienced them the night before. And he added a new self-observation. Looking away to one side, he quietly, almost under his breath, said he had found himself "sucking like a baby." Generalized obfuscation followed this admission. Everything he said was vague, rambling, and indefinite. The therapist hoped this new information could be kept conscious and available to awareness. It would be important for later interpreting the infant-to-mother transference; *i.e.*, that the patient was experiencing urgent need for sustenance from the therapist as he had continued to experience with his mother since infancy—a need to suck milk from the breast-penis.

Later in the hour he returned to his experience the night before. Once again his narration became clear as he described his longing for the therapist and seeking homosexual contact. But he omitted any mention of his infantile feelings and sucking activity. The therapist suspected that the patient had mobilized some method of avoiding, perhaps denial, perhaps simply withholding. In an attempt to counter this defense, the therapist made a confrontation. When the patient seemed to have finished retelling the story, the therapist directly, with emphasis and with minimal inflection, said, "And you found yourself sucking like a baby." The patient winced, turned his face away, and was briefly silent. Then he said, "Yes, I know." In another short silence he turned his head back towards the therapist; then he continued his association. He did not directly pursue the matter that had been forced to his attention, but it was clear that he had fully acknowledged it and was also aware that his therapist knew about it too. Because of the patient's fear of feeling close to the therapist, the therapist chose not to confront any further. He felt that any further attempt to hold the patient to the subject in that session would now be more threatening than constructive.

Work with borderline patients can be quite different from that just described. By contrast, some hours are characterized by intense involvement in one, several, or all aspects of life at the borderline level. Help may be urgently needed at these times to deal with two multiply determined problems: (1) the patient's becoming overwhelmed with the belief and feeling that he is in danger and (2) his unwitting action through which he puts himself in real danger. At these times he needs help to recognize (1) the actual safety afforded by reality, especially the reality of his relationship with the therapist, and (2) the actual danger involved in using certain pathological relationships, in taking action on instinctual pressures and fear, and in failure to acknowledge that what he fears arises only from within himself. Ordinarily one would expect a patient to accept reassuring reality-oriented help of this kind. Paradoxically, the borderline patient may resist it, even fight it, mobilizing avoidance for that purpose. Then confrontation is required. We shall now consider this situation in detail.

The borderline patient's feeling of being in serious danger no matter which way he turns is of utmost importance. A brief resumé of leading determinants of this fear would begin with his belief he will be or is abandoned. It would then include his impulses, which he feels threaten destruction of the objects he depends upon. This in turn means to him aloneness or being destroyed. Self-esteem at these times is demolished; his primitive superego threatens corporal or capital punishment. Simultaneously, reality gains little recognition and holds little sway.

When overwhelmed or about to be overwhelmed with this complex experience, the patient needs the support of reality. Most of all he needs the real reassurance that he will not be abandoned and that no one will be destroyed.[4] If the therapist tries to respond to this need with simple clarification or reality testing, he often meets resistance. The patient avoids acknowledging the safety provided by reality, especially the reality of his relationship with his therapist. Confrontation is needed to meet this avoidance.

Why does the patient sometimes avoid acknowledging the safety afforded by reality; e.g., that his relationship with this therapist is secure? There are three reasons. (1) The fear of being abandoned (and destroyed) arose, for most borderlines, out of real experiences over prolonged periods of time with primary objects. Through certain complex mechanisms this experience was perpetuated throughout their lives in subsequent relationships that they formed in the quest for sustenance. A large part of their experience, then, speaks against the therapist's version of reality. The patient fears to risk accepting the therapist's offer as if the therapist were leading him to destruction. (2) The force of the patient's raging hunger and his partial fixation at the level of magical thinking convince him that he really is a danger to people he cares about and needs. Even though he may acknowledge them to be of no danger to him, he fears using relationships when he so vividly believes that he will destroy his objects. (3) These patients use projection to avoid

---

4 Of course, we are not advocating empty reassurance. If control is so tenuous that a threatening situation really exists, steps in management are required to provide safety. For example, hospitalization may be indicated.

the recognition that the supposedly dangerous, raging hunger arises within themselves. The patient's acknowledgment that his object is safe rather than dangerous threatens the breakdown of this defense. These three fears may be experienced unconsciously, or they may be preconscious, conscious but denied, or even conscious and acknowledged.

Now we will turn to the problem of the borderline patient's putting himself in actual danger. Of course, danger in his life can spring from many sources. But the one germane to discussing confrontation is his use of avoidance mechanisms so that he remains insufficiently aware of the dangers as he acts. Specifically he employs avoidances against recognizing (1) the real danger in certain relationships, (2) the real danger in action used as a defense mechanism, and (3) the real danger in action used for discharge of impulses and feelings.

(1) The potentially dangerous relationships are those he forms with other borderline or psychotic persons; *i.e.*, persons who seek primarily exclusive possession and succorance. These people are also ridden with fears and destructive urges upon which they tend to act. The patient may throw himself into togetherness with some one like this, believing he has found a wonderful mutual closeness, perhaps feeling saved and exhilarated. In fact, the reality basis for the relationship is tenuous, if present at all. It simply provides the illusion, partially gained vicariously, of gratifying each other's needs for supplies of infantile closeness. Belief in the goodness and security of the partner may be maintained through the mechanism of splitting. Along with it, denial and distortion may serve to obfuscate his real ambivalence, instability, and untrustworthiness. Inevitably the partner will act destructively, independently, or in concert with the patient's own destructiveness. The least noxious outcome is desertion by one or the other. In all events, with their high hopes they ride for a fall, one that precipitates the full borderline conflict, often in crisis proportions. The therapist must realize the risk in these relationships and try

to show it to the patient. Failing that, he must set limits. Often the patient will not acknowledge the reality his therapist tries to bring to his attention and will not heed the limits set down. The lure of infant-mother closeness is too great. Furthermore, acting upon it with the "friend" may relieve by displacement his similar urges towards his therapist. But most importantly, acknowledging the real danger in such a relationship would mean giving it up. That would feel like an abandonment following close on the heels of wonderful hope. So the patient avoids the reality, and the therapist must turn to confrontation.

(2) Borderline patients are inclined to endanger themselves by resorting to action as a defensive measure. For example, if psychological avoidances become insufficient, they may take refuge in literal flight, perhaps running out of the therapist's office, failing to keep appointments, or traveling to some distant place. If in the process they deprive themselves of needed support from the therapist, they may be unable to check their frightening fantasies and impulses. Decompensation or other forms of harm may result. Another means of defensive flight is offered in drugs and alcohol—the dangers are obvious to the therapist. Some patients use displacement in order to allow their destructive impulses towards the therapist to be expressed in action. While avoiding acknowledgment of rage at the therapist, the patient can be unleashing it on the outside world. He might break windows, verbally attack policemen, incite brawls, etc., mobilizing various rationalizations to justify his behavior. All the while he keeps out of awareness his bristling hostility towards his therapist.

(3) Endangering action may also be used simply as a means of discharging a variety of highly pressing impulses. All of the borderline's various sources of destructive urges can be expressed through harmful activities, including self-destruction. Wishes to incorporate and merge can likewise be expressed in ways that endanger. Drugs, alcohol, promiscuity, suicide to gain Nirvana, pregnancy, and obesity

form a partial list. The patient resists giving up both the destructive and the incorporative activities. To do so would mean bearing the pressure of unrelieved impulses.

In all these instances of using action in the service of defense or impulse discharge, the patient to some degree avoids recognizing that his actions are in fact dangerous to himself. If he knows it intellectually, he is likely to say that he has no feeling about it, that it does not seem real, or it does not matter. This avoidance allows him to pursue the endangering activity unchecked. Mere reality testing and limit-setting will not induce him to recognize that he endangers himself and must work to give the activity up. However, by combining confrontation with reality testing and limit-setting, one can often break through the denial and accomplish this aim.

There remains one more danger in the use of avoidance mechanisms, one that was mentioned in an earlier section. It involves massive denial of intense feelings and impulses. It is true that much of the time there is no need to force a patient to face denied feelings and impulses. But there are occasions when it is urgently necessary to do so. For example, the patient may be under the extreme pressure of wanting to kill his therapist and, as a defensive alternative, be on the verge of actually killing himself. In order not to be aware of such unbearable emotional and impulse pressure, these patients are capable of employing denial and other avoidance devices massively. They may avoid to the point of literally eclipsing all feelings from their subjective view. Distressing as it is for them to face what they avoid, non-hospitalized patients cannot be allowed this much denial. It is too dangerous. It is dangerous because totally denied intense impulses and feelings are especially subject to expression in uncontrollable, destructive action. This action may take place with a sudden burst of feelings, or it may occur in a robot-like state of non-feeling. Clarifications and reality testing are to no avail against massive denial. Confrontation is required. In doing so the therapist's aims are (1) to help the patient become aware of his impulses so that he need not be subject to action without warning, (2) to help him gain temporary relief through abreaction, and (3) to help him gain a rational position from which he can exert self-control or seek help in maintaining control.[5]

All facets of the urgent need for confrontation cannot be illustrated in a single clinical example—two are involved in the vignette which follows. One involves the patient who is overwhelmed with the belief that he is in danger of abandonment. The other is the patient who puts himself in danger by discharging feelings through action. The patient to be described is the one we referred to once already. This episode took place a few weeks after the one previously discussed.

It had become clear that this patient used considerable repression and that he also depended heavily on avoidance devices, especially denial. But these were not enough to meet his needs for defense. He also consciously withheld thoughts and affects, was vague, and nearly all the time avoided looking at the therapist. Details of a traumatic childhood had emerged. For periods of up to a year he was abandoned by his mother and left to the care of a domineering but emotionally cold grandmother. His mother fluctuated widely in attitude towards him. At times she was intensely close in a bodily seductive way. At other times she was uncaring or coldly hostile. She and his father made it a practice to sneak off for evenings after he had fallen asleep. To ensure that he would remain in the house, they removed the door knobs, taking them with them. Repeatedly he awoke, finding himself alone, trapped, and in prolonged panics.

To summarize the earlier description, the most prominent quality of his transference was the belief that his therapist did not think about him or care about him. Outside

---

[5] We should include here the importance of providing the patient sufficient sustaining support to enable him to bear the otherwise unbearable. It may not be possible to support adequately with the relationship alone. Temporary hospitalization may be needed as an adjunct.

the treatment hours he frequently felt that the therapist did not exist. He suffered marked aloneness, yearning, and rage—increasingly centered on the person of the therapist. The therapist's work had primarily involved clarifications of the emerging transference and relating it to early experiences and life patterns. The therapist also repeatedly implied that in fact he, the therapist, was not like mother, not like the patient felt him to be; rather, he was solidly caring and trustworthy. The patient's feelings, however, intensified; and he began to seek relief by occasionally discharging them through action. It was at this time that he increased his homosexual activities, and the previously reported hour occurred. At the same time more rage was emerging. Many times his therapist interpreted that his impulses and rage were so intense because he believed he was really alone, absent from the therapist's thoughts, and uncared about. Each time, the reality of the relationship was also implied. But the patient seemed unable to accept it.

Before long, the patient put himself in serious danger. Rage with the supposedly abandoning therapist dominated him. He got drunk and purposely drove recklessly across a bridge, smashing his car on the guard rail. He himself was manifestly little concerned for his safety. He was concerned about how the therapist would react. That is, would the therapist be uncaring, as he expected?

Clarification, interpretation, and showing him the reality of the relationship had not been effective before. They would be less effective now. Certainly mere pointing out of the danger of his action would make little impression. The therapist elected to include confrontation in his efforts. First, he repeated the interpretation: the patient's erroneous belief that the therapist did not exist was the source of his intense anger. Next, the patient was confronted with the actual danger he had put himself in by discharging his rage in action. With emphatic concern the therapist said, "You could have been hurt, even killed! It was very dangerous for you to do that, and it is important that it does not happen again." Now the patient tacitly acknowledged the danger. Confrontation had succeeded. It was followed by a second confrontation, a confrontation designed to gain the patient's acknowledgment of the therapist's really caring about him. The therapist said, "The way to avoid this danger is to work with your feeling belief that I do not care or do not exist. By all means, whenever you approach believing it, whenever you begin to feel the intense rage which naturally follows, call me up. Call me, talk with me, and that way find out I really do exist, I am not gone." Superficially this maneuver would seem to have been a manipulation, but in fact it was a confrontation, presented very concretely. Its message was that the therapist was in reality a reliable, caring person whom it was safe to trust. The patient responded with what seemed to be half-hearted acknowledgment and agreement. But he did not again endanger himself in any similar way.

However, about three weeks later he was again experiencing the same very intense transference feelings and impulses. He drank heavily and made contact with a group of homosexuals who were strangers to him. He went with them to a loft in a slum section of the city and awoke there the next morning. He found himself alone, nude, and without memory of what had happened. He was frightened at the time but not when he told his therapist about it. The therapist responded by first showing his feelings of strong concern as he agreed that it was a dangerous experience. This amounted to a confrontation against rather weak denial of danger and fright. Then he clarified the psychodynamic pattern along the lines already described, showing the patient that he had put himself in danger by taking action to express his yearning for and rage with his frustrating supposedly uncaring therapist. Next came a combination of limit-setting and confrontation. "This is much too dangerous, and you must not allow yourself to take such risks again. You felt so intensely because you believed I did not care. Anytime you feel this way and are in danger of acting on it, contact me instead. It would be much better, much safer, to talk with me on the phone. Please do so, whenever it is necessary, at any time of day or night. See that I exist and that this relationship is real."

The patient gave the impression of neither agreeing nor disagreeing. He never called. But there were not further recurrences of discharging intense feelings and impulses in any dangerous actions. Two months later he was overwhelmed with fears of closeness with his therapist, and he felt suicidal. But he took no action, instead requested brief hospitalization. He was discharged at his own request after five days.

SUMMARY

It has been useful to us to define confrontation as a specific technique for dealing with avoidance defenses. Because borderline patients rely heavily on these avoidance mechanisms, we have found confrontation to be necessary in their treatment. In routine work confrontation is helpful in order to bring into view and keep in view therapeutically useful material. At certain difficult times it is needed as part of the therapist's effort to help his patient regain an experience of security and avoid actual dangers towards which he is inclined.

Bibliography

Balint, M. (1968), *The Basic Fault. Therapeutic Aspects of Regression*. London: Tavistock Publ.

Bibring, E. (1954), Psychoanalysis and the dynamic psychotherapies. *J. Amer. Psychoanal. Assn.*, 2: 745–770.

Bibring, G. L., T. F. Dwyer, D. S. Huntington, and A. F. Valenstein (1961), A study of the psychological processes in pregnancy and of the earliest mother-child relationship. Some propositions and currents. *The Psychoanalytic Study of the Child*, 16: 9–72. New York: International Universities Press.

Chase, L. S., and A. W. Hire (1966), Countertransference in the analysis of borderlines. Read before The Boston Psychoanalytic Society and Institute, Mar. 23, 1966.

Freud, A. (1936), *The Ego and the Mechanisms of Defense*. New York: International Universities Press, 1946.

Grinker, R. R., Sr., B. Werble, and R. C. Dry (1968), *The Borderline Syndrome*. New York: Basic Books, Inc.

Guntrip, H. (1968), *Schizoid Phenomena, Object Relations and the Self*. New York: International Universities Press.

Jacobson, E. (1957), Denial and repression. *J. Amer. Psychoanal. Assn.*, 5: 81–92.

Kernberg, O. (1966), Structural derivatives of object relationships. *Int. J. Psycho-Anal.*, 47: 236–253.

———— (1967), Borderline personality organization. *J. Amer. Psychoanal. Assn.*, 15: 641–685.

———— (1968), The treatment of patients with borderline personality organization. *Int. J. Psycho-Anal.*, 49: 600–619.

Khantzian, E. J., J. S. Dalsimer, and E. V. Semrad (1969), The use of interpretation in the psychotherapy of schizophrenia. *Am. J. Psychother.*, 23: 182–197.

Lewin, B. D. (1950), *The Psychoanalysis of Elation.* New York: W. W. Norton.

Little, M. (1960), On basic unity. *Int. J. Psycho-Anal.*, 41: 377–384.

Murray, J. M. (1964), Narcissism and the ego ideal. *J. Amer. Psychoanal. Assn.*, 12: 477–528.

———— (This Volume), The purpose of confrontation.

Myerson, P. G. (This Volume), The meanings of confrontation.

Semrad, E. V. (1954), The treatment process. *Amer. J. Psychiat.*, 110: 426–427.

———— (1968), Psychotherapy of the Borderline Patient. Conference held at Tufts University School of Medicine, April 4, 1968.

———— (1969), *Teaching Psychotherapy of Psychotic Patients.* New York: Grune & Stratton.

Vaillant, G. E. (1971), Theoretical hierarchy of adaptive ego mechanisms. *Arch. Gen. Psych.*, 24: 107–118.

Webster's New World Dictionary of the American Language (1960), New York: World Publishing Co.

Winnicott, D. W. (1969), The use of an object. *Int. J. Psycho-Anal.*, 50: 711–716.

Zetzel, E. R. (1971), A developmental approach to the borderline patient. *Amer. J. Psychiat.*, 127: 867–871.

The Misuses
of Confrontation in
the Psychotherapy
of Borderline Cases

GERALD ADLER, M.D., AND
DAN H. BUIE, JR., M.D.

Although we are convinced of the importance of confrontation in treating borderline patients, we are also impressed with the vulnerability of these patients to the misuse of confrontation. Misuse can arise from faulty clinical understanding as well as from the therapist's transference and countertransference problems. In this chapter we shall convey some of our thinking about these matters.

In the preceding chapter we discussed some crucial characteristics of borderline patients relevant to the issue of confrontation. We stressed their vulnerability to feeling abandoned, their life and death destroy or be destroyed position, and the serious threats to self-esteem that their fury and infantile wishes pose for them. We also described their brittle defensive structure and the particular importance in understanding their use of avoidance defenses. We then presented the thesis that confrontation was needed in the therapy of borderline patients in everyday treatment as well as in crisis situations because of the specific characteristics we described in these patients.

Borderline patients, by definition, have areas of strengths as well as areas of great vulnerability. In part because their

149

vulnerabilities can be masked by their higher level defenses (Kernberg, 1967), and in part because of what they can provoke in the therapist (Adler, 1970; Adler, In Press), they are particularly prone to the misuse of confrontation. We shall approach the subject of misuse of confrontation from two vantage points: (1) the borderline patient's vulnerability to harm from confrontation and (2) the countertransference issues that lead therapists to confront in destructive ways.

THE BORDERLINE PATIENT'S VULNERABILITY
TO HARM FROM CONFRONTATION

The borderline patient's psychic equilibrium is tenuous because of his intense impulses and inadequate defenses. For him, confrontation is a powerful instrument that can be as harmful as it can be helpful. Confrontation is most useful in a setting that takes into account the tenuous working alliance present with most borderline patients. A good working alliance requires that the patient be able to trust in the therapist's judgment and constructive purpose. We are referring not only to basic trust, but also to a trust gained through experience that the therapist will not harm the patient by placing him under more stress than he can tolerate and use. Since the trust is tenuous for a long time with these patients, the therapist must observe certain restrictions and precautions in using confrontation in order not to undermine that trust. We shall list and discuss these restrictions and precautions about the use of confrontation with these patients, not as a set of rules, but as matters to take into account in order to decide how, when, and about what to confront:

(1) *Assess reality stress in the patient's current life.* When a patient is under more serious stress in his life—e.g., when a loss is impending—we do not want to load him with even more stress in therapy. Clinical judgment of the amount of stress a patient is bearing is often difficult and requires

thoughtfulness as well as a mental status examination and empathy. This task is particularly difficult in this group of patients who can employ avoidance devices as defenses. The patient can be near a breaking point and yet feel and show little evidence of it. Only with the additional aid of thoughtful appraisal of his life situation and psychological makeup can the therapist reliably evaluate how much stress his patient experiences as a result of various real life traumata and how much more he can stand. He can then decide whether or not a confrontation should be made at that time and, if it should, how much support is needed along with it.

(2) *Avoid breaking down needed defenses.* This precaution applies to all types of patients. However, when working with borderlines, these defenses, especially denial, are brittle. While they may at times be massive and formidable, they are inclined to give way to confrontation all at once. The patient may be overwhelmed with impulses and fears as well as with a sense of worthlessness and badness. All sorts of confrontations can have this effect—not only ones aimed at awareness of impulses, but also those promoting acknowledgment of the therapist's caring and valuing the patient.

(3) *Avoid overstimulating the patient's wish for closeness.* In the feelings and beliefs of these patients, closeness always carries with it the threat of destroying and being destroyed. Showing strong feelings of any type can stimulate the wish for or feeling of closeness. So can being personal in any way; *e.g.*, telling a personal anecdote. At certain times these patients can be overstimulated quite easily. Even the therapist's leaning forward in his chair for emphasis can be too much. Heightened oral-level urges, fear, and defensive rage can ensue; flight or some form of endangering action may result. The outcome may be that the tenuous working alliance will be lost in the course of the rage. In his anger the patient can feel he has destroyed the therapist within himself, or he can feel he has evicted the therapist from the premises of his person (Frosch, 1967; Adler, In Press). In

this way his rage sets up a chain reaction: he is now alone within, and the intense borderline experience is precipitated —fear of abandonment and aloneness, raging destructive oral urges to get the therapist back inside again, panic over the destructiveness and expected retaliation, and efforts to protect himself by rejecting the therapist further—thus only increasing his aloneness.

(4) *Avoid overstimulating the patient's rage.* Confrontation may involve deprivation and frustration for the patient. It may also involve a show of anger by the therapist. In either case these patients, who much of the time labor under considerable pressure of denied and suppressed anger, are easily stimulated to overburdening levels of rage. Usually the patient's rage also brings fear, panic, and ultimately a sense of annihilation. The ensuing dangers are the same as those evoked by overstimulation with closeness.

(5) *Avoid confrontation of narcissistic entitlement.* As long as a patient is borderline, he feels and believes his entitlement to survive is threatened. We have already described the similar ways in which narcissistic entitlement and entitlement to survive are manifested (Buie and Adler, Chapter Six). One can easily be mistaken for the other. Some therapists believe they must help borderline patients modify their narcissistic entitlement. For these therapists it is important that they not fall into the error of misdiagnosing entitlement to survive as narcissistic entitlement. If they make this mistake, they will believe they are confronting therapeutically a wish to which the patient feels entitled when actually they are threatening him with harm by attacking a fundamental need, his entitlement to survive.

It is, however, our opinion that direct work with narcissistic entitlement should not be undertaken at all until the patient has emerged out of his borderline state into a character neurosis. Our experience indicates that as long as entitlement to survive is not secure, narcissistic entitlement is needed as a source of feeling some self-worth, power, and security, even though it is at the level of infantile omnipotence and liable to give way transiently to its obverse. We are emphasizing that the patient's narcissistic entitlement may be a significant force that is keeping the patient alive. The confrontation of narcissistic entitlement can demolish self-esteem and security, leaving the patient feeling worthless, helpless, and evil for having made inappropriate demands. He is thereby made more vulnerable to threats to his entitlement to survive; *i.e.*, to aloneness and helplessness against annihilatory dangers. The patient cannot be exposed to danger this way without reacting with rage. If the patient is strong enough, this rage can lead to redoubled insistence on his narcissistic entitlement along with some degree of protective withdrawal. If he does not have the strength to reassert his narcissistic entitlement, he will probably have to reject his therapist in his rage and in fantasy destroy him or become seriously suicidal. Desperate aloneness must be the result; with it comes the panic of being overwhelmed, with the rest of the borderline conflict following.

COUNTERTRANSFERENCE ISSUES THAT LEAD TO THE
MISUSE OF CONFRONTATION

We have stressed the intense dyadic relationship that these patients crave and that they often begin to feel rapidly with their therapists. And with this relationship the issues of living or dying can be experienced by these patients with great urgency. These feelings in borderline patients inevitably arouse a response in their therapists. The patient yearns for holding, touching, and feeding; and he often becomes increasingly angry, helpless, and despairing when these infantile demands are not gratified. The therapist, in response, may feel that his patient literally has to be rescued; and, therefore, tends to give the patient more and more; *e.g.*, time, support, reassurance, and touching. For some patients, this giving by their therapist may fill them up and remove the emptiness and despair temporarily or even for long periods of time. At its best, it may offer a corrective emotional experience in contrast to the deprivations of the patient's earlier life. But more often than not, this giving with the feeling of having to rescue the patient opens the door for increasing regressive wishes and angry demands by the patient. For this group of patients, nothing is enough, and the therapist's nurturant response may lead to further regression. Balint (1968) describes this phenomenon in therapy as a "malignant regression." The therapist, facing these persistent demands in spite of how much he has already given, may feel helpless and depleted, as well as increasingly furious that his giving does so little good—indeed it seems to make the patient emptier and angrier. The therapist at this time may also feel envious of a patient who seems to feel free to demand so much and apparently is successful in arousing an intense rescuing response in another.

At such a point, a confrontation may be used by a therapist as a vehicle for expressing his fury and envy. Rather than being a confrontation that attempts empathically to put the patient in touch with something he is avoiding, it may be an angry assault on the patient's narcissistic entitlement. As we shall discuss, the therapist is in reality using a hostile manipulation. For example, the therapist may angrily state that the patient has to give up these outrageous, infantile demands. As described earlier, asking the patient to give up narcissistic demands at the time he is struggling with an entitlement to survive can be disastrous for the patient whether or not the regression to the life and death position may have been provoked by the therapist's initial rescuing response to his patient. In addition, these patients have a primitive, severely punitive superego that they easily project onto others and reintroject. The therapist's anger as he attacks is readily confused by the patient with his own and may redouble the destructive self-punishing position the patient already is in.

Even when the therapist does not respond to his patient by acting on wishes to rescue him, the patient will often feel increasing anger during treatment as he expects nurturance from the therapist and envies all that the therapist possesses. At times these angry attacks can be provoked by something in the therapist that makes him less accessible; *e.g.*, an illness or preoccupation with a personal issue. The patient's anger at such times may take the form of a devaluing, sadistic assault on the therapist. As part of this attack, the patient may minimize the importance of the therapist in his life or in his anger may destroy anything the therapist attempts to give. This destruction can be manifest by the patient's devaluing anything the therapist says as incorrect, inadequate, or inconsequential (Adler, 1970). For the therapist this can be a painful, dehumanizing experience in which he may feel isolated, helpless, and totally unimportant to another human being especially when he has had little experience with these patients and does not recognize it as part of the transference. Since wishes to be helpful and competent are important strivings in all therapists, such behavior by the patient can be particularly distressing. A "confrontation" by the therapist in this setting may in fact serve as an attack in order to cut through his intense isolation and sense of abandonment by his patient. It may also be retaliatory. What the therapist overlooks in his distress is that what he is experiencing so intensely at the hands of his patient is what the patient feels at the roots of his psychopathology and has usually experienced repeatedly and severely early in his life. Such oversight by the therapist also means loss of potential therapeutic work.

We want to illustrate the treatment of a borderline patient "confronted" about her narcissism at the time that her concerns were about her ability to survive. The patient was a 23-year-old single secretary who had been hospitalized following the termination of four years of psychotherapy. She had felt her therapist to be aloof, ungiving, and uninterested in her personally. Though the therapy ended by mutual agreement, the patient began to feel increasingly abandoned, empty, desperate, and suicidal. During her hospitalization the tenuous life and death quality of her life was spelled out, including a long history of abandonment by important people and her inability to tolerate her fury and disappointment when this occurred. While in the hospital she began therapy with a new psychiatrist whom she felt was empathically in tune with her. Though there were many tense moments for the patient, therapist, and hospital staff, the patient gradually became more comfortable and was able to leave the hospital to return to her job. Shortly after this, her therapist had an accident in which he sustained a serious comminuted fracture of his leg. Not only did he suddenly miss several sessions with the patient, but he felt less emotionally available, preoccupied with himself, unable to talk about the accident with his patient, and experienced a sense of personal vulnerability. The patient began to complain angrily about his not caring enough and his lack of understanding of her feelings. The relative vulnerability of her therapist to these devaluing attacks led the patient to talk increasingly about her love and admiration for him while she covertly nursed her fury and concern for his vulnerability. The therapist later acknowledged he found the patient's love gratifying and relieving. Gradually, however, the patient became increasingly suicidal, requiring readmission to the hospital. During her sessions with the therapist in the hospital, her angry complaints reappeared with increasing demands that he be more available, give her more, and stop using her treatment for so much personal gratification for himself. She also acknowledged her concern for her therapist's physical condition and how important he was to her. The therapist was still unable to respond adequately to this, which led again to the repeated complaints. Without his awareness his anger grew. After several more sessions of these complaints, he responded most angrily, asking the patient why she considered herself so special that she felt entitled to so much—even more than he gave any other patient. The patient then became more frightened and became increasingly suicidal.

Following that session, the therapist obtained a consultation in which he could readily spell out his feelings of vulnerability since his accident, his discomfort about it when the patient brought it up, and his relative emotional unavailability and discomfort with the patient's demands and attacks. He felt that his preoccupation with his injury had made him feel helpless, passive, and less resilient in the face of the patient's concerns and angry attacks. Now he saw his angry statement as a retaliatory gesture to counter his helpless rage during the patient's assaults. He was then able to go back to the patient and help her to explore her feelings about his accident; he could also tell her some of the details about it. Both the patient and therapist felt relief— and the patient could then speak angrily about her disappointment in her therapist for not being omnipotent, her concern that he was vulnerable, her belief that she had magically harmed him, and her fear of expressing her fury toward him once she felt he could not take it. After these sessions, the patient could return to her previous more integrated level of functioning.

We also want to stress the sense of helplessness and hopelessness in a therapist who struggles to work with a patient, but who finds the patient seemingly unresponsive in spite of his every effort (Adler, In Press). The patient's unyielding passivity may arouse a defensive activity in the therapist who tries to clarify or interpret away the patient's regressive position with increasing effort. Balint (1968) and Little (1960, 1966) have stressed the reliving and working through of this position as important in the treatment of such patients and the difficulties arising when therapists feel they have to make it disappear. If the therapist is to help the patient resolve this regression, he must come face to face with prolonged unbearable feelings of depression, emptiness, despair, loneliness, fury, and a sense of annihilation, both in the patient and in himself. For long stretches, empathic listening with clarifying questions may be the only activity required of the therapist; but the burden the therapist has to shoulder may be overwhelming as time passes. And the angry attacking pseudo-confrontation is often the means chosen by the therapist as a way of seeking relief and as a demand to the patient to give up such behavior as he becomes increasingly overwhelmed by what his patient is experiencing, especially as he senses that often his words mean so little to the patient.

We now want to summarize three tyes of countertransference difficulties that may occur in the treatment of the borderline patient that are relevant to the issue of confrontation: (1) the therapist's wish to maintain the gratified position of nurturant mother, (2) the therapist's response to the biting attacks of the patient, and (3) the therapist's wish to have a well-behaved patient.

(1) Though the wishes of these patients to be one with their therapist can frighten both patient and therapist, there are also gratifying aspects to such longings. The omnipotence that these patients ascribe to the therapist as they recreate the mother-infant dyadic tie can give the therapist much pleasure. In fact, the therapist may wish it to remain forever, in spite of his commitment to help the patient to grow up. As the patient works through the infantile regression, he may begin to take steps away from the therapist-mother as more mature choices become open to him. At this point, a bereft therapist can repeatedly "confront" the patient with the lack of wisdom of the choice or with the therapist's feeling that they have not sufficiently explored the step the patient wants to take. At the same time he ignores the patient's healthy side and its growth in therapy. Consciously, the therapist sees himself as being helpful and cautious, but in effect he is manipulating to maintain the gratification of infantile tie with his patient. The result is a patient stuck in this dyadic tie to his therapist because of countertransference wishes of the therapist—and under the guise of "confrontation," manipulation or suggestion is used to keep the patient from growing up.

(2) Since these patients' wishes for nurturance cannot be totally gratified by the therapist, the patient ultimately

has to shift from warm sucking to angry biting in his relationship to the therapist. The patient's rage may destroy the sense of gratification the therapist had been receiving from the previous positive relationship with his patient. Rather than accept the rage as a crucial part of the treatment (Winnicott, 1969), the therapist may "confront" the patient repeatedly that he is running from his positive feelings for the therapist. When correct, such confrontation is useful but in the situation we are describing, it is not true. Again, it is instead a manipulation and part of the therapist's attempt to return to the positive dyadic tie. This manipulation, or pseudo-confrontation, serves primarily as a defense for the therapist, this time because of his discomfort with the patient's fury. It also works in the service of his wish to maintain the gratification of the positive dyadic tie with his patient. The therapist's manipulations we have just been describing also make a demand upon the patient. When they are about the patient's entitlement, they tell the patient that if he chooses to retain a piece of behavior, he is bad and not in the therapist's favor.

(3) The issue of the patient's "badness" is important in the treatment of borderline patients. Many of these patients present it initially with their neurotic defenses and adaptive capacities more in evidence. However, the stress of some outside traumatic events, or the intensity arising through the psychotherapeutic situation can be sufficient to lead to a regressive unfolding of the borderline defenses and the primitive wishes, demands, and fears we have described. The therapist may feel that there is a deliberate, manipulative quality to this regression and view the patient as bad. This response occurs most intensely in therapists who are inexperienced in working with borderlines or in those who are frightened by their patient's regressive manifestations (Frosch, 1967). An angry pseudo-confrontation by the therapist may be his countertransference response to punish the "bad" patient and to get him to give up his bad behavior or face losing the therapist's love and approval. Needless to

say, this therapist's position is extremely threatening to the borderline patient, who has blurred ego and superego boundaries, a primitive superego, and fears of abandonment, engulfment, and annihilation. It intensifies feelings that his own sense of worthlessness and badness is indeed correct.

Even in the experienced therapist some anger is almost inevitably provoked in his work with regressed borderline patients. Is it possible for him to use it constructively, when necessary, in forceful, appropriate confrontations? We think it is. However, it is our feeling that a therapist can best make a useful confrontation, even though angry, when he has no wish to destroy the patient, not even his sick side. We recognize this as an ideal. In practice the therapist inevitably has some destructive wishes, and he must be consciously in touch with them if he is to avoid putting them into action. These wishes, if no harm is to come from angry confrontation, need to be balanced by the therapist's desire to be helpful to his patient as well as by his struggle to master his own destructiveness. The therapist's capacity to maintain his empathic touch with his patient enables him to monitor how forceful he can be without actually venting destruction on his patient or having the patient subjectively experience the force as an attack. That is, he is aware of the character structure of the patient, with its vulnerabilities, and of his own sadistic, destructive urges; this awareness places him in a position to use confrontation constructively, even when angry.

Throughout his work with his patient, the therapist can demonstrate his reliability and caring by using appropriate clarifications and confrontations of the potential self-destructiveness of the patient. The therapist's reliability and caring are also communicated through his attempts to demonstrate the concept of two people working collaboratively over time—that the patient can count on the ongoing relationship with his therapist and will not be abandoned by him. In spite of our statements about presenting a dependable relationship to these patients, many borderline patients do not easily learn that we can be trusted and relied upon. For them, as we have discussed earlier, the frightening experiences of their rage and the projection of it onto the world may result in perpetual distrust and isolation no matter how trustworthy the therapist is, behaves, or states he is to the patient. We feel that the experiencing of the murderous rage in the transference (Frosch, 1967; Winnicott, 1969) and the non-retaliation by the therapist are crucial for many of these patients. Only then can the corrective emotional experience occur that ultimately removes the terror of aggression and the primitive ways of getting rid of it that are so frightening to these patients. When it happens that the patient observes his therapist struggling with his own countertransference fury, he has the opportunity to learn how another person can master murderous rage. The therapist's successful struggles provide the patient with an opportunity to internalize important new ways of tolerating fury and using its derivatives constructively. If the therapist fails in his struggle, the patient may then comply helplessly as a victim of an attack; and his view of the world as untrustworthy is further confirmed. Through this mutual observation and struggle the patient can learn most effectively that neither he nor the therapist need destroy each other in spite of mutually destructive urges. Hopefully, the therapist also gains something from the successful encounter with his own fury—moving toward a direction of never wanting to destroy, but only to catalyze growth.

Bibliography

Adler, G. (1970), Valuing and devaluing in the psycho-therapeutic process. *Arch. Gen. Psychiat.*, 22: 454–462.
——— (In Press), Helplessness in the helpers. *Br. J. Med. Psychol.*
Balint, M. (1968), *The Basic Fault. Therapeutic Aspects of Regression.* London: Tavistock Publ.
Buie, D. H., Jr. and Adler, G. (This Volume), Confrontation in the psychotherapy of borderline patients, I: the use of confrontation.
Frosch, J. (1967), Severe regressive states during analysis: summary. *J. Amer. Psychoanal. Assn.*, 15: 606–625.
Kernberg, O. (1967), Borderline personality organization. *J. Amer. Psychoanal. Assn.*, 15: 641–685.
Little, M. (1960), On basic unit. *Int. J. Psychoanal.*, 41: 377–384, 637.
——— (1966), Transference in borderline states. *Int. J. Psychoanal.*, 47: 476–485.
Winnicott, D. W. (1969), The use of an object. *Int. J. Psychoanal.*, 50: 711–716.

Aspects of
Confrontation

ROLF ARVIDSON, M.D.

This chapter aims for a brief and simple statement of ideas and observations on two aspects of confrontation. The verb, *to confront*, is defined in *Webster's New Twentieth Century Dictionary* (1962) as "to face, to face defiantly, to set face to face (as an accused person and a witness)," and "to set together for comparison." In common psychiatric usage, the term has acquired a valence of aggression. In this essay, the last meaning about a friendly comparison of views is implied in my definition of confrontation. I see confrontation as a regular but unobtrusive technical manuever that, without drawing attention to itself, assists in the elaboration of content. Its form in the actual therapeutic dialogue or interchange is expressed thus: "It seems to me that . . . and I wonder how it seems to you." Such a confrontation will be contrasted with confrontation as a style that dominates and shapes the therapeutic relationship and the patient's vision of the therapist; that is, the structure gains dominance over the content. I shall first discuss my own concept of confrontation.

Confrontation is the first in an orderly sequence of steps (confrontation, clarification, interpretation, and work-

ing through) by which the therapeutic work is carried out
(Greenson, 1967). Its purpose is to show the patient what he
or she is resistant to talk and feel about. It is not an attempt
to uncover unconscious fantasies and motivations. Although
the therapist is prepared to admit that he is wrong or only
partially correct in his assumption, nevertheless his statement reflects his dynamic formulation and therapeutic
strategy of the moment. It goes without saying that progress
in therapy, be it five times weekly psychoanalysis or once a
week casework—*i.e.*, regardless of the level of discussion and
the nature of the dialogue—a pertinent and productive issue
must be sorted out and its built-in resistances appreciated.
However, by virtue of this preparation, any confrontation,
whether directed towards a minor omission or a painful
revelation and in spite of the fact that it was based solely on
a genuine concern for the patient, also expresses the therapist's authority over him. By confronting any one link in the
material, the therapist leaves out something else; through
this selection he controls the situation. The greater his skill
and the more careful his assessment of the state of the ego
and the therapeutic alliance, the less anger and resistance
he stirs up and the more successfully can he lead the
development.

I shall now describe a clinical episode that illustrates
the relationship between confrontation and content. The
patient is a thirty-year-old graduate student from a poor
background who has been in analysis for about two years. He
is married to a woman who comes from an illustrious family
and who is wealthy and accomplished in her own right.
During a particular stretch of the analysis two observations
were noted. He was not talking about his studies, which
earlier had been a regular fixture of his hours. He was
increasingly expressing anger at his wife, accusing her of
making him into an appendage of herself; for example, letters
concerning their properties and finances were addressed to
her and not to him. She had also reminded him that his
spendings had increased. He wanted to quit his field and go

into politics. I sensed from him at this juncture an enormous pressure to comfort him, to take sides, and to become engaged in a battle or a crisis. I was aware of being annoyed. I realized that he had regressed into a familiar pattern of crisis and that behind his aggressive shouting about becoming a political figure was his passivity, which had always escaped clear focusing. However, I restrained myself and simply confronted him with my observation that he was no longer talking about his studies and that maybe this indicated that he was no longer working at them. If that was so, maybe we should talk about it. He had indeed stopped working and was several papers and exams behind schedule. In the associative material that followed over the next few hours, his resistance against telling me about the studies became clearer. He wanted to avoid a clarification of the obvious fact that by failing to pursue his academic studies, which promised him some independence and self-esteem from his own efforts in his own field, he put himself in the position of becoming an appendage.

Now, a more direct confrontation of the "face it as it is" kind, but probably heavily infected with my anger, would have been: "Stop the shouting and don't let us waste more time. It is clear that you want to be dependent on your wife's money and be passive and taken care of. If not, you would have done your homework." I believe I would have been shoooting straight from the hip and certainly would not have been fussy. My confrontation, "You want to be dependent," would have been correct and would no doubt have stirred him up. There would have been some obvious advantages to this position. I might have emerged as a strong person—the "awakening father" would be a good phrase for it—who is not afraid to stick his neck out and to tell the truth and if necessary to battle over it. In addition to gaining a clearer definition of the image of the therapist, some analytic time might have been saved.

Naturally, there would have been drawbacks. The creation of guilt would have burdened the ego, and a sense of attack would have interfered with the working alliance. However, the greatest drawback to this approach might have been that the patient's own initiative was bypassed and that this confrontation contained an admonition to behave differently and not simply to talk about something in order to explore and elaborate a system of fantasies. But in telling somebody to be different—and telling someone that he is passive is to tell him that he should not be that way—there is a subtle and implicit assumption of responsibility by the therapist to get the patient to do his homework. The ideal aim of therapy might not be to get the patient to work and be active. After all, the patient alone can do that and assume that responsibility himself. Instead this ideal aim might be to interpret an unconscious fantasy, in this case, to be a woman's phallus and hence to satisfy his passive wish of being part of her.

Any one confrontation in the sense used here is wedded faithfully to the content of the patient's associations. Once the therapist departs from the text of the hour and instead dips into his general pool of impressions of the patient, the authority inherent in the dynamic theme itself is broken and is replaced with the authority of the therapist's own motivations. It is reasonable to ask how the idea of associating freely to the patient's material and of maintaining a free-floating attention fits into this approach. The answer is that these activities issue strictly and honestly from the material and that a successful practice of them is dependent upon the therapist's having a clear and full comprehension of his own narcissism and that his self-centeredness does not rate high on a scale.

A bind or resistance is particularly apt to develop when the confrontation is formulated and delivered as if in tune with the patient; i.e., the therapist was in form only trying to figure out where the patient was at, while in fact he was ambiguously and covertly telling the patient where he should be at. This is an example: A resident is reporting an hour with a patient. The patient had started the hour with a long silence that had made the resident impatient; at the same time he was preoccupied with the content of the previous hour, which had interested him partly for personal reasons and partly for reasons that he was to see his supervisor. He had become eager to get started but did not direct his attention to the silence as a source of information and study. He then had said, "It seems to me that you are reluctant to talk about . . .," and he mentioned the issue that was on his mind. The patient answered, "I don't know, maybe so," and then she went on to talk with much feeling about something else, which disappointed the therapist but which nevertheless contained her unconscious comments upon the therapist's maneuver. She told about her mother, who always controlled her and never really considered the patient's own needs. For example, her mother always insisted upon the kind of clothes she should wear, which were never coordinated and never matched. She put one kind of plaid on top of another kind, and it looked confused. Nothing fit her. But she could never tell mother because she would get impatient and angry.

This is not confrontation. Rather it is an awkward and clumsy way to get a patient to talk about something and the form itself creates resistance. And rightly so! Now the resident would have been much better off even if he ignored the silence by frankly stating that he did *not* know where she was at, but that such an issue was on his mind. Did she think it might be useful to talk about, or was she really concerned about something else?

I shall next discuss the second category of confrontation, which is not an unobtrusive part of a total approach but is a major technical tool whose aim is to have the patient face how he feels and where he is at as quickly and as thoroughly as possible. The ramifications of such an approach are many for the transference, the countertransference, and the vicissitudes of the self in the therapeutic encounter. In this small essay only a few aspects will be studied.

We probably can agree with the view that in therapy we want to enlarge the patient's awareness of the self to the point that the patient as he knows himself is recognizable as the person interacting with others. This self-awareness to be achieved needs, first of all and as a start, a full acceptance by the therapist and a respect for the patient as he presents himself and feels about himself. Confrontation of the kind, which is only a part of a larger therapeutic encounter, attempts to remove the resistances to such a self-revelation. Ultimately and ideally, the patient takes responsibility for revealing it, and he has a choice. In contrast, confrontation as practiced as a style might tend to tell the patient how he feels and what he is like. He has less of a choice and less authority. Importantly, the transaction of self-revelation is personified in the therapist himself; his voice and his words come to stand for the truth, however accurate the truth might be. The other kind of confrontation ultimately forces the patient, if he is able, to reveal himself; and at least for a moment, he has to face himself alone. To be poetic, but with some justification, he has to face himself from the inside.

The following brief description of a therapy case will serve as a basis for discussion. A twenty-seven-year-old man was referred to me as a patient by his wife, who knew of me through a friend. His chief complaint was that he did not always tell his wife the truth; e.g., he was on a diet and had bags of cookies secretly hidden in the house. He also failed to pay small bills, which he stated upset his wife. He presented himself as having a psychopathic personality although there were no real clues to such a diagnosis. Clinically he seemed to be a compulsive-obsessive person with great personal charm and considerable warmth. The issue of control seemed a fundamental problem. I saw him for about eight interviews with the goal of evaluating the need for therapy as well as his wish for it. He idealized his wife and referred to her authority in all matters psychological. During these interviews I did not come on strong, but mostly listened. When I did make a comment about his behavior, he usually told me in a seemingly approving fashion that his wife had suggested the same. In general the case puzzled me, and I felt that something was missing in my comprehension of it.

One night I got a phone call from his wife telling me that my patient had left without telling her his whereabouts and that the "game was up." The "game" was that he was a financial speculator and that for the third time in their marriage, his plans had failed, his money was lost, etc. When I asked her why she had not told me the true state of affairs earlier, she answered that she had wanted me to find out for myself and not to interfere. After many crises, he returned but still told me very little about what was going on. He then left for a stay in another city and while there visited with an old friend of his. During that trip, he was introduced to a well-known therapist whom the friend himself had consulted and who was a proponent of active therapy. Spontaneously, the patient referred to him as a "confronter." The friend had told the therapist about the patient's difficulties, both in business and in his personal life. Over a short period of time, the patient was exposed to what seemed a marathon-like confrontation. The therapist obviously knew the content of a compulsive-obsessive neurosis very well and was able to confront the inventory of the patient's behavior, thinking, and feeling with an amazing clarity, which impressed him. Truly, the accused came face to face with the evidence and the witnesses to his neurosis: his smiling revealed his insecurity and hostility, as did the picking of his fingers; as for his low voice, "You really want to scream." From the way he sat in the chair, it was predicted (accurately) that the patient urinated against the sides of the toilet bowl and not into the center. Although much of the therapist's activity seemed a caricature, some of his statements were based on the patient's actual accounts and were coldly to the point. The patient, who had a pilot's license, told him that he felt comfortable flying commercial airlines because he always knew by the "feel" of the plane what the pilot was doing. The therapist carefully explained to him that he was living an illusion and that his sense of control was a denial of the fact that if something happened to the plane, he could do nothing about it. He tied this to other aspects of his living.

His confrontations had a large element of provocation and an insistence that the patient interact with him. His relationship with me was carefully scrutinized, and he was told that I too knew all these things about him but that I had not told him, the moral being, I believe, that I should have. The patient felt very elated leaving the friend and the therapist. However, when he boarded the airplane, he suffered an acute anxiety attack and had to leave the plane. After the third attempt, he was able to stay and fly.

He eventually returned to tell me the story. The patient thought the experience meaningful and helpful and admired the therapist for his honesty and fearlessness and for having "shot straight from the hip." He wanted to do likewise. I thought he would now be looking for a "confronter," and I was wondering to whom I could refer him. To my surprise, he told me he wanted to thank me for having stayed with him in spite of all the bad things I had known about him without telling him and that I really must have liked him. He had been looking forward to talking to me again. He seemed very relieved, almost happy.

I selected this case both because it affords a close description, perhaps a caricature, of confrontation and its meaning to the patient and because it is representative of a special group of patients who tend to attract persistent and forceful confrontations. He has a basic compulsive-obsessive personality structure with considerable isolation of affect and a pleasant remoteness. Subtle but distinct passive and masochistic trends are paired with real and often impressive accomplishments. There is a diminished sense of self in the face of an apparent sense of ease and fluency in dealing with people. In other words, there are rough incongruities that invite responses.

In any beginning therapeutic relationship, I consider these phenomena to be regularly observable in the patient:

(1) A deep dread of self-revelation and change that

evokes hostility and sadistic fantasies because of the psychic work demanded.

(2) Concomitant wishes for closeness, a sense of communion, and the bridging of the gap between him and the therapist.

(3) A reaction to his hostility and these wishes with anxiety and fear of rejection.

The therapeutic task is to reduce the affective distance between the therapist and the patient while at the same time to foster independence.

When the patient tries to orient himself to the above psychic phenomena, his responses can be traced on an imaginary continuum that is progressively marked with these defining psychic states:

(1) The patient has the belief that there is a lack of separation between himself and the therapist; hence, neither can hurt the other. The sadistic impulses are then controlled. This state can also be described as a fusion between self and object representation. There is a maximum sense of sameness and a minimum of separation anxiety.

(2) The patient tries out real and imagined qualities and aspects of the therapist partly through imitation but always in the service of pleasing and maintaining the object; there is also high narcissistic return for the patient.

(3) The patient actively and *selectively* (that is, he has a choice) takes on qualities of the therapist in his efforts to cope with conflicting ideas and affects. There is a minimum of fusion and confusion between the self and the other. The working alliance is maximal and the gratification comes from the competence in exercising psychological skills.

It is my contention that the behavior of the therapist, his style and tone of approach, tends to influence selectively these three modes. I would propose that the less authority you give the patient the more primitive the mode of identification tends to be. A passing comment on cognition and feeling in therapy might be useful here. I do not imply that therapy is mainly cognitive, but confrontation as a practiced style can be provocative and seductive in its magical expectations. What is often confronted is what the therapist *thinks* of the patient and the patient's mode of handling feelings with the implicit demand to be different: be and act differently with the covert message (and promise), "Be like me." Sensitivity and encounter group techniques have alerted us to the "here and now" feelings of the patient, but it must have its start and basis in the patient's own feelings.

I shall turn to a study of the actual case. When this patient returned from his therapeutic experience, much had seemingly been accomplished. He certainly was a different person in specific ways when he returned to consult me. His speech was more direct and animated, and he expressed a convincing wish to involve himself in our work. But what was the nature of the change? On the surface it was a change in style and approach. Central to his account of his other therapeutic experience was that image of the therapist's constantly intruding into his thoughts and feelings, constantly pursuing and prodding him. It over-shadowed the content. His remarks are illustrative: "He made me sit up straight. I no longer felt like a shit-ass who knew nothing. I felt great. Before, I felt like nothing. Man, he was strong!" This from a patient with considerable learning and sophistication. He expressed openly and almost enthusiastically that his pleasant personality was apparently unreal and that it really expressed badness. I shall not concern myself with the superego aspect of the material and the existence of an identification with the aggressor. Instead, I shall take the material as evidence of the patient's dawning awareness that these were psychological forces and factors of which a person might not know. But this awareness seemed predicated upon the barely existing alliance that had been established between us before he interrupted his therapy with me. I state this because he had eagerly looked forward to returning to tell about the things that were being pointed out to him.

The maintenance of his belief in his newly gained

strength seemed to have depended upon the continued presence of the "confronter." Away from him, the belief tended to shrink. For example, when he collapsed at the airport and was afraid to fly, I doubt that his anxiety resulted simply from the therapist's having exposed his defenses against the feared loss of control in and of an airplane, but just as much from the failure to maintain the belief issuing from the fusion between the self and the therapist, expressed overtly as being and feeling like the therapist. Needless to say, this psychological state is precarious and unstable and depends for its maintenance on the appropriate object.

I shall next investigate another meaning of the therapeutic encounter with the "confronter" and suggest that the "confronter" had also been tricked and further that this type of patient might characteristically do so. On the surface, then, it seemed for a long time as if that therapist had overpowered the patient's defensive positions and gained entrance to his inner feelings. However, further therapeutic work suggested an alternative picture characterized by the question, "Who had seduced whom?" Had the "confronter" gotten beyond his defenses or had his style simply made room for the patient's deeper neurotic needs. In actuality, it turned out that the patient's wife was also a "confronter." He clearly had added to the inner representation of his wife part of his own self; namely, his phallus. Unconsciously, he believed her to be his phallus and source of strength. He harbored the same belief in regard to the therapist except that the instinctual mode for the transaction was different in the two cases; for the wife, it was predominantly oral; and for the confronting therapist, it was anal as well. She had very much encouraged in him the belief that she had rescued him from the ghetto in which he had grown up and that without her he would still be there aimlessly living an indifferent existence; without her, he was fuzzy and without a straight goal. In many ways, she was correct. His relationship with her had enabled him to be aggressive and socially and financially successful. But it was unstable and fluid, highly sensitive to the vicissitudes of the same relationship. He very much felt that without her he would fail and she, on her part, literally insisted that if she left she would take his success with her. She had what he needed to do it. No doubt to be helpful, she had regularly confronted him with the fears behind his pleasant and bland exterior.

When he had first come to me, my approach had worried him, and he had been afraid of my technique or absence of it. I had constantly stressed his own talents and initiative. The discontinuity between his wife and myself had been noticeable and had enhanced his fear of separation, essentially a separation from his own phallus bestowed on his wife. The style of the other therapist readily filled that void and need. Hence, the encounter, while it lasted, had been in some way reassuring and comforting, because he had lent him his phallus.

We can assume that the gratification of an unconscious wish to be penetrated by the confrontation, even though it might momentarily give a sense of strength, ultimately interferes and limits the effectiveness of the therapist in his task to expand the awareness of the self. The patient's smiling insistence that he was *bad* reflected the gratification of a forbidden wish. Naturally, this is not self-revelation but rather a contraction of self-awareness. That is, the chances for confronting the wish, giving it up, and mourning it had been bypassed.

I shall last and briefly indicate a problem that perhaps is not readily discernible.

We talk a great deal about the therapist's influence upon both the patient and the pattern of progress in therapy based on what he says to the patient. However, it may also be legitimate and educational to inquire about its effect upon the therapist himself.

To that end, simply to stress the complexity of the apparatus, I shall roughly schematize the ways and methods through which a therapist gathers information about the patient.

(1)   He inquires directly about the patient's feelings, ideations, and historical data. He listens to what the patient actually tells him and draws inferences from what is not said.

(2)   He empathizes with the patient, which means that he imaginatively and affectively contemplates the patient's internal and external psychological situation.

(3)   He examines carefully and continuously the feelings, ideas, and tendencies that the patient's words, affect, and behavior now generate in himself.

For the average therapist the task of maintaining these channels of information free and unpolluted by self-centered reveries, bad tempers, and fatigue requires attention and a special psychological state that I shall briefly sketch for the sake of my subsequent argument. The ingredients are a maximum level of passive receptiveness, patience, and a capacity to tolerate uncertainty and not to jump to conclusions.

Now, any kind of confrontation that the therapist truly believes in and is not merely thrown at the patient requires a certain amount of aggression in its execution. When we observe ourselves carefully and honestly we sometimes might discover a flush of sadistically tinged affect even in the most timely and correct confrontation. It often requires self-discipline to prevent belief from becoming conviction and instead for the therapist to return to an ego state when *listening* is again possible. There is a need in most therapists to be active, to intrude, and to control; and there always lurks a tendency to grandiose and impatient narcissistic manipulation. In the holy name of interacting with patients and of being involved, we, at times, try to exercise off our restlessness and frustrations.

I am not saying anything novel. I am merely stressing the problem of aggression, the constant threat it poses to the ego state of passive receptiveness, and the need to control it in its manifold manifestations.

I believe it is legitimate to ask how active a therapist can be, how intent upon being "in there," and still remain reflective, fully listening, and judicious in his assessment of the therapeutic possibilities. I believe there are limits in most therapists and that excessive involvement contaminates both the therapeutic field and the therapist's own cognitive processes.

Finally, it probably is healthy to remain doubtful about the correctness of one's conclusions and to leave the door open for new possibilities and problems; that is, one must safeguard one's curiosity. Is it possible to maintain that curiosity while at the same time constantly to point out to the patient with aggressive conviction what he or she feels or thinks?

Confrontation as a technical maneuver subordinated to an overall therapeutic strategy has been compared and contrasted to confrontation as a major style characterizing the therapy and aiming less for content and more for *getting to the patient.*

These ideas are framed by a view of psychotherapy that has as a primary goal the expansion of self-awareness and independence. Crucial for the success of these tasks is to provide the patient with choices and to *help him confront them.* In this chapter, the question is raised whether confrontation as a style interferes ultimately with this goal in these ways:

(1) Fostering magical attitudes like being the therapist or being or feeling like the therapist.

(2) Gratification of unconscious wishes; *e.g.,* related to penetration.

Both interfere with self-awareness and the mastery of separation even though behaviorally there is the superficial suggestion of greater emotional freedom.

Finally, in addition to dealing with the effect of confrontation as a style upon the patient, the effect upon the therapist has been discussed. I feel this is a neglected area of inquiry. Naturally, participation with the patient is a significant part of the observation of him, but there has to be a harmonious balance between these two modes for the sake of an ego state conducive to optimal thinking and reflecting about the patient.

Bibliography

Greenson, R. R. (1967), *The Technique and Practice of Psychoanalysis*, Volume I. New York: International Universities Press.

Webster's New Twentieth Century Dictionary of the English Language, 2nd Edition (1962). Cleveland and New York: The World Publishing Company.

Confrontation in the Analysis of the Transference Resistance

HAROLD N. BORIS

The practice of psychoanalytically oriented psychotherapy has by now accumulated a wealth of very useful technical precepts. Among these, one is to work from the surface downward. Another is to analyze defense before impulse. A third is to fashion a working or therapeutic alliance before going on to interpret certain material, particularly aspects of the transference. And there are, of course, others.

The value of these principles lies in their capacity to achieve certain ends. But in the course of time a kind of displacement has occurred in which these means to those ends have become valued almost more than the ends that they were originated to serve. The result of this displacement is that the principles such as I have mentioned have been given a weight unbecoming to a bit of technology, with the further consequence that alternative precepts that serve the same ends have become controversial. Such is the case, I think, for the technical device of confrontation.

At the same time, it is equally true that, of the variety of measures the psychotherapist can employ, not every one of them will prove interchangeable with others; not all roads lead to Rome. Nor is a hodgepodge of eclecticism likely to serve the ends in view. Technical approaches work their effects in close complementation to one another. An integrated approach will accomplish more than a simple assembly of mediations. It is such an approach, with confrontation as its centerpiece, that I shall present here.

Departures from "standard" practice become most attractive when, of course, standard practice is least able to induce its effects. One such circumstance obtains when the patient is experiencing little or no inner conflict. This circumstance has two aspects. One is in effect when the patient, in mourning or in love, experiences matters as if all that is good and important is outside of him. The other, in essence the opposite side of the same coin, is the one that shall interest us primarily. This is when the patient feels that all that is bad is outside of himself. People who have failed to internalize one side of a potential conflict such that superego lacunae are notable and people who have all too well contrived to re-externalize conflicting factors come within this category. When either aspect of this circumstance exists, the people so arranged do not ordinarily present themselves for treatment. Instead, they direct their energies in attempts to do business with the environment. Those for whom the badness lies without will generally be busy either with psychopathic carryings on or with attempts to effect massive changes in and of their environments respectively.

But from time to time, "externalizers" do find their way into treatment, sometimes under a misapprehension, sometimes out of moral or legal requirement, but sometimes too, out of an experience of inner conflict, if one that is expended by the very application for assistance. Once there, however, such patients are by no means a breed apart, but stand in a matter of degree from probably all patients. Ignoring for the moment the countertransference implications of the phrase, the problem they pose for the therapist is that the patient so arranged cannot fathom the business of looking at and into himself. As such, the patient and therapist will both feel a distressing absence of something to meet about, indeed a degree of potential conflict over what there is for them to do. The therapist may feel the patient a threat to his therapeutic intents and procedures, and the patient almost certainly will experience the therapist as a most frightful (if potential) threat to his particular arrangements. If the therapist does not get rid of the patient on grounds of a lack of motivation or a deficit in psychology-mindedness, then what to do?

Clearly the therapist will attempt to induce the patient into undertaking that subdivision whereby part (the observing ego) of the patient joins with the observing therapist in a scrutiny of the remainder, or alien part, of the patient. But this, we must by definition assume, is not proceeding well enough to give the therapist reason to hope; and the itch to tell the patient, "Look, you're the one who is crazy, sick, impossible, wrong," is getting stronger.

If the therapist does finally convey something of this sort to the patient,[1] he will be employing, to use Eissler's term (Eissler, 1953), a parameter additional to and different from his usual clarifications and interpretations. He will be using one form of confrontation, the form that I think of as social confrontation.

Unlike interpretation, the function of which is to *resolve* internal conflicts by bringing unconscious fantasies or feelings to the patient's attention, social confrontation is designed to *induce* internal conflict.

The ego, as Freud observed, is Janus-shaped. One face looks outward to the external, real, or social world. The other, if only to avert its gaze, looks inward to feelings and fantasies, acting upon these as if they too had the hard, incontrovertible substance of fact. If interpretation presents to the inner face what it has failed to see of what is within and behind, social confrontation exposes to the outer face what it has failed to see of what has been externalized or left

---

[1] For an instance of actual use, cf. Franz Alexander's use as described by Myerson, Chapter One.

external. Both attempt to convey to the attending ego information that it has failed to acknowledge, assimilate, and take account of. In that sense, the undoing of a projection and a piece of a repression or the undoing of a denial and a reaction formation have much in common, the only difference consisting of the face, inner or outer, to which the information is conveyed.

And yet there is an important, even fateful, difference between an interpretation and a social confrontation. It is the difference between saying, "This is the third session you have wasted this week," and "You are once more reacting as if only bad can come from our work together." Although both statements deal with how the patient is using the sessions, the first derives from the judge's bench, the second from the translator's booth. The first unmistakably proscribes, the second describes something of which the therapist tries to make sense. To assent to the first, the patient must accept both the fact and the therapist, since the statement inextricably contains both. To assent to the second, the patient need only acknowledge the fact.

Social confrontation, then, is intended to oblige an internalization of the therapist. The patient is to identify his ego with the therapist's or, perhaps, to introject the therapist into his superego. Now it is true that patients sometimes receive an interpretation in the same way. But when the patient does regard an interpretation as conveying some design or intent of the therapist, it will be out of some motive of the patient's own; and, as such, the confusion can be clarified and the motive analyzed at any propitious time. A social confrontation, however, far from being a fantasy on the patient's part, is on the therapist's part an entirely deliberate fusion of content and intent, specifically contrived to convey particular force. As such, even supposing the therapist might subsequently wish to analyze its effects, it will prove far less susceptible to analysis. For though the patient may, in time, come to feel the confrontation to be far less assaultive than he initially felt it to be, will he have equal luck in understanding the meaning and function of his internalizing-externalizing propensities? It is with these propensities, after all, that the therapist felt himself to be confronted. Yet it was precisely these vehicles on which the therapist counted. Faced with the patient's use of externalization as a vehicle to keep truths out and away, the therapist turned the vehicle around and sent it right back, with himself now in the driver's seat.

Will it come clear to the patient, assuming it to be true of the therapist, that the therapist was not endorsing the patient's internalization-externalization dynamic? Or will the patient believe that the therapist was hoping only to reverse the flow of traffic and perhaps the choice of what the patient takes in and sends out?

Much of the undoubted effectiveness of social confrontation will be of value only to the extent that one also prefers or is prepared to risk its rather special sequel. Putting aside the more obvious possibilities—among which is that the patient may redouble his need first to externalize, then keep his distance from the external badness, and so leave therapy —one outcome may be that not only the alliance but the subsequent "cure" is effected via introjection. If the tough but good therapist is used internally to overshadow previously established internalizations, the patient may go on to conduct so ardent a relationship with the internal therapist as to so manically triumph over his previous introjects. Under these circumstances, it is clear that therapy of the ordinary sort may subsequently prove impossible. Like the transference "cure," cures by introjection, even identification, are coin-flips of the original neurosis. In the latter two, the cast of characters in the internal drama may change, changing the effect *upon* the ego; but the helplessness of the ego *in regard to* the scenario will not have changed at all.

These special sequels to confrontation may or may not be acceptable to the therapist, depending, one supposes, on the degree to which the patient's symptomatology and previous inertness in therapy pose a technical or personal problem for the therapist. To the personal issue, there is little to say beyond asking why the problem a patient poses to the therapist becomes the therapist's problem; but to the technical issue posed by the relative absence of internal conflict, there is an alternative beyond social confrontation. This is confrontation of a different sort, the usages of which I propose to consider first where it is least necessary and then where, in my view, it may prove quite necessary indeed.

Let us suppose that we accept for treatment a twenty-year-old girl who comes complaining of a general depression, growing difficulty with her school work, and an uneasy relationship with her roommates. Let us further suppose that in taking the history the evidence becomes clear that her roommates stand for her sister who, in turn, stands for her mother and that the uneasiness in those relationships is of a fairly typical Oedipal nature, with the problem in school work participating, at least to some extent, in the form of a success neurosis in which to succeed means to out-do mother and thus constitutes a strong source for guilt.

The precepts I alluded to earlier would translate into a course of treatment something like this. We would begin with the derivatives, on which the girl's affect is most strongly centered and out of which would flow the initial motivation for her willingness to work. Initially she would express her feelings about her roommates and convey her complaints. Encouraged by our respectful attention, those feelings would tend to heighten and broaden, taking on at times a mildly paranoid flavor. Transference feelings toward us would begin to emerge, casting us as the father, who must spurn these bad, jealous, and envious women. As this happens, her demands on us would increase to the point that listening and mildly commenting would not be enough. The situation now would increase in intensity, bring more painful affects to the surface. We would then begin to engage her further in an alliance, the thrust of which would be to have her look with us at the meaning and function for her of what she is and has been going through—to turn inward. As tactfully as we could, we would help her focus attention on the work of those attributes in herself that she found most alien. Fairly soon self-understanding, still vis-à-vis the roommates as derivatives, would begin to ease some aspects of her overinvolvement. As a result, she would begin not only to experience some relief but also to come further toward accepting the alliance for self-study that we are the while fashioning and exercising with her. In time, we would begin to demonstrate the displacements, on the one hand, and the derivatives of the conscious feelings, on the other. We would point out connections between perceptions of and feelings about the roommates and her sister and help her to move, thereby, toward a consideration of father's role in those latter feelings. As she became more immersed in this undertaking, we would show her the gaps in her feelings toward her sister that have been left by repression, splitting, or denial. The recovery of these lost feelings would bring the initial object, mother, more into view. And so it would go on until, depending on our assessment of her needs and vulnerabilities, we either took some of these issues further with her or began to taper the process off before further regressions could take place as the heirs and preludes to earlier experiences.

In the procedure I have just outlined, confrontation has found no place. But it is worth considering whether it could have a place. On the face of it, the answer would seem to be no. If, for example, we directly confronted this patient with the fact that it is her mother who is really at issue, we would likely be met either with massive disbelief, which would be a credit to her defenses, or with profound outrage. Outrage would, among other sources, come from her narcissistically well-wrought conviction that she has outgrown mother and all those old, dreary preoccupations with father; and we would be flying head on into an already fragile self-esteem. Indeed if we pressed the interpretation, it is not unlikely that the patient would abruptly terminate treatment. We are thus well cautioned against wild interpretations.

But if we go back over these consequences, we see the

depressive and persecutory anxieties to which the patient would be subject were we to in fact make interpretations from, as it were, the id. Let us focus on these anxieties for a few moments. It is plain enough that we could have aroused these anxieties by wild interpretations, interpretations from the id. But are they not there in potential anyway? So what if, rather than beginning with where the patient is in terms of the real-life situation, we began with where the patient is in terms of her apprehensions about therapy—the very apprehensions we have been so carefully allaying or treating with so delicately in the use of our usual principles?

Now we can be sure that we are not the only ones who are trying to find ways around the encounter with these anxieties: the patient is too. She will be doing so in the material she presents, the way she presents it, the means she uses to offset the potential threat we could present—in short, by the actions she takes.

If we race headlong into making wild interpretations, we would mobilize these anxieties and see these anxieties all too clearly for the brief moment before her emergency countering action would take place. But we do not need to see these anxieties directly. They are easily inferred from the precautionary actions the patient is taking in, round, and about the manifest content of the therapy. And though they occur instantly in the first session—really because they occur so immediately—only to recede in the face of the reality of our presence, they are transference anxieties. Their capacity to give way as our presence becomes felt and the alliance becomes wrought argues generally for the good reality functioning of the ego. But before the ego does its work, the anxieties and the fantasies that accompany them are very nearly delusional even in so basically neurotic a patient as is the young lady we have been considering. Her capacity to act appropriately obscures this for us, as the success of her active responses to her anxieties enables her to barely feel them and even less to become aware of the fantasies about herself in relation to us, and vice versa.

Now in time, were it a searching psychoanalysis we were assisting her in, these would reemerge at the depths of the transference neurosis. But there are patients, borderline and frankly psychotic, where these anxieties are foremost and are not susceptible either to delay or to therapeutically appropriate countering actions. I shall deal with these instances later. The point I wish to make here is that such anxieties are immediately present and in good evidence with any patient and that they can be dealt with immediately, should one wish to confront the patient with them.

Now the device of confrontation too has its principles, because the use of confrontation in therapy, however unfamiliar it is to therapists generally, is by no means unique. Winnicott (1962) subsumes the process as one that "leads from the Unconscious" (p. 297). Others of a more rigorously Kleinian bent suggest interpreting the psychotic anxieties first (cf. Klein, 1957). But notice that when we are going to deal with psychotic anxieties or unconscious material we have to talk the language of the unconscious and of psychosis. This, as most of us know, is a very concrete language, and one with very active verbs in it. Its syntax is never elliptical, conditional, nor does it contain any negatives. It is causal and effective, in which the subject does something active to the predicate because. Action is the essence of the experience; real or fantasied countering actions are the defense.

Now as to the anxieties themselves. They will be of two basic sorts: (1) the talion anxiety, out of which the fearful, underlying wish is projected and the threat experienced as originating externally and (2) the depressive anxiety, in which the source of the fear is experienced as internal and originating from an internalized object. I would call this, with Anna Freud (1965), a superego anxiety, were it not for the archaic nature of some of these anxieties, which are more reasonably termed superego precursor anxieties. These two anxieties, though phenomenologically different, are, at root, really one. But projections and introjections do relocate the object that is experienced as the source of persecution and hence, the felt experience. It is of considerable importance to determine who the persecutor is, or at least where he, she, or it is located, and hence, the kind of anxiety—depressive or talion—that is being experienced or warded off.

If the principle of confrontation involves interpreting the patient's anxieties in terms that describe the unconscious fantasies that engender the anxieties, let me now go on to say why.

In confrontation, as I am using the term, one does without the usual therapeutic alliance. Insofar as one does fashion an alliance, it is not, as in the more familiar procedure, with a part of the patient's conscious, observing ego. It is rather with the repressed unconscious, that pathway to the id.

The ego, after all, is at least partly the agency that offers resistance to the repressed aspects of the impulse life, which transfigures them with its defensive maneuvers and which, in its narcissistic preoccupations and love-hate affairs with the internal objects, diverts them from realization and discharge. Rather than attempting to allay its vigilance with an alliance built up of the patient's identification with us and our therapeutic procedures, confrontation interferes with the defenses and bypasses that aspect of the ego. In using confrontation, the therapist reaches across to what lies beneath the ego. This is, of course, the restless stirring of the impulses, which, as much as they are held siege by the ego, hold it, in the symptomatic or characterological impasse, no less captive. That state of affairs reduces the autonomy of the ego, the restoration of which constitutes our therapeutic goal.

The autonomy of the ego, as Rapaport (1957) among others has shown, is comprised in two directions. As it tries to gather strength against the upward, outward push of the impulses, it throws itself into the arms of social reality for proscriptions, limits, indeed frustration. But once there, its autonomy threatens to be compromised from that direction also, for to be a "good" person all too often means excessive renunciations of the impulse gratifications that enrich and enliven the ego and give it a base of strength of its own. Thus, it must retreat and defend against the strictures of reality too, usually via denials and introjections, ultimately the formation of the superego. This increase of distance and hence autonomy from the social world can preclude impulse gratification, thus raising inner pressures again.

In effecting the usual therapeutic alliance, we offer a professional and sometimes a more explicitly real self together with a set of ego procedures to a patient whose own self and ego have been too well compromised in its mediative attempts to adapt impulses to reality. The benefits of this are obvious.

Not so obvious are the costs, for in fashioning the alliance we palliate the pressures the patient experiences and hence deprive him of the need to bring forth essential material. The balance between amelioration and cure is too much in favor of salving. But more questionable even than that is whether the identification with the therapist, the therapy, or the social values of the therapeutic system, so adaptive to us and our needs, is not at the same time a symptom for the patient that fails to get analyzed. In asking the patient to take a given attitude or in demanding he renounce one, in being real for the patient or even thera-peutic, do we *unnecessarily* compromise his autonomy? Social confrontation seems to me to contain more of this risk than the inculcation of the alliance in usual ways. But, on the other hand, it is so pronounced a measure that it stands out and calls both therapist's and patient's attention to it. As Bion (1966) has observed, it rather is the countertransfer-ences that the profession shares that escape recognition and analysis; surely the widespread, unquestioning belief in the therapeutic alliance is one of these.

Thus, if it is not necessary to inculcate identifications, we may do more for the patient by not doing so. The question is, then, can we avoid the traditional alliance?

With confrontation one can and does. As I noted with

the patient we were considering, the effect of bypassing the ego is an immediate rise in anxiety. But there is also another effect. The transference-rooted longings immediately gravitate to the therapist, so much so that they directly occupy center stage; and it is his sense of this propensity that all the anxiety is warning the patient against. But the transference longings themselves can form a bond stronger and more adhesive than the usual therapeutic alliance. Thus, while the patient may consciously resist, he unconsciously cooperates with treatment. The easiest example of unconscious cooperation is the slip of the tongue, which, in indecent haste, infiltrates the ego's machinery of wary vigilance. But that kind of infiltration is not the only pathway; the ego is filled with interstices. Nonverbal behavior, silences, transitions, gaps in secondary process communication all reveal in their absences the presence of unconscious cooperation.

By attending to this, despite the disinclined ego, one cements the allegiance from the patient's unconscious. The resulting anxiety, however, must continually be interpreted. Its interpretation marks the difference between the "wild analysis" of the unabashed beginner and the careful crafting of confrontation.

The conscious aspect—the observing ego—listens in on these interpretations. Nothing more is asked of it in the way of participation. In this sense, its autonomy is respected. Though it will find some measure of relief from anxiety and guilt from understanding what it experiences, the object of the procedure is to enable it to assimilate the wishes it has warded off.

When it does assimilate and integrate the impulses, its captivity by social reality, internalized and external, is reduced. It can act more autonomously, with greater true distance and perspective. One need not, then, concern oneself with matters and experiences external to the analysis of the transference. One need only—and that just in the first stages of treatment—actively interpret the anxieties that constitute the resistance to the transference neurosis or psychosis. After that, the transference becomes the sole preoccupation of the patient.

It is, however, important, even vital, not to provoke, induce, or elicit the transference actively. One does not replace one alliance with another, but remains impartial. So however active one may be in clearing the way for the development of the transference by the interpretation of the meaning and function of the anxieties that comprise the resistance, the interpretation of the transference wishes themselves must closely follow the patient's own material. Wild interpretations, as I noted, are out.

In confrontation, then, one bypasses defense analysis, goes to the analysis of those anxieties that resist the full flowering of transference, and then goes on to interpret the transference (and only the transference) in the ordinary way. Thus it brings one to where one is going on behalf of the patient via allegiance from the unconscious, achieving the same ends by almost inverse means.

With these alternative precepts in prospect, let me now return to the young lady we were considering earlier. But this time we will eschew the procedure I earlier supposed—and with it, taking the history and making an evaluation. Instead, we shall get, as it were, right down to work.

The first thing one will notice is that she is experiencing some anxiety, and so one quite gently calls this to her attention. She gives a half laugh, allowing some of the tension to discharge and acknowledging that she feels a little nervous. Something frightening could happen here? One half says, half asks. This, however, she denies and then instead offers her story. But now one interrupts: "Talking about being frightened is frightening?" one asks.

Her response to this is a fugitive move of impatience, a hesitation, during which one may well imagine she is deciding how best to deal with one's intrusion; and then having decided another denial would put her in a bad light, she says merely, "I guess so," and prepares to go on with what she came to do.

She goes on, then, with her story; and this time one does not interrupt, at least for a while. Interrupting directly would be experienced as so assaultive as to make the transference and the reality too difficult for her to distinguish.

As one then briefly retires to listen to her story, one listens less to the facts and figures (for we would hear all this again, and anyway, it is likely to be quite distorted in its present rendition) than for what effects her narrative is designed to have on one. Her narrative is a countering action to what she imagines one to be up to and about. It has its defensive components, designed to forestall or allay, and it has its courtship components, calculated to allure and entice. From these we can fairly readily infer what her anxieties are, especially if one, on his part, fails to comply with the intentions she has of her narrative. The restraint one places on his own inclinations to respond with um-hums, questions, nods, or the taking of notes, will bring his own impulses more clearly to mind. And, adding these data to what one has inferred from what the patient is attempting, will make matters reasonably plain.

As the patient proceeds and as one makes no compliance, one will soon see the eruption of anxiety once again; and this will serve as a cue. The eruption will be experienced by the patient as ego-alien, as if an undesirable symptom; and so one's intervention at this point will be experienced as less intrusive than if one had not waited.

One might say, "You are disappointed." If she tentatively acknowledges this, one would add, "You had hoped for better?" If she denies that she is disappointed, one deals with the anxiety that prompts the denial: "It is better not to care—one could get hurt." Or, "It is better not to care, because one can hate oneself for not succeeding."

She is likely to give either of these a mixed response, as if to say, "Yes, I care but don't want to." And one says, "For fear of disappointment." If she acknowledges this, one will say, "From whom?" She will say, "From myself." One then will say, "It is not right to hope for better from me?"

With this the anxiety that was temporarily allayed by our empathic clarification of her disappointment will rise again with the guilt over what will seem to her our permission to let loose her transference wishes. And so, with this the issue is joined. The anxiety is high, the defensive maneuver curtailed, and the only thing in the circumstance that will offer some relief is the further emergence of the unconscious transference wishes.

From this point on, with one reaching backward, not into her history, but back to the beginning of this first session, there will be a counterpoint between the expression and interpretation of anxieties and then the expression and interpretation of wishes. The first will open the way to the second, and the second will engender the first. One can feel that the alliance has been really joined when she tells of the fantasies about this first session that she had before even the initiating phone call.

If I am correct that, though in cases like that I have described, the choice between approaches amounts to six of one and half dozen of the other, such may not be the case in procedures open to us in working with borderline and psychotic patients. For there we have, on the one hand, approaches that attempt to buttress the besieged ego through doses of reality, supportive relationships, and facilitative interjections of counsel or limits—all of these intermixed with the painstaking elicitation of affects; and then, on the other, we have a confrontative procedure that reaches beyond the strenuated ego to the fantasies and feelings it so valiantly, though quixotically, is attempting to ward off. Both may be said to strengthen the ego: the first, by support, as it were, from the outside and above; the second, by facing the averted ego inward, from within and below. But beyond this shared strategy, through implementation, a difference may exist. Supportive approaches tend, generally speaking, to reinforce defenses against the return of the repressed, and intervene primarily with such troubling defenses as denial and projection. But confrontation here too tends, by and large, to facilitate the emergence of the unconscious by attending to the anxieties that induce not only the denials, regressions, and projections but the repressions as well. This can only have an outcome different from traditional ego-supportive measures. If, therefore, there is controversy over means here, it is likely to be a displacement from convictions about either their comfort or the possibility of the achievability of the ends.

However, since the prime medium of all therapeutic work is the therapist himself, his position in respect to the patient will be the governing factor in the workability of this, as of any procedure. The method I am discussing must be rooted in the absence of a very particular sort of countertransference. It requires that to the largest extent one can, one wants nothing for or from one's patient. Only under these circumstances can confrontation escape being a preemption in which "one strolls about the other's mind as if it were one's own flat."

On the other hand, such austere neutrality conveys in great potential the possibility of exciting the patient to a very considerable envy of the self-contained therapist. Once aroused, envy's urgent need to be quenched and its no less imperative need to bite the hand that feeds it can foil or despoil any therapeutic attempt until the entire therapy is frozen in an unending stalemate.

One can forestall envy sufficiently to appease it by becoming partisan—by caring, feeling thwarted, getting angry, and, in the end, socially confronting the patient's confrontation of oneself. Or one can analyze envy in the measure to which it arises and, by so doing, maintain the neutrality upon which confrontation of the transference resistance so utterly depends.

This point is illustrated in the example of confrontation I shall shortly describe. The case is one where the choices among approaches might each have led to different ends—a foreclosure of fuller effects in the more usual approach and what continues to look like an opening to a reasonably thorough therapeutic analysis through confrontation. But note, too, the effect of my countertransference reaction in the fourth session.

Since I am interested in conveying what I can of the feeling of the encounters that comprise the vignette, I shall not present background or historical material except as it was presented to me.

Miss Gallet phoned one evening to tell me that she was about to commit herself to a state hospital because she was very fearful of hurting herself but wanted, before doing so, to see me and thereby arrange for treatment that she could return to on her release some ten days later. I agreed to see her between appointments the following day, and she duly presented herself for the twenty minutes I could arrange.

I was at once struck by her eyes, which were almost flamboyantly made up. The next of her features to catch my attention were her teeth. For the rest, she was a somewhat statuesque young woman in her middle or late twenties who, though dressed with some style, had outgained her clothes.

Since the meeting was to be simply one in which to make arrangements, I simply sat back to hear what she had to propose.

She told me that she had just broken up with her boy-friend, on whom she had been very dependent; and she was afraid that unless she did something else, she would do what she did the last time she had broken up with a boyfriend and withdraw into a corner, as she put it, in a very masochistic way, for four years; and she just couldn't do that again.

But having said that, she interrupted herself to ask me what I thought of "Thyrozine," as she called Thorazine.

I said: "You have some thoughts about it."

She said: "What do you think of Preludin?"

I said: "Preludin and Thorazine."

She said: "That's just it!" And laughed.

It then developed that Preludin, which is an appetite suppressant, and Thorazine were felt by the patient to be at odds. Her medicine was Preludin, but the doctors (five psychiatrists, it turned out, had been involved in the last several weeks) gave her Thorazine, which she felt to undermine Preludin.

I said: "What kind of doctor am I? One who puts into you the wish to grow fat and sleepy and fill yourself up with mother and food, or one who will help you become independent?"

She sent her high arcing peal of laughter up again and then said simply, "Yes."

The second session was held two days later. The patient said that she had gone to the state hospital, but without an admission slip, and was therefore not admitted. She had then returned to her second psychiatrist, who filled out the paper; but now, handing me the paper, she came to ask me what I thought.

I said: "What kind of doctor I am?"

She said: "Yes."

I said: "You are asking because you are afraid."

She said: "Yes."

I said: "Of?"

She said: "That you think I should go into the hospital."

I said: "Like who?"

She said: "Them."

I said: "Them?"

She said: "The people."

These, it developed, were a considerable assembly who were testing her, giving her messages, and otherwise controlling her life.

I said: "You are worried about testing me with your questions, about giving me messages about taking me over. Doctors have Thorazine and hospitals and other things to put into people, and you are worried that you don't. So that you are worried that I can hurt you with my things worse than, in self-protection, you can influence me with yours."

She responded to this with another question: Could I do two things for her? One, go to Children's Hospital and get the records of when she was a patient at age four or five; two, find out if her birth certificate is authentic.

I said: "What do you wish?"

She said: "I just want you to see if they did something to my head. And I want you to see who my parents really are."

I said again: "What do you wish? What do you hope I would find?"

She responded to this then saying that her parents wouldn't be her real ones and that something had been taken out of her head.

I said: "That is the other side of what you said before. Sometimes you feel that you are missing something and want people to put it back into you, and sometimes you feel you have ideas that you wish were taken out of you. And these feelings have to do with your parents; sometimes you want to put ideas into them and sometimes to take them out, and always you are afraid of what you believe they can do back to you."

The patient then went on to elaborate on the meaning of the wishes concerning her head and her parents, something that was to occupy her for some weeks. Later, while she was in the hospital over the severe depression the abandonment of the splitting and projection introduced, she reconstructed the experiences of incest that had taken place between herself and her father, and the delusional material stopped abruptly.

But before this could happen one other episode had to be confronted. This took place before and then during what was to be our fifth session. The fourth had been in my office at home at six o'clock meeting time. There was an aura of reticence throughout, which I could not properly identify, partly because during that week I was preoccupied with certain occurrences in my own family. These were much with me, and I kept nodding to them and telling them I would hold an audience for them later. I didn't manage to see that their presence had also to do with this patient.

On the Friday of the fifth session the patient's mother called to say that the patient had barricaded herself in her room and taken "a whole lot" of sleeping pills and tranquilizers, had gone to sleep, but had wakened to tell her to call me to say that she wasn't coming.

But I insisted that she come and, when the mother said she didn't feel her daughter was in a condition to drive, told the mother to put her into a cab.

And so the patient came, looking bloated and pasty and altogether hag-ridden. Her mouth was dry and she had difficulty working it. She sat slumped in silence, but I noticed that she looked at the clock from time to time in an intent sort of way.

I had the fantasy that she had swallowed my clock, so I said: "You have feelings about the clock—it worries you."

She nodded.

I asked her what worried her, but she seemed confused and shook her head.

I said: "You hate the idea you had about the clock and have attacked the idea and so confused yourself."

She sat up straighter and said, "Something about six o'clock."

"Six o'clock," I repeated, "and about swallowing."

"It's suppertime," she said.

"Whose?" I asked.

"Yours?" she asked.

"So you are keeping me from my supper?" I asked. "That worries you?"

She nodded.

"Tell me," I said.

She tried to work her mouth, but gave up and sort of shook her head.

"You are worried that I might eat you," I asked, "instead of my supper?"

Now came the sudden peal of laughter. She sat forward now.

"I suppose you think that that's because I want to eat you," she said. "Is that why I took the pills?" "Is it?" I asked.

It then developed that she was valiantly trying to diet, had been feeling starved, had envied my ability to eat, had wanted to deprive me of my supper, had felt some compunction, had felt hungry for me in an endless sort of way—being afraid of the long-seeming weekend—was afraid of these feelings, had put them into me, was afraid to come for fear that she would experience them again, and so had eaten her doctor-pills and spared me.

Further working through of this material opened the way for an emergence of more genital wishes and the intense depressive anxieties she experienced in relation to them. The regressive maternal transference shifted somewhat and new material came to the fore. But of particular note is that though the patient's life situation has been very difficult—including a two-and-a-half-month hiatus in treatment—she has managed to maintain the depressive position and keep her paranoid proclivities at bay.

Now, in conclusion, I thought I would like to say what brought me to try to learn the confrontational approach to begin with. It was not the task of working with neurotic patients where it is a six-of-one-half-dozen-of-the-other option, nor even that of working with borderline or psychotic patients, where it is often the approach of choice. Nor was it to work with groups, where I myself use it quite extensively, even exclusively. It was, of all things, to meet the task of trying to begin work with what statistically speaking is the normal person: the people of the community with whom, if anything is to be done, one must take the initiative and painstakingly develop a working relationship. For in such work, the consultant himself often becomes the epi-problem for the consultee. If one is not, therefore, to settle for working with the self-referred, the self-selected, and the coercively referred, one must, or so I feel I have learned, develop a method very like that I have been discussing; for analysis of transference anxieties, which would otherwise induce in the consultee massive sorts of resistance and be managed, most usually, by avoiding the relationship altogether, proved to open the way to reaching and engaging with the very hardest of the so-called hard to reach (Boris, 1971).

Bibliography

Bion, W. R. (1966), Book Review: Eissler's *Medical Orthodoxy and the Future of Psychoanalysis. Int. J. Psychoanal.*, 47: 575–581.

Boris, H. N. (1971), The Seelsorger in rural Vermont. *Int. J. Group Psychotherapy*, 21: 159–173.

Eissler, K. R. (1953), The effect of the structure of the ego on psychoanalytic technique. *J. Amer. Psychoanal. Assn.*, 1: 104–143.

——— (1958), Notes on problems of technique in the psychoanalytic treatment of adolescents: with some remarks on perversions. *The Psychoanalytic Study of the Child*, 13: 223–254. New York: International Universities Press.

Freud, A. (1965), *Normality and Pathology in Childhood.* New York: International Universities Press.

Klein, M. (1957), *Envy and Gratitude.* London: Tavistock Publ.

Rapaport, D. (1957), The theory of ego autonomy: a generalization. In *Collected Papers*, ed. M. M. Gill. New York: Basic Books, 1967, pp. 722–744.

Winnicott, D. W. (1962), The aims of psychoanalytic treatment. In *The Maturational Processes and the Facilitating Environment*. New York: International Universities Press, 1965, pp. 166–170.

Confrontation

with the

"Real" Analyst

LEON N. SHAPIRO, M.D.

This chapter will address itself to the issue of the real person of the therapist as a critical variable in treatment outcome. For neurotic patients with a solid reality sense, the person of the analyst does not appear to be of central importance to our understanding of treatment outcome. An expectant interpretive technique that pays primary attention to intrapsychic issues should lead to adequate conflict resolution. As we deal with patients with a less firm hold on reality, however, we run into limited ego capacities based on structural defects. In general, these are patients who do not have a stablized sense of self based on introjections, incorporations, and identifications formed out of solid experience with real, responsive, caring, and important people in their developmental past (Zetzel, 1971). For these patients, real characteristics of the therapist may be critical elements in the restructuring of the internal objects necessary for adequate ego functioning; and the confrontation of these characteristics in the therapist-patient interaction may be a major aspect of the treatment process.

Patients who have had unstable early object relationships are not ordinarily accepted for analysis because of their

209

predictable difficulty in maintaining a functional psychic distance from their regressive transference wishes. Diagnostically, some are grouped as "borderline," others as acting out character disorders. Eissler (1950) has suggested that a phase of psychotherapy in which the therapist functions as a primary object can be a preliminary to later analysis. In such cases, the real gratifications and confrontations of the first relationship provide a basis for continuing reality sense in the face of the later transference regression. More or less extended preliminary psychotherapy has become a standard technique in cases where suitability for analysis is in doubt.

In some cases a period of psychotherapy after analysis may be necessary to consolidate the formation of "the capacity to bring before the mind once more something that has once been perceived, by reproducing it as a presentation without the external object having still to be there" (Freud, 1925, p. 237). Freud (1925) defines such a capacity as a necessary prerequisite for reality testing. The case to be reported here was referred for a second analysis after the first analyst had reached a regressive impasse. The most striking feature of the post-analytic phase was the inclusion of the figure of the therapist as a participant in a changing masturbatory fantasy. The development and organization of this fantasy was accompanied *pari passu* by marked changes in clinical behavior.

A male analyst terminated with a thirty-five-year-old female unmarried architect who had been in analysis for four years. Before termination he had obtained several consultations because of the patient's increasingly regressive behavior. Following each consultation the patient showed some transient improvement, and the analyst was encouraged to continue the case but with the introduction of several parameters (Eissler, 1953). The parameters revolved around his efforts to differentiate himself from intense regressive expectations. To this end he revealed to the patient many aspects of his own life and interests. As will be noted, the patient had experienced gross rejection at the hands of both parents and saw the analyst and the analysis as promising to make amends for her deprived childhood. The analyst, an unusually kind and giving man, was unable convincingly to confront the patient with the hopelessness of these expectations. Ultimately, on further consultation, he was advised to transfer the patient.

The argument that I will make here is that this kind of confrontation must be consistent with the real state of the analyst's attitudes. The capacity to be lovingly interested, while it may be of enormous therapeutic value for some patients, can become for others an unbearable temptation to ego regression. With this patient the regressed behavior persisted accompanied by increasing demands for time, attention, and displays of affection.

The patient had her first appointment with her new analyst, also a man, one week after termination. Her appearance was neat and well-groomed, but she was clearly frightened to the point of near mutism; her movements were uneven; her behavior furtive. She glanced at the therapist, then kept her eyes riveted on the floor, alternately shaded her eyes and covered her mouth, twisted in the chair, turned to the wall, and answered questions with monosyllables.

This state of near panic had been her condition for at least the past year. She had been taking 400mg. of meprobamate per day for several years. She had stopped working over a year before, rarely left the house except to go to her hour, had stopped seeing all of her friends except for one boyfriend with whom she had been "going steady" for ten years. She claimed that she had gotten increasingly worse during the analysis and confirmed that her analyst had obtained four consultations on the question of whether to continue the analysis. Although the patient had been referred for further analysis, her condition seemed sufficiently unstable so that some initial psychotherapy seemed in order.

The second analyst saw her for almost two years in twice a week psychotherapy. She worked regularly for a year, was off medication, was seriously considering marriage to her boyfriend, and was relatively symptom free at termination.

In attempting to reconstruct what happened, several possibilities should be considered. The psychotherapy can be seen from one point of view as the termination phase of an analysis that had been unsuccessfully terminated. In spite of her increasing anxiety and the persistence of her regressive behavior at the time she left the first analyst, the patient was in possession of considerable insight. She had remembered with appropriate affect her earliest experiences and recognized the persistence of the early struggles in her current difficulties. For example, although she was relieved at the termination, the first analyst had been kind to her and apparently in the course of the analysis had tried to be "real" and supportive. She felt she knew a great deal about his life—his family, his child, his interests. She believed, however, that his periodic illnesses made him too fragile for her to attack. Her anger focused on her transference convictions that he didn't like her, that he liked his other patients better, that she was ugly and awkward and uninteresting. She recognized clearly that the transference feelings were in direct continuity with her struggles to find some kind of stable relationship with her father, a relationship that had remained highly seductive on both sides and had strong anal overtones; but during her first analysis she was unable to use this insight. She remembered the ways she would provoke her father to spank her and the sexual excitement involved. The development of her anal preoccupations were well delineated in memories of earlier struggles around toilet training. Her mother had turned her early care over to a sadistic nurse, who tried to control this hyperactive little girl by rubbing her nose in feces whenever the child soiled. She recognized in the analysis how many of the early themes interwove themselves in her subsequent development and the way they distorted her relationship to her first analyst. It was interesting that she was fully aware that she expected Dr. A. to treat her as the favorite child she had longed to be.

She was able to recognize that her accusations that he liked his other patients better were identical to and continuous with her sibling jealousy. It was not clear at the time either to her or to her former analyst that he was conveying in his style a promise of actually fulfilling her wishes.

In contrast to the coherence of historical themes, the nature of her current experience seemed totally fragmented. On medication (which she recognized as the magical incorporation of her former analyst) she could function for hours with limited anxiety. She could and did read a great deal, went for walks alone; then an incident like the following would occur. A man whom she had met many times at a fruit stand said "hello" to her. She answered. They chatted for a moment and she continued her walk. Within minutes she was flooded with anxiety. She recognized that the anxiety was a response to exciting feelings in her vagina and anus. She knew that it must have to do with the man she met, but there was no fantasy.

The fact that the feeling was partially or dominantly in her anus, she felt was shameful, had to be hidden, and "showed" on her face, which she would hide. The sexual excitement stood in isolation from fantasy or feeling about people, an isolation that was characteristic of most of her moods or affects. She would have flashes of anger at her boyfriend for no apparent reason or she could become suddenly depressed or anxious or terribly suspicious that everyone hated her. The episodes might last for minutes to days; but all had a strange unrelated quality for her, unrelated in the sense that the affect states were devoid of content (fantasy or memory). Her responses to these unpredictable rushes of feeling had been an increasing restriction on her life and inhibition of her behavior so that she appeared withdrawn and almost frozen.

Her second therapist compared his work with the patient to knitting together the strands of torn fabric and used this analogy with her. She clearly knew the historical strands. The fabric of her life was, however, in tatters. It was clear that she had done a great deal with analyst A (which she persistently denied) and that she had access to many primitive feelings that she had spent much time rediscovering. The second therapist suggested that she might play with the feelings, get to know them in a different way. They then might not need to be so isolated; maybe she could use them. In his approach to the patient, the new analyst took up the shame and guilt aspects of her response to sensuous feeling. He questioned her condemnation of the anal eroticism and reminded her that this could be an important component of "sexuality." He suggested that she enjoy the anal aspects of her sexuality as a means of integrating these experiences into her life. He also asked her to try to construct fantasies that might correspond to the bodily sensations she was having. The maneuver gave permission to the patient not only to allow the anal fantasy into consciousness but also to confront and explore the anal activities as a means of stimulating the fantasy. The approach had the intent of modifying the intensity of the superego response (Strachey, 1934). The resistance in the first analysis had centered on the patient's inability to maintain sufficient hold on reality in the face of a regressive transference. In Strachey's discussion of the nature of therapeutic action in psychoanalysis he states that the superego occupies a key position in analytic therapy and is a part of the patient's mind that is especially subject to the analyst's influence. Or, to state it another way, variations in superego attitudes toward impulse expression vary to a significant extent depending upon current object relationships. In this case there appears to have been a significant difference between the two analysts on the matter of expression of anal impulses. The first analyst tended to treat the patient as someone who had indeed been so rejected that only some kind of "corrective emotional experience" could be reparative. His "accepting" attitude was intended to provide a new kind of relationship in which she could develop. In effect, he agreed with her superego attitudes that the shittiness was bad and had to be put aside. The second analyst was more comfortable with her anal pleasures and preoccupations and encouraged her to accept them as important libidinal components of her life.

The therapist's presence in the face to face encounter served to modify the potential seductiveness of this intervention by confronting her with the realities of the treatment situation and with the reality of his inability and unwillingness to "make up" for her early deprivation. Thus there were (1) significant differences in the formal aspects of the treatment situation, (2) significant differences in the specific attitudes of the two analysts toward a central issue of conflict in the patient, and (3) differences in therapeutic intent, with the second analyst deliberately offering himself as an object in fantasy in an effort to stop the regression.

During the two years with the second analyst, each shift in the patient's clinical behavior was accompanied (or perhaps preceded) by a modification of the structure of her sexual fantasies. The most significant changes in the fantasy included the therapist as an increasingly active participant. During most of her adult life and persisting throughout the analytic phase of her treatment, the patient was able to achieve orgasm only by means of a masturbatory ritual in which she would defecate on paper in the middle of her living room and then lightly spank herself. The ritual was accompanied by enormous shame and guilt, but there was no attendant fantasy.

After the therapist encouraged her to "play" with her anal sensations, she gradually shifted to direct anal stimulation with a carrot (still without fantasy). The changes in the ritual seemed to be followed by her having more freedom to get out of her apartment. Her increasing freedom appears to have been based on a shift of attitudes in relation to her "shameful" anal preoccupations. Part of her withdrawal to her apartment was based on a concern that people could tell by looking at her face that she was "shitty"; *i.e.*, preoccupied with the ritual. Several months later, she reported another shift in the ritual in which the therapist appeared in fantasy.

At this point, she would lie on her back in bed, masturbate by clitoral stimulation, spank herself lightly, saying "You are a constipated girl" (a phrase the therapist had used in describing her difficulty in talking) while the therapist watched her "without moving." She also reported that she was now able to have orgasm by clitoral masturbation during intercourse. The therapist's position and function in the fantasy seemed to reflect his introjection as a superego modification. He is now a functional part of a fantasy that allows the patient to integrate into more genital eroticism, previously isolated and condemned aspects of her anal preoccupations.

With this shift, she experienced a significant lifting of her chronic anxiety and depression and began to cut down on her medication. She also reluctantly returned to work. Several months later she was off medication and struggling actively with angry feelings toward her boyfriend, father, and therapist. The therapist by this time had raised the issue of termination as a further device for maintaining the reality of the situation: "You may incorporate my attitudes and keep the memory, but you will have to say good-bye to me in reality." At that time the fantasy had undergone further modification. The change was primarily in the position and function of the therapist. He was no longer rigidly immobile but was engaged first, in giving enemas, filling her with water, and later, in having anal intercourse with her. The shift in the masturbation fantasy was accompanied by transient episodes of abdominal distention and later by the wish to have the therapist's child—a part of the therapist she could always keep. (The memories might not be enough.)

Why was she unable to use her first analyst in the same way to stablize her functioning? The repeated consultations reflected his concern about the progress of the analysis. His efforts to be "real" with the patient, however, seemed to add to the difficulties. The more he showed of his "real" self the greater the regression. The analytic situation at the time was quite clear. The patient was demanding that the analyst love her and devote himself to her in a way that would fill the sense of emptiness left by what she felt was her parents' rejection. In spite of his efforts to confront her with the limitations of the treatment situation, she had managed to elicit his great capacity for *real* devotion. In the face of an impasse, he insisted on continuing with the conviction that he could in fact somehow fulfill these infantile needs. I am suggesting that the confrontation could not work because it was "out of character" for the first analyst. To be effective a confrontation with an aspect of reality (in this instance—the therapist's refusal to provide unlimited love) must reflect the convictions of the therapist.

Analyst A is an intuitive and gifted man who has a capacity for conveying socially a sense of welcome to people that makes them feel close even on short acquaintance. He is always "available," setting no sharp limits between his work and personal time. These personal characteristics of the first analyst were increasingly revealed in his efforts to halt the transference regression and subverted his efforts. An important aspect of the patient's anxiety was her fear that she would "fall into" people, that she would like them or be stimulated by them and want "too much" from them. At meetings she would often have to leave the room to avoid physically falling off her chair—as if pulled into the arms of the person she was talking to.

The real intuitive openness of her first analyst made it difficult for her to use him to structure primitive impulses. When she tried to use him in fantasy the real promise of gratification pulled her further into a regressive flight from the threat of fusion. The more "real" he became, the more frightened she was.

Her second therapist states that even in her present state of good functioning, the patient is clearly borderline. She has great difficulty in placing the origins of affects; her anger shifts back and forth easily from self to paranoid perception of others. There is persistent anxiety about fusion alternating with feelings of rejection. The welcoming, warm, intuitive quality of her first analyst, which contributes to his unusual talent in the treatment of neurotic patients, seems to have militated against his usefulness in this situation.

The patient also reported a striking difference in "firmness" of the two therapists. She felt it was easier to be angry with the second because he seemed to insist on her growing up and treated her angry outbursts as important aspects of herself in her everyday functioning. She also felt that the physical differences in the two analysts were important, the "healthy" aura of the second analyst reassured her that her anger could be contained. He is at the same time less "open and accepting" in his approach to patients, tends to wait and see before allowing a patient to develop a close relationship. He keeps sharper limits between his work and personal life.

The formal differences in the setting and real differences in the "persons" of the two analysts were reinforced by significant differences in therapeutic style. A recent vignette from her second analyst reveals a confrontational aspect of his style that the patient found useful in putting her current life into perspective.

The patient often cried in the office and would wait until she was quite wet with tears and would then ask for a paper towel, which the therapist would hand her. After several months, during which time the anxiety had diminished, the therapist did not hand her the towel immediately but asked instead why she wanted to use his towels. The patient became frightened, felt she was being attacked and criticized. If that's how the therapist felt, she didn't need his "damned towels." She'd bring one in from the bathroom from now on. He pointed out that she'd still be using his towels to wipe herself and that seemed important to her. At this point her anger subsided sufficiently for her to express the fantasy: "Maybe I want you to wipe my ass!" The therapist reminded her that she felt that her shittiness showed on her face. The anger subsided further, and she associated again to the memories of messing her pants and the conviction that her father couldn't stand her.

The next hour she reported that she had less anxiety than she'd had in weeks and that the weekend with her boyfriend had gone much better than it had in a long time. She was less angry at him, felt closer and more sexually responsive. She also reported that the therapist, who had previously been "rigid," was now seen as moving in the fantasy that accompanied the anal perversion.

The therapist's confrontation about the towels contained not only his positive wishes that the patient rely more on herself but also a statement that his tolerance of her dependent wishes had limits. "What is the meaning of your wish to lean on me?" was a clear message. This aggressive aspect of the therapist's confrontation seems to have been similar in some respects to her perception of her rejecting father. In effect, the therapist, though very different, was enough like the father to allow the further completion of an early identification. The father appears to have been highly seductive with both affectionate physical contact and frequent exciting (to both?) spankings. At the same time he was (and still is) extremely critical of any signs of clinging or dependence in the patient or displays of physical sensuality. The quality of the towel incident appears to have been a regular characteristic of the therapy. Her response was to include the therapist as an increasingly active figure in the masturbatory fantasy, where he represented a superego modification. The second therapist also confronted the patient quite early with the limited nature of the therapeutic commitment. Aware of her regressive response to the open-ended psychoanalytic situation and cognizant of the potential dependency relationship that might accompany his incorporation into the fantasy, he took up the question of termination as soon as her reality situation was reasonably stable.

During the termination, which lasted for eighteen months, she had recurrent episodes of return of anxiety that she would characterize as having "lost the therapist" (a sense of his not being with her). In what sense did she "have him" when she was feeling well? The therapist quotes her as follows:

> I have a sense of how you are with people. You tried to think with me about what we are doing. As if it were a puzzle that could be figured out. . . . I try to think through my anxiety now, the way I figure you would if you were there. It wasn't that you cared so much about me . . . but you seemed to assume that I could get better. I told my boyfriend that you (a male therapist) were just the kind of mother I needed. . . . There are times that mothers just expect their kids to grow up.

Those characteristics of the therapist that allowed him to be used as the "mother of separation" (Stone, 1961) seemed to permit the later fantasy development in which he became the father of her "anal" child. He had first to be delineated as a person separate from herself, a process that involved repeated confrontations around the therapist's unwillingness to respond to her demands, before he could be incorporated into the fantasy structure.

Several issues in this case stand out because of the opportunity to contrast not only the formal aspects of psychoanalysis and psychotherapy but also the style of the two therapists and the use of their real qualities by the patient.

(1) Definition of the therapist as a real person separate from the transference depends on his capacity to position himself as a modified part of the patient's superego. The early maneuver in relation to her shame and guilt about anal impulses was to this end.

(2) The psychic distance normally assumed by the second therapist appears to have allowed the patient to accept his independent reality. These real qualities appeared to be a necessary substructure for effective confrontation and limit setting. She was then able to identify with and incorporate

some of his attitudes while maintaining her relationship to him as a separate person.

(3) In other cases such psychic distancing might be inappropriate and be seen as "cold" or rejecting. The welcoming, accepting attitude of the first analyst in contrast might be more appropriate.

(4) We need to incorporate the notion of the therapist's style and personal qualities as a major element in the evaluation of patients for psychoanalysis and hopefully in time we can develop a typology of "fit" between patient and therapist, which would be a useful addition to the arts of referral patient selection.

Cases like this one make the point that for some patients to be able to create ego and superego structures in therapy highly specific real qualities may be required in the therapist, such as specific character attitudes toward impulse expression. The patient's capacity to use those qualities was certainly enhanced in the therapy situation (in contrast to the psychoanalytic situation) and was also influenced by the technical interventions described. Characteristics of the analyst like the welcoming attitude and the general quality of psychic distance are probably not subject to more than minimal change in the course of training. They represent permanent features of the personal terrain of the analyst, aspects of his development that interpenetrate all the facets of his life. They are certainly not subject to very much conscious manipulation on the part of the therapist as a matter of technique.

Each therapist develops techniques around his core attitudes and hopefully selects those patients with whom he can work best. The style of the second therapist says to the patient, "I am no crutch. You can grow up and lean on yourself." The other says, "I accept you, warts and all." Every clinician will recognize that neither model is appropriate for all cases.

The development and subsequent modification of psychic structure are dependent on the age and appropriate responsiveness of the environment to shifting instinctual demands. Critical elements in the environment of the psychotherapy session, viewed as a maturational experience, are the real personal qualities of the therapist (less so in analysis). Confrontation with these qualities may also influence the way a patient can dare to include the therapist as a participant in erotic fantasy. The elaborated fantasy, in turn, reflects a growth in ego structure that can modulate instinctual expression. This process is described in a border-line patient whose perversion-related fantasies were modified in the course of post-analytic psychotherapy. The progressive appearance of the therapist in the fantasy was accompanied by a marked improvement in symptoms and each change in the activity of the therapist in the fantasy was accompanied by significant changes in mood and function.

Bibliography

Eissler, K. R. (1950), Ego psychological implications of the psychoanalytic study of delinquents. *The Psychoanalytic Study of the Child*, 5: 97–121.
————— (1953), The effect of the structures of the ego on psychoanalytic technique. *J. Amer. Psychoanal. Assn.*, 1: 140–143).
Freud, S. (1925), Negation. *Standard Edition*, 19: 235–239. London: Hogarth Press, 1961.
Stone, L. (1961), *The Psychoanalytic Situation: An Examination of Its Development and Essential Nature*. New York: International Universities Press.
Strachey, J. (1934), The nature of the therapeutic action of psychoanalysis. *Int. J. Psychoanal.*, 15: 127–159.
Zetzel, E. (1971), A developmental approach to the borderline patient. *Amer. J. Psychiat.*, 127: 867–872.

The Place of
Confrontation in
Modern
Psychotherapy

LESTON L. HAVENS, M.D.

In this chapter I will describe the place I see for confrontation in modern psychotherapy and psychoanalysis. Because this is a "difficult" subject, both to exposit and in the extent of controversy it provokes, I want first to reach for perspective, in particular on the various psychiatries occupying the contemporary scene.

Today psychiatry is badly fragmented, new people coming into the field find themselves bewildered, and by nothing more than the issue psychotherapy, active or passive? I remember Ives Hendrick's saying that when he began to teach psychiatry, the great need was to stop the doctors from talking and start them listening. So completely was this achieved that by the time my generation arrived, the great need was to start them talking again. Today they are talking again. Indeed we are in a time of active therapies that stand in the sharpest possible contrast to psychoanalysis, both in their techniques and in their therapeutic claims.

Psychoanalysis has proved itself remarkably adept at understanding patients, down to the smallest details, through formulations of great clarity and completeness: the whole compromises a wonder of present intellectual life. At the same time psychoanalysts point to extraordinary difficulty *changing* the patients, despite prolonged and frequent contact. Indeed some of the patients appear to get worse, the well-known regression in treatment; and this conclusion is supported by the few good statistical studies there are.

All the while the active therapies, existential analysis, social psychiatry, behavior therapy, biological treatments, marital and sexual treatments, such as those of Masters and Johnson, claim to be greatly changing the patients, a claim they support with often impressive statistics. What is more remarkable, these schools present little evidence of understanding the patients; often they disdain the painfully arrived at understanding of more traditional psychiatry. The younger generation of psychiatrists, for example, turns away even from familiar history taking and psychological examining procedures in its eagerness to get to therapeutic activity.

In short, we have the contemporary spectacle of doctors who understand much and make modest claims of effectiveness standing against doctors who appear to understand little and claim to effect a great deal. Admittedly these remarks caricature a situation more complicated and overlapping, but they do reflect significant parts of present reality. It is as if knowledge were impotent and action blind.

How are we to understand this paradox? Sometimes, it is claimed, the statistics refer to different sets or levels of data. For example, analysts may be changing character, defenses, or patterns of behavior admittedly chronic, while behavior therapists affect only symptoms, social psychiatrists act on the external environment, and existentialists restrict themselves to the patients' values or expectations. The difference in results is said then to be due to these differences in goals.

It is also argued that the active therapists do effect change, but that the change is temporary or purchased at such a price that wiser heads would avoid it. Indeed, the present era of active therapies can be compared to psychotherapeutic trends seventy to eighty years ago. At that time education (which can be compared to behavior therapy), manipulation (which overlaps with social psychiatry), and value reorientation (which suggests existential therapy) were widely advocated and practiced, only giving way, and then not everywhere, to the psychoanalytic effort to reach behind symptoms and syndromes to the historical events and psychopathological processes behind, with the goal of modifying these.

The two solutions are at root one: that psychoanalysis appears to be less effective because it attempts to be more profound; or, from the standpoint of the other schools, these claim to be more effective because they are less "profound"; that is, less patient of historical reconstruction and less gingerly about therapeutic intervention. I doubt that any meaningful reconciliation is likely among many of the viewpoints, certainly not among some of their leaders, because the schools have become polarized, at least in their writings and teachings, though probably not so much in their practices. Psychoanalysis has separated itself very sharply from syndromic, descriptive psychiatry, despite the great need for accurate diagnosis in the determination of analyzability; it has separated itself from the interpersonalists or Sullivanians, despite their contributions to the management of psychotic defenses. (We see in Harold Boris' Chapter Nine the discussion of techniques similar to those of Sullivan, 1940, and Frieda Fromm-Reichmann, 1950.) And psychoanalysis has kept apart from existentialism, despite the work of Avery Weisman (1965) and a very few others; I can find in psychoanalytic writings almost no understanding of existential analysis. These are matters of particular importance in psychoanalytic training, for there is no assurance today that candidates have had adequate training in descriptive psychiatry, for example. Often they have read only in psychoanalysis itself. The result is that today many ambulatory cases of mania, psychopathy, and schizophrenia are taken into intensive psychotherapy or analysis out of diagnostic ignorance. The clinician's surprise is often registered by use of the term so popular today, "borderline."

Partly as a result of the isolation of psychoanalysis, perhaps even more as a result of its growing sophistication and self-consciousness, there has been a tendency to replace the psychoanalytic therapist by the analytic technician, a path so much followed in the whole of medicine. While the analytic technican may have great deftness, while he may even justly pride himself on not doing obvious harm, one suspects something critical is missing.

It was not missing early in the development of psychoanalysis, when Freud brought himself body and soul to the work. I suspect it began to disappear when the criticism of bias or suggestion was leveled at Freud's scientific claims and when transference and countertransference phenomena began to come clearly into view. Then psychoanalysis entered a second phase, one more like a smooth, slowly moving lake than the wild rapids of its beginning. Analyses lengthened; the doctors fell more silent and gradually quiet; unobtrusive men took the place of conquistadors and conquerors. It was like the consolidation of a new province: after the generals come the administrators, bureaucrats, lawyers. One result was that the old charge of suggestion had largely to be dropped (it was transferred to the patient's having *read* psychonalysis), for these analysts waited and listened for the transference neurosis to unfold; they were like scientists in their laboratories, painfully checking and rechecking, not discovering but confirming. A neutral, passive, almost aseptic technique developed appropriate to the scientific task in hand. Who could doubt that the transference neurosis occurred spontaneously or that every attempt had been made to avoid the great artifacts of countertransference? Some well-trained and experienced analysts broke out of this mold, Franz Alexander, John Murray, others; but an attitude of caution or even delicacy prevailed. We can compare it to the Halstead era in surgery, when the emphasis fell on technique and respect for the tissues.

The reaction against the era of consolidation has been strong. Social psychiatry has attacked the analytic concentration on individual patients: must not the social context change, too, if gains are to be kept; or what happens to marriage and family when one person changes and the others don't? Existential psychiatry, for its part, attacked the intellectualism, the attempted separation from value judgments characteristic of psychoanalysis: how real is the scientific neutrality proposed? Behaviorism sought to bring reality gradually but *forcibly* to the patient's attention; otherwise will not his extraordinary capacity for avoidance triumph over every verbal effort? And, in many instances, is not the neurosis in the transference either a pale imitation of the natural neurosis or so overwhelming as to be unmanageable? The behaviorists have asserted that, like the psychoanalysts, they want to attack the neurosis as the patient experiences it in treatment; but that we need more precise control over the exposure of the neurosis and its confrontation by reality.

Analysis has not stood by helpless while these active therapies have more and more caught professional, as well as public, attention. Analytic literature has increasingly discussed parameters of treatment, alliance formation, and perhaps most important, working through. If I catch the music of recent technical developments, I hear therapists becoming stronger, more personal, more active, even insistent; for does not the neurosis, even clarified, clarified, and clarified again, seemingly bored to death, *remain*, like that legendary guest, the Bore? It is the therapist who more often than the neurosis grows bored and leaves.

Now I do not want to suggest any turning back of the clock. There is no return to the childhood of analytic technique recapitulated in these well-known words (Freud, 1914):

In its first phase—that of Breuer's catharsis—it consisted in bringing directly into focus the moment at which the symptom was formed, and in persistently endeavouring to reproduce the mental processes involved in that situation, in order to direct their discharge along the path of conscious activity. Remembering and abreacting, with the help of the hypnotic state, were what was at that time aimed at. Next, when hypnosis had been given up, the task became one of discovering from the patient's free associations what he failed to remember. The resistance was to be circumvented by the work of interpretation and by making its results known to the patient. The situations which had given rise to the formation of the symptom and the other situations which lay behind the moment at which the illness broke out retained their place as the focus of interest; but the element of abreaction receded into the background and seemed to be replaced by the expenditure of work which the patient had to make in being obliged to overcome his criticism of his free associations, in accordance with the fundamental rule of psycho-analysis. Finally, there was evolved the consistent technique used today, in which the analyst gives up the attempt to bring a particular moment or problem into focus. He contents himself with studying whatever is present for the time being on the surface of the patient's mind, and he employs the art of interpretation mainly for the purpose of recognizing the resistances which appear there, and making them conscious to the patient. From this there results a new sort of division of labour: the doctor uncovers the resistances which are unknown to the patient; when these have been got the better of, the patient often relates the forgotten situations and connections without any difficulty. (p. 147)

No, the issues we need to discuss are not suggestions and the radical shaping of analytic content practiced at the turn of the century. The issues concern the "forgotten situation," the relationship of doctor and patient, and, of course, the resistances. To what extent are we able to *enter*, not merely have the patients "relate," the past, those "forgotten situations"? Should we not speak of a need for the doctor and patient to confront one another? And to what extent must we also confront the *resistances?* Harold Boris has already discussed this last brilliantly (Boris, Chapter Nine); I will only add some remarks about resistances that lie in the character.

In summary, I will argue that the vigorous pursuit of all three confrontations, with the past, between the persons, and of the resistances, underlies successful application of the *traditional* therapeutic techniques, such as clarification, abreaction, and transference interpretation; these last *depend upon* confrontation with the past, person, and neurosis. Finally, I will emphasize that this confrontation process cannot be depended upon to occur spontaneously, however elegant and pure the technique or the neurosis; in fact the whole neurotic process is against it. The neurotic process wants to hide or disguise the past, separate the persons of doctor and patient, and protect the neurosis.

The order in which I discuss these three types of confrontations is not random. I believe that confrontation with the past is the first to be undertaken; this is necessary in order for the therapist to place himself within the patient's world and to overcome the resistances to historical reconstructions. If this is not done initially, the resistances will too much delay and often prevent the work. (Successful confrontation of the past also reduces the need for some of the very subtle and difficult techniques that Harold Boris, Chapter Nine, describes.) On the other hand, confrontation of the persons involved and of the neurosis occurs simultaneously.

Confrontation of the past may seem at first glance the most obvious aspect of all therapy and any emphasis on the word confrontation little more than gilding the traditional lily. God knows, therapy is an historical investigation; it means to uncover the past; the whole procedure aims at a reconstruction of the past into the fullest possible conscious thought and feeling. One aim is to put the past truly behind but not in the sense of a repressed or dissociated forgetting.

The past is to be with us but as a companion, not a hidden, secret master. We argue that those who forget or ignore the past are doomed to repeat it.

For what reason, then, do I emphasize *confrontation* with the past? I remember hearing many times in my residency that it did not matter whether a past experience was real or fantasied, that what counted was the experience's psychic reality, the conviction or investment a memory commanded. Much was said about Freud's discovery that reports he had taken to be realities were at least in part fantasies, but less about Ferenczi's (1949) hint that with many of the cases Freud had been right in the first place, that indeed real experiences probably strengthened if they did not initiate the fantasies.

I myself came to a conclusion very similar to Ferenczi's on the basis of comparing psychotic and neurotic perceptions, with a generous assist from Adelaide Johnson (1956). I will not review the whole train of, to me, impressive evidence that I presented elsewhere (1964), but give the conclusion: the old teaching, psychic reality, rather than reality or fantasies, conceals the empirical findings that, where psychic reality becomes so strong that it overrides even contemporary reality (as in hallucinating), such psychotic reality seems more often than not to have behind it a past real experience. I would go so far as to suggest that, in the absence of brain lesions or toxic states, people cannot distort reality to the extent we call psychotic, unless they have actually experienced a similar distortion (presented to them as outward reality) in the past. In essence, the claim is that the psychotic person does not have a distorted reality sense in the way that particular expression is usually used, does not have a weak ego, so to speak, so much as a strong past. Along this same line Dr. Vicki Levi and I have been drawing together case material from a paranoid man that carries the Schreber argument one step further: not only does the paranoid person suffer from massive amounts of repressed and projected libido, but past experiences of an aggressive nature against the patient have also provided a real basis for the concept of an external persecutor, who at the same time must be loved. (This is surely the conclusion to be drawn from Niederland's (1963) discoveries about the Schreber case itself.) And the patient's appearing unrealistic or psychotic is a function of intrusive past perceptions that must be partly disguised, because the patient still cannot face the reality of the incredible past history.

It is not necessary here to review in any detail the impact of family studies on contemporary psychiatry. Suffice it to say that much more pathology has been observable in even apparently well families than was suspected up to now. For example, much more family violence occurs than was believed possible, more children annually in this country dying at the hands of their own parents than of many physical diseases. We are essentially being asked to make as radical a shift in our views of the normal, as we did when Freud clarified the nature of primary process mental life. Not only do our minds teem with perverse thoughts, and violent ones as well; but the *Ladies Home Journal* picture of ideal family life is as far from reality as is the Norman Rockwell picture of young Americans full of clean thoughts. Obviously many family relationships are as dangerous as many viruses and cancers, so that external reality as well as internal reality calls for a radical reshaping of our expectations.

We should not, therefore, be surprised to find that our patients' fantasies are matched by their past realities, in many cases. Most of us are not so squeamish, as our profession was a hundred years ago, as to reject the patients' "bad" thoughts; but many of us are still very reluctant to acknowledge the extent of their "bad" homes. This reluctance added to any denial by the patients of the reality of their parents may prevent the historical reconstruction.

The revision of our expectations is important. Too often we may attempt to reach the patient's unconscious conflicts before the parental realities are enough explored and accepted. Such a mistake was implicit in Freud's view of Schreber's experience with his father, radically at variance with what Niederland (1963) discovered. An earlier generation of psychiatrists was, perhaps out of habit or defensiveness, too ready to make the assumption of parental normality. It is not a mistake we should continue.

I appreciate that parents characteristically "change" during psychotherapy and analysis, that some of the initial condemnation of parents during treatment springs from the disappointments of the child, and that patients must gain perspective on parents, often to the point of reconciliation. This should not obscure, however, any partial justice of the child's complaints, only because it is easier to make a solid peace with parents if their real features are acknowledged, and not just by the *patients*. Parents may appear to change during treatment precisely because their negative features have been acknowledged. In short, I believe therapists should beware of putting themselves too much in the position of parents by automatically lofty or neutral attitudes toward patients' complaints, lest realistic aspects of the patients' complaints harden the transference neurosis immutably. From such attitudes too, in part, flows the condemnation of analysis as the guardian of society and the "adjuster" of patients.

I make this point at such length because it brings us directly to the issue of confrontation. As long as Vicki Levi's patient remained in doubt about the reality of his past persecution, his reality sense was clouded. A doctor's inability to accept the past reality or, at least, the doctor's insistence on remaining neutral as to whether it was reality or fantasy, assisted in that clouding. When, however, the doctor grew increasingly sure it was real and insisted on the patient's confronting that reality, the contemporary clouding of the reality sense cleared (cf. Rosen, 1955). How is the patient to get help with his "defective reality sense" if the doctor won't believe the truth?

Now, I want to argue that this lesson is not applicable

to psychoses alone. Neuroses, too, present us with a clouding of the reality sense, although much more limited and less profound than in psychoses. More often than not, this loss of full reality sense in neuroses is shown by an over-investment in certain objects or by assigning special feelings to them; for example, the phobic patient is not "realistic" about the phobic object, although he may have *intellectual* insight. Similarly, the fetishistic patient *experiences* the shoe as if it were a penis, even though intellectually, even perceptually, it remains a shoe. In every neurosis one comes upon bits of psychosis, what I call neurotic delusions; *i.e.*, misconceptions very heavily defended; the resistance is of psychotic proportion. In these instances I have always found heavy reality contributions. As long as the neurotic person, as well as the psychotic person, remains in doubt about the reality status of these early perceptions, as long as the therapist remains neutral on the issue—early experience, fantasies, or reality?—the patient cannot complete the historical reconstruction and take that first step toward freeing up the fixations. He is unable to gain perspective on the past; for in any *historical* construction, the issue, fact or fancy, is central. The historian has a vital interest in the *truth value* of assertions.

Even more important, the therapist is repeatedly called upon to push through, against the patient's denial or other resistances, an accurate account of early experience. Some part of the patient's feelings is isolated or repressed by means of denial or distortion of some part of an early experience. There cannot be an abreaction of those feelings until the reality distortion is corrected. We encounter the vigorous correction of such distortion in all Freud's case reports. I am not speaking now of interpretations; instead I mean such statements as, this must have meant so-and-so happened. How can we deal with, even recognize, *fantasies* until we have a clear grasp of *reality?*

This is the essence of my point. Past reality must have its day in court. The delineation of ideas, complexes, conflictual fantasies, and the ego measures brought to bear against them have been the traditional materials of psychoanalysis. I am saying that a third material must stand equally beside them, the patient's historical past; and that this historical reconstruction will not occur spontaneously, even in neuroses. We can truly speak of three analytic tasks; fantasy work, ego work, and historical work.

Now it can be argued that the word confrontation does not belong here, that I am merely describing "clarifications." Certainly it could be cogently argued that to get a bit of reality past many of the resistances we meet a quiet clarification will do better than bombastic insistences; the latter are likely, with many patients, to excite more resistances than they overcome. That is plain enough. And throughout I never mean to equate confrontation with bombast, screaming, or emotional outpourings of any particular sort. Someone said that Lincoln could make a fool stop and think with a joke or a glance. Many of the most effective confrontations are that quiet or that homely. The goal is to get the message across, not to be ourselves defeated by the resistances, whatever the method. We want the patients to confront their inner and outer realities, and in the long run it is the therapist alone against the resistances.

Much analytic remembering fails to reconstruct the past; perhaps it is too intellectual or too purely perceptual a recollection, and this failure fully to enter the past opens the way to acting it out. For these reasons, *confronting, meeting, encountering*, such words as these, seem to me to represent better the work to be done in relationship to the past than such a word as *clarification*. I believe, further, that with some patients, whose pasts have been extraordinarily difficult, it will be impossible to indicate an understanding of their pasts without participating in the correction of their presents, whether by general social or local family interventions. To stand idly by discussing the difficulties of the past while these continue in the present is to convince the patient you have no real grasp of the past.

Of course, as the transference neurosis develops, we will be blamed for the past. That is precisely what we want to have happen. My point is that transference interpretations cannot be convincing if the interpreter does not really understand, first, what he is being blamed for and, second, whether his neutrality and passivity indeed make him resemble in actuality any unfeeling figures of the past.

So much for confrontation with the past. Of course a great many questions remain. We have to ask ourselves, for example, to what extent we *ever* reconstruct the past, to what extent we can speak at all of reality in the past. To me these are philosophical questions, and I can only hope the metaphysicians will not upset irretrievably our rough clinical categories. One clinician I have found useful on this subject is the analyst Samuel Novey. His little book, *The Second Look* (1968), deals entirely with the issue of reconstructing personal histories; further, he has a special interest in those confrontations with the past that occur when a patient returns to the actual scenes of his childhood. He indicates, too, that not only does the transference present us with the past, as do such accidental events as encounters with childhood scenes, but also with *present reality*, which so often matches the past closely enough to trigger off inner confrontations.

The place of confrontation with the person of *doctor and patient* is, of these types of confrontation, the most difficult to discuss and certainly the most controversial. Psychoanalysis prides itself on a technique relatively free of suggestion, personal influence, charlatanry of any kind, despite the abuse it takes on all these counts. Am I suggesting that we return to the time of Mesmer, deepen our voices, and darken our rooms? No, but I do want to suggest that not every personal encounter is quackery or charisma.

We are all well aware that the hidden element in much psychotherapeutic success is the personality, the character of the therapist. We take pride in this, as well as some scientific embarrassment. I am going to argue that the personality or perhaps better the person of the therapist—where it has not been inhibited out of existence—is a necessary element for applying the traditional psychotherapeutic techniques, that these techniques cannot *take hold* in a completely neutral or passive solution.

We have in our Boston community several very able therapists who do not appear to confront their patients with their persons, who would in fact vehemently deny such aggressive behavior, but whose very presence is itself a great confrontation. One I know seems just to sit there, in his benign quiet way, hardly breathing, but all the while bringing to bear a vast silent request for relevance, feeling, sharing. Many others of us have to raise our voices, kick, or scream to come across one half as much, to encounter so extensively the patient and his neurosis or psychosis.

There is another therapist among us, a Toscanini of psychoanalysts, who is so self-effacing, neutral, objective, so *spare* that the word *personality* hardly applies to him at all. Yet stay a little longer, feel a little more, as the patient must. How many of you could be less than honest with him; would it be possible to find anything in him on which to hang distrust; would not his most casual interpretation sound to you more deeply than the rest of us in chorus? Or, one last example, I know a distinguished woman therapist whose patience and strength are literally like mountains. Oh, call this literary or hysterical hyperbole all you want, but then be with her a while. Do you mean to tell me that when she makes a "clarification" it is not as different from your mealy-mouthed passive therapist's clarification as Beethoven's *Ninth* is from my whistling "Dixie"? No, there is almost that much difference between them.

I am saying that the medium must carry the message, and if the medium is wrong, or if the medium is missing, there will be no message. The anesthetic is perfect, the diagnosis correct, the nurses skilled, the patient ready, but too often the psychiatric surgeon has no knife.

I think the lesson is clear. We must be careful how we teach objectivity and neutrality, for with many students we will too readily suppress what personalities they have. Of course some need to put away parts of their personalities; but on the whole most psychotherapists are hardly an aggressive lot, not particularly loaded with what the world calls personality; and what capacity they have for confrontation is too readily snuffed out.

I predict that, if we do allow both our knowledge and our capacities for sharing what we know to flourish, both our objectivity and our capacity for intimacy, the tiresome and seemingly endless debate about the value of psychotherapy, will soon expire. Psychotherapy is effective; it can be remarkably so; it often remains only to do it.

Only with the development of the transference neurosis do the precise nature and full extent of the patient's illness become apparent; the doctor then confronts the illness, in both its fantasy and ego components. Those active therapies that do not allow such a development keep themselves from anything like a full knowledge of psychological illness.

The therapist's passivity and neutrality are the essential elements for this full unfolding of the neurotic process. It is true that in psychoses and in borderline and some character states transference (indeed transference psychosis) may develop so rapidly, if the doctor is too neutral and passive, that the treatment situation is irretrievably overrun. It is to such situations that Harold Boris (Chapter Nine) is addressing himself. But with less severe conditions, there is general agreement that some degree of passivity and a considerable neutrality make possible understanding of any particular illness. These are the lenses by which we focus on, we could almost say enlarge, the patient's neurosis. They are truly diagnostic instruments.

Essentially we *lure out*, you might say, unconscious material into the treatment relationship; the result is transference; we replace a repression with a projection. Hysterical types do this most rapidly, with their penchant for dramatic projections; but paranoid people provide the same treatment opportunity, if the doctor can keep ahead of the loss of reality sense. More literal minded obsessional types take longer to develop the projections but may then have a sharper reality sense to dissect them. A blank screen provides the most faithful and visible reproduction, the blankness demanding neutrality and the screen passivity. All this seems clear and well established among us. It is essentially an experimental method in the best scientific tradition. The doctor arranges for the production of the experimental or transference neurosis so that he can take its measure and determine its treatment.

What am I contributing by using a forcible, affective-seeming word like *confrontation* for the quiet intellectuality of the usual words, *analysis of the resistances?* Of course there are *intellectual* confrontations, but I think we mean by interpretation or analysis something different. It suggests giving the patient a translation or understanding of this piece of his behavior; the implication is that he can take it or leave it. As Paul Myerson (Chapter One) indicates, the word *confrontation,* on the other hand suggests force or blockade, the *imposing* of a counterforce to the neurosis. Alexander's example (Myerson, Chapter One) illustrates this: the patient is irritating; the doctor gets irritated; the two, as it were, cancel each other out, neutralize each other perhaps, so that the progress of the treatment can continue.

Presumably Alexander did not *analyze* his patient's resistance but, instead, attacked it because the patient did not accept that it needed analysis, indeed that it was anything but perfectly justified and sensible. Alexander's attack made this piece of the patient's behavior ego-alien; it set up an internal conflict, as Boris (Chapter Nine) puts it. Now we are moving toward the heart of the matter.

Attitudes of neutrality and passivity allow the neurosis to emerge in front of the doctor, *provided* the patient's defenses allow such an emergence. If not, only that part of the neurosis consisting of the ego defenses emerges. The doctor is then confronted by the outer structure of the neurosis; his efforts to get *inside* are frustrated, or he is given only bits and pieces. Or, still another variant, the patient allows the doctor detailed, genetic insight, but without affective accompaniments; the patient agrees the doctor may be right, but so what? The patient's main investment remains in himself as a superior being, above anything the doctor can say.

I think many students of psychoanalysis would agree that some of the most important contributions to resolving these difficult situations came from Wilhelm Reich (1933). He highlighted the presence of the neurosis in the character. If I understand the way Reich found he had to make these interpretations, they seem more like confrontations than clarifications. And the reason is obvious. By definition *symptoms* are brought to the doctor for remedy; *character*, on the other hand, is equally much by definition, silent to the patient. The characterological aspects of ourselves are like French glass; others can see in, but we can't see out. What is the passive neutral doctor to do about these silent aspects of the patients?

One answer is to say, as I have often heard it said, that the psychoanalyst cannot deal with any problem that the patient does not bring him; that is, he must wait for a problem to become *symptomatic*. In this way of thinking, any effort to approach the non-symptomatic is looked on as specifically nonanalytic and thrown into the limbo of para- meters. Patients are "analyzable" only if their character problems are very slight or self-resolving. Personally, I believe the declining impact of psychoanalysis in psychiatry, general medical practice, and elsewhere, springs from this self-imposed restriction.

But how is the doctor to remain passive, neutral, and at the same time to take arms against a sea of characterological troubles? In asking this we arrive at the heart of the diffi- culty. If the doctor leaves his neutral, passive position, does he not prevent the development of the very transference neurosis that successful treatment requires? Or, from the other side, if he remains passive and neutral, do not the patient's characterological problems block either the doctor's view of the transference neurosis or his ability to interpret it meaningfully? I believe this is the central issue of the analyzability problem.

Or the doctor springs on the neurosis, wrestles it down, feels triumphant, only to discover that the neurosis comes back for more and more. The neurosis has seemingly gained fresh strength from its exercise with the doctor. Again, we can all think of many examples of this too, where the patient's rationalizations match point for point the therapist's interpretations, like a battle spreading along ever-widening fronts. Here there is confrontation all right, but no resolution. We do not want every skirmish to turn into a war.

The neurosis is an active force—it is not simply as Charcot and Janet believed—a weakness of the personality. We know that treatment is a struggle. We would *like* to keep it intellectual; we may be smarter than some patients, even smarter than their neuroses, and have sharper ideas. But we know the voice of reason is weak; it rides a great archaic mount, so we expect to struggle. But grabbing something from a person's grasp seldom prompts them to give it up; the whole force of the reaction is opposite.

Like children lost in the forest we would all wish here for a magic wand to guide us out of this forest. The magic wand would say, "Therapist, yes, you must be passive and neutral and passionate all at once, or all in succession, without any one posture muddling the others." That would be a magic wand! And perhaps the wand would add, "Considering all your training and teachers, and the amount of money you are paid, you should be able to do it."

Well, we *are* in the forest; but we are not children, and there is no magic wand. Perhaps we encounter here one of those basic natural antinomies Kent wrote about, inherent conflicts that admit of no resolution. Or perhaps we have some psychological equivalent of the Heisenberg principle; we can no more be both passionate and objective than we can know both the velocity and position of certain particles.

I am tempted to leave the whole matter there, confident that most of you will insist upon being both active *and* passive, neutral *and* passionate, letting the devil take antinomies and Heisenberg principles. It did not require this discussion to teach us that psychotherapy calls for both objectivity and intimacy, freedom and goals, passivity and activity. I believe, myself, that only the long period of psychoanalytic confirmation I referred to earlier, with its necessary emphasis on neutrality and objectivity, is a period we are leaving behind. And only our having stayed so long there and drunk so deep of those waters can explain our ever having needed to question the necessity of confrontation in the first place. Of course, psychotherapy and psychoanalysis require both clarification and confrontation; of course each is helpless without the other; and of course there must be inherent conflict between them—hence, the art and perhaps never the science of psychotherapy.

But how, in fact, are we to move the characterological to the symptomatic without destroying the treatment? Often we wait for life to do it—by forcing insight on the patients, through the pressure of circumstances or the criticisms of a friend. Of we may act as Alexander did, by a flash of anger that overrides the patient's resistances and establishes the characterological trait now as a symptom.

The commonest method is neither of these. It is the method Elvin Semrad (1971) succinctly calls "the right hand and the left hand." We give with one hand, or we spend the credit we have in hand, while at the same time something unpleasant is pointed out. At the moment of special closeness we chance the separation of the patient from a bit of his character. The closeness makes seeing it the doctor's way possible, a transient identification; and the greater that closeness, the more likely the insight will be kept long enough to be useful. Then the work of understanding can begin. This is not intimacy for its own sake, but to make possible a confrontation and, in turn, analysis.

What this method and Alexander's have in common is

feeling, one positive, the other negative. Perhaps that is what is meant by the existential saying (Jaspers, 1900) "Nothing happens until the doctor is touched by the patient" (p. 676). Or perhaps it was said even earlier and in Boston by the old words (Peabody, 1927) "The secret of taking care of the patient is caring for him." We see here a reconciliation of those polar positions of psychotherapy, objectivity and intimacy, reason and feeling, each so vital, each so helpless without the other: intimacy makes objectivity usable, while objectivity justifies and spends the gained intimacy.

Bibliography

Alexander, F. Cited in Paul Myerson's paper. Op. Cit.

Boris, H., Confrontation in the analysis of the transference resistance. This Volume.

Ferenczi, S. (1949), Confusion of tongues between the adult and the child. *Int. J. Psycho-Anal.*, 30: 225–230.

Freud, S. (1914), Remembering, repeating and working-through. *Standard Edition*, 12: 147–156. London: Hogarth Press, 1958.

Fromm-Reichmann, F. (1950), *Principles of Intensive Psychotherapy*. Chicago: University of Chicago Press, 1960.

Havens, L., Psychosis and the concept of ego defect. Presented before the American Psychoanalytic Association, New York, 1964.

Jaspers, K. (1900), *General Psychopathology*. Chicago: University of Chicago Press, 1963.

Johnson, A. (1956), Observations on ego functions in schizophrenia. *Psychiat.*, 19: 143–148.

Myerson, P. G., The meanings of confrontation. This Volume.

Niederland, W. (1963), Further data and memorabilia pertaining to the Schreber case. *Int. J. Psycho-Anal.*, 44: 201.

Novey, S. (1968), *The Second Look*. Baltimore: Johns Hopkins Press.

Peabody, F. W. (1927), *The Care of the Patient*. Cambridge: Harvard University Press.

Reich, W. (1933), *Character Analysis*. New York: Orgone Institute Press, 1949.

Rosen, V. H. (1955), The reconstruction of a traumatic childhood event in the case of derealization. *J. Amer. Psychoanal. Assoc.*, 2: 211–221.

Semrad, E. (1971), Personal communication.

Sullivan, H. (1940), *Collected Works*. New York: W. W. Norton, 1965.

Weisman, A. (1965), *Existential Core of Psychoanalysis; Reality, Sense, and Responsibility*. Boston, Little Brown.

Confrontation

in the

Therapeutic Process

DOUGLAS F. WELPTON, M.D.

For some time I, like others, have felt the need in our field to develop a two-person psychology of the therapeutic process, a theory that includes the psychology of the therapist as well as that of the patient. While we have learned a great amount from focusing on the psychology of the patient, I have been concerned that efforts to conceptualize the therapeutic process in terms of a one-person psychology distort what really happens in such a way that we will not be able to advance our understanding of what helps patients grow and change unless we broaden the scope of our study to include the therapist. This is, I have found, easier to say than to do.

The complexities of trying to describe and comprehend the intricacies of the therapeutic interaction are considerable, especially when it is often the nonverbal behavior, or the tone of voice rather than the content of the words that counts. To be able to capture and render to someone else how the therapist knows what he does, how his empathy and his free-floating attention actually operate so as to enable him to be open to his own feelings, fantasies, and unconscious processes is a considerable task. To study the two-person psychology of therapy also requires that we relate these psychological events in the therapist to those in the patient to study the interplay between them. Finally, and this is what I have found most difficult, such a study requires that the therapist open up aspects of himself and his work that he would prefer to keep private. Here, for example, I have found it difficult to describe an intervention that I regard as a mistake and far from ideal. Revealing more openly what we really say or do is most difficult, and yet I do not know how we can truly study or advance the process of therapy unless we describe actual experiences from treatment for study. In the course of doing so, our own personalities inevitably emerge, since we do convey ourselves and our values to our patients and we are not blank screens. Many years ago Alice Balint (1937) wrote: "The character of the analyst is an integral factor in the analytic situation and with the best will in the world it cannot be eliminated" (p. 13–14). The consequence of our knowing this fact is that most of us turn to our trusted colleagues or to other friends to get help in our struggles to be therapeutic, and this is understandable. It has, however, left us without a complete theory of the therapeutic process because we have focused on the patient and tended to exclude the therapist.

There is another problem with all efforts to understand and theorize about human behavior, which is that theories by their very nature are simplistic and reductionistic; they tend to simplify experience in their efforts to describe and understand it. This simplification of experience is true whether the theories are based on a one-person or a two-person psychology. It is probably an inevitable limit of psychological knowledge that it is easier to fit people into theories than to develop theories that do justice to the complexities of people and human behavior. In spite of these difficulties, this paper is an effort toward a two-person psychology of therapy. The issue of use of confrontation in therapy is a timely one in developing this interactional psychology, since confrontations are interpersonal processes and are an aspect of the patient-therapist encounter that is the very heart of the therapeutic process.

TWO KINDS OF CONFRONTATION

In my clinical work, by my paying special attention to my confrontations during the last several months, I have observed that confrontation is more than one thing and cannot be talked about as though it refers to one single type of intervention. All confrontations do involve a moment of intense encounter between the therapist and the patient, one in which forcefulness is a crucial aspect of the experience as Myerson (Chapter One) has observed. My thesis, however, is that we should distinguish two different kinds of confrontations; namely, what I would call the angry confrontation to be compared with the empathic confrontation. In making this distinction between two different kinds of confrontations, I am aware that I am being reductionistic and contrasting the extremes of the confrontation process for heuristic reasons, and that the real experiences of therapeutic confrontations may lie anywhere along a continuum between the angry prototype, on the one hand, and the empathic prototype, on the other.

The Angry Confrontation

An angry confrontation is one in which the therapist is annoyed, angered, or even enraged at something he does not like that the patient is doing. Frequently the therapist feels unfairly and unjustly treated by his patient, and his feeling dislike for this behavior of the patient invariably underlies his anger and his confrontation. It is the anger of the therapist that produces the forcefulness of the confrontation; whatever the therapist says in his confrontation, the patient experiences as the basic message: "I don't like your behavior when you are this way, and I have my limits in tolerating it." When I have been made angry in this way by a patient, I have usually found myself sitting on my initial angry feelings for a little while in an effort to be calmer and more restrained when I bring the matter up; and I have observed that at other times, when I have avoided being confronting, I have treated the patient to an angry silence. When an angry confrontation of this sort was successful, the patient got the message and stopped behaving as he had been toward me. I felt relieved that our relationship had improved, at least in this regard. The difficulty with which I was left, even after such a "success," was my concern that the patient had changed out of submissive compliance. Because of his wishes to remain in treatment with me and to have me like him—and these are very powerful motivations for most patients—he had given in and submitted to my wishes by giving up a part of his behavior, at least in his relationship with me. He had changed for me, not for himself—this is what has troubled me most. His adaptation to me had fostered his feeling like the underdog and identifying with the victim. I was in the position of feeling I had forced someone to change, perhaps against his will, and of having to cope with my guilt for having done so. I was further troubled by my thoughts that I had fostered the patient's dependency on me through his changing for me and my approval, with the result that I found myself reinforcing a dependency pattern that patients generally need help to free themselves from.

In my observations, there are two basic processes in the psychology of the therapist that lead him to make an angry confrontation. One is that he dislikes the way the patient is behaving; he disapproves of it. The second, and this is the more important element, is that he feels a need to change the patient's behavior. The more he dislikes the patient's behavior, the more driven he may feel to have the patient change it; and his anger conveys with force this expectation to the patient. His disapproval of the patient for his behavior may border on rejection of the patient, conveying to the patient explicitly or implicitly that he does not want to work with someone who behaves as the patient is behaving. The patient may well change in the face of such forceful anger and disapproval; but if he does so, it is inevitably out of his need to please the therapist and to hold on to him, which forces on the patient a need to submit and comply with the therapist's expectations. It comes as no surprise to me, when I review my experience, to find that the patients who have elicited angry confrontations from me are those who have the greatest problems with passive submission, who unconsciously provoke angry attacks from others, who complain characteristically of feeling like victims, and who are torn between identifications with the aggressor and with the submitter (victim). Brenman's (1952) observations on the teaser and the teasee describe the sadomasochistic interactions in these processes, while Loewenstein (1957) has captured the psychology of provoking angry confrontations most cogently when he speaks of "the seduction of the aggressor," which is the masochistic patient's role in these interactions.

I remember with some embarrassment an episode in the analysis of a phobic and compulsive engineer who was constantly feeling guilty and struggling with his masochism with his parents, whom he experienced as demanding perfectionists. He felt he could never fully please them and meet their standards for success, especially since he came from a highly successful family. In the analysis we had worked on his highly demanding and aggressive superego, with some alleviation of his guilt and self-inflicted suffering during the first year of our work. The bind that we got into developed around the issue of the appointments, since he had to change the hours of our meetings three different times during our first year. Part of his need to change arose from his inability to tell an employer that he was in analysis, for fear this would prejudice them against hiring him on a permanent basis. In my efforts to provide him with a less rigid and compulsive model about these matters, I had indicated to him that I had some flexibility in my schedule and I thought we should be able to shift hours if necessary. By the time we had come to discussing our third schedule change, however, I had begun to feel very put upon, not so much because I thought the changes impossible to make, but because I felt the whole burden for working out these changes had fallen on me. In my effort to free myself from my burdened feelings, I indicated to the patient that my schedule was not infinitely flexible and that when it came to this latest change I would be able to offer him one new hour each afternoon (we were switching from morning to afternoon appointments because of his work schedule) when I could see him. He took this to mean I could offer him only one possible time each day, probably partially communicated by my somewhat terse tone, for I was feeling much less flexible at that moment than I had before. He reacted with an explosive outburst, telling me that such an arrangement was unacceptable and a breach of faith. In a most provocative tone he asked what would happen if he could not meet at those times, and I responded with restrained but obvious anger that then we could not continue with his analysis. This was an angry confrontation produced by my dislike for his rigid and demanding behavior about the appointments and my need to have him change it immediately. I not only was disapproving of his behavior but was indicating to him the possibility that I could reject him (no longer see him as a patient) if he did not change. He responded with more anger by threatening to sue me for malpractice; and since I had by then gotten over my anger, I said to him that I thought we both hoped we could work out mutually acceptable appointments but that I felt he was expecting from me more flexibility about the schedule than I had. After he left the hour he evidently cooled off and began to feel quite guilty for his exploding, a pattern of which he was well aware. He called me and offered to meet at the morning hours we already had even though he had told me earlier that these would be very difficult for him. I heard in this his readiness to submit to me in a compliant identification with the victim, and I told him that I remembered he had said these hours would be very difficult and I thought we should give the whole issue more consideration in our next appointment.

In the subsequent hours we were able to work out mutually acceptable appointments. I found that all my inclinations were toward forgetting this angry confrontation, since I felt that it was a mistake on my part, that I had clearly acted on countertransference, that I had played my role in the seduction of the aggressor; and I felt guilty for it. I did not, however, follow my inclination to forget it and instead pursued the episode with the patient, who confirmed my observations of how victimized he felt; he spoke of feeling "bullied" and needing to "bully me back" with his threats of malpractice, for which he felt embarrassed. He said that he kept wanting to bring up this episode because he felt I had made a mistake and he wanted to make me pay for it. I acknowledged his honesty about his wishes for revenge and told him that I agreed with him that I had made a mistake, that I was not above making mistakes, but that I had said what I had because I felt he needed to know that there were limits to how far I could go to meet his demands on time changes. He was quite surprised that I could admit to making a mistake and went on to make clear that he never felt free to do so, especially with his family. I felt that we had made a therapeutic gain of my mistake through this work. After my admission of how I saw what I had done and why, he was free from his need to get revenge and could pursue the issue of how he came to put me under such pressure as he felt under himself, which led us back to a very alive analysis of his unfriendly and aggressive superego.

Indeed it often seems that when an angry confrontation can be pursued fully by both therapist and patient, it opens up for discussion a previously obscure aspect of the patient's behavior, and the force of the confrontation enables the patient to see something he would otherwise ignore. This shared investigation is possible, however, only when the therapist has gotten over his anger and ceased to experience the patient as someone who is tormenting him. The therapist's return of empathy requires that he realize the patient is not behaving the way he is just to torment his therapist, but behaves this way with others as well and restricts his personal relationships by doing so. When I was able to return to a more empathic position with this patient, I realized that I had gained a deeper understanding of this man's demanding superego for having felt under the pressure of it myself; I really knew how he felt when trying to meet what he experienced as his parents' demands. In his own way the patient had unconsciously fostered this understanding in me by treating me as he does himself with his demands.

The Empathic Confrontation

I would now like to contrast this angry confrontation with the empathic confrontation, a process that is no less forceful but that comes from a very different psychology on the part of the therapist. I find that I am able to confront patients in this caring way when I feel free from the need to change them. Instead of feeling under pressure to make them different, I find myself accepting them for what they are and then in a free position to take up whatever behavior interferes with their capacities to form close, caring relationships with me or the others in their lives. When working this way, I follow my own feelings of liking or disliking the behavior of the patient very closely, for this is my best guide as to where we are and what is important to the patient at that time. Not only is it important to the patient, but it is also what counts most in the treatment at that moment since the patient and I have to work out those things we dislike about one another if I am going to be of help to him. I have found that there is no better indicator of my potential helpfulness to a patient than my feelings of like for him: that if I can truly accept him for who he is and what he is and like him whatever his drawbacks, then I can be my most helpful self. If I cannot work out a relationship with a patient in which I like him, I cannot be of much help and should send him to another therapist. I offer the following example to help clarify what I mean by an empathic confrontation in which I attempt to make use of my feelings of dislike within the framework of an accepting attitude.

A married nurse had been seeing me in twice-weekly therapy for two months during which she had talked a lot and conveyed a good deal of emotion. In spite of this I was feeling that I was not really getting to know her better or feeling closer to her. I liked her and had been working to help her with her depression, which was linked to her demanding, perfectionistic standards for herself, which she had taken over from her hard-driving, upwardly mobile mother. We had discussed her anxiety about therapy and particularly her intense concerns about what I would think of her if she revealed to me the things she did not like about herself. My comments had been directed toward questioning why she thought so poorly of herself, what she expected of herself, and of likening her own harsh demands of herself with those of her mother in the past. I attempted to help her toward a position of being open to understand herself rather than one of constantly judging herself as good or bad, right or wrong. In this discussion she said that she had an even greater fear of meeting me outside my office for fear I would not talk to her and would want nothing to do with her.

I had noted from the start of our work her tendency to bolt into and out of my office so as to avoid real greetings and partings. Based on my feelings, and the information from her, and my observations, I made the following confrontation. I said that, while I knew how afraid she was of me for fear I would not like her and had observed how she bolted into and out of my office, I felt that she was really keeping distance between us in a way that made it harder for me to like her. I said this in a calm, gentle tone because I felt general acceptance and liking for her and because I only wanted to understand with her why she behaved in a way that elicited from me the opposite feelings from what she wanted, and I said this to her in our discussion that followed the confrontation. I did not feel under any pressure to change her; I just wanted to understand her. She responded with a sigh of relief that she knew she had been keeping me at a distance and felt some relief to be able to discuss it. She repeated how afraid she felt of me and said that her bolting into and out of the office represented her efforts to avoid dealing with me in a real situation, akin to our meeting outside the office. In the following interview she told me how upset she had been since last time about her need to keep me at a distance and especially with my comment, which she mistook as my telling her I did not like her. I reminded her that this was not what I had said, although I could understand her tendency to take it this way. I said that I had told her she made it difficult for me to like her more when she kept such distance. She fell silent, then began to weep and almost inaudibly said, "Why did I have to have such a crazy father!" I asked what she meant, and she then began to convey with intense sadness what a difficult time she had had with him.

She had been born while he was away in the armed service and when he returned she was three years old. From the start he rejected her almost as though she were not his child. He showed obvious preference for her older sister and not only treated her coldly but told her she was "ugly." The most difficult part came during her early teens (at this point her embarrassment and hurt were conveyed through her remorse) when he had crawled into her bed to wake her in the morning until one time when she thought he was naked and jumped out of bed. He stopped this behavior, and she felt even more hurt when her mother would not believe her about her father's behavior. It was these events that caused her the greatest pain, and she related them directly to her inability to trust me and her fears of developing more closeness with me. She also said during this hour that she had come to realize that she had chosen her husband because he did not threaten her sexually. All of this history came forth with deep feelings, and at the end of it, when she said that she did not know how to get beyond her problems with men to form a closer, friendlier relationship as, for example, with me, I replied that I thought she had already started to do so in what had just been happening. Indeed I knew that I felt closer and more friendly toward her for knowing what she had been through in her past and for sharing with her these experiences with genuine feeling.

What I am calling the empathic confrontation, as shown in this example, is based on facing myself and my patient with a vivid, here and now, mutually shared experience that has been happening between us in the therapy. While it may be something that the patient is doing that frustrates me in my efforts to be a special kind of friend, which is how I think of myself as a therapist, I am not angry with the patient nor do I feel that he or she has to change. I feel instead that I am accepting of their behavior but ready to question it with them so as to understand them better. If the confrontation is successful, I have found that it deepens my empathy for them and how they have come to be the way they are. The empathic confrontation places a premium on here and now experiencing, for I am impressed that it is the first-hand experiencing of new or different ways of being with the therapist that truly facilitates change. My observations confirm those of Hobbs (1961) that patients change first through their experiences and that the insight gained from such a change follows it rather than precedes it. With this patient, for example, the change in her behavior toward more closeness with me appears to have come from the experience of the confrontation, in which I was saying and showing her that I was interested in developing a closer and friendlier relationship with her. She had already mentioned, as part of telling me her history earlier in our work, her father's advances toward her; but now it came with intense and believable feelings and led to what I felt was a real insight for her that her experiences with her father sexually were interfering with her relationship with me. The transference was no longer an intellectual understanding but had become a real and alive experience.

I must say that when I approach patients through these empathic confrontations I feel somewhat anxious and not just because of how I am confronting the patient, for I have usually assessed through my inner senses that the patient is prepared for it, but because I am also confronting myself. I am putting myself on the line about our mutual relationship and where it stands as I see it, and I believe that I must be open to examining what I have thought and felt about it as I hold the patient to doing. This empathic confrontation is really an open clarification to the patient of my countertransference responses, and I have to be open to discover how much they have been elicited predominantly by the patient (patient-induced countertransference) and to what extent they arise within me without much stimulus from the patient (self-induced countertransference). For example, if this patient had asked me if something were interfering on my part from my liking her more, I would have taken the question seriously and done my best to answer her. This would have required my efforts to be as open as possible with myself about my feelings toward her, including my self-induced countertransference, if present. I had already gone through this process and knew that I liked her and that I felt blocked from liking her more; this concerned me because I felt that I could be of more help to her if she could safely get closer to me and if I could like her more.

To return to the issue of confrontation, I am saying that my experience has led me to distinguish two types, one made out of anger and the other out of empathy. Between these two types lies a continuum on which a given confrontation may fall in proportion to how much it has elements of the angry type, on the one hand, and how much of the empathic type, on the other. The angry confrontation involves some behavior of the patient's that the therapist dislikes and feels a compelling need to change. His anger and force communicate to the patient that he must change what he is doing if he wishes to continue with the therapist as well as that the therapist does not like him for the way he is behaving. The danger inherent in these angry confrontations is that the patient changes out of a submissive compliance in which his needs to have the therapist stay with him and like him win out. Change on these terms means that the patient is changing to please the therapist rather than changing for himself. The potential therapeutic gain from such a confrontation appears to lie in the openness on the parts of both the patient and the therapist to look at this episode together for mutual self-understandings.

Like the angry confrontation, the empathic one also centers on the here and now experience between therapist and patient, but the therapist feels in a different position. Instead of feeling angry, he feels anxious about bringing directly to the patient and himself a piece of their shared experience that reflects on his own feelings about the patient. He is basically accepting of the patient's behavior, which he is not when making an angry confrontation. His anxiety, as I understand it, comes from the direct experiencing not only of the patient's feelings toward him, but even more so from experiencing and having to examine his own feelings toward the patient. In my example with the nurse I had taken up her transference although in doing so I had brought my own countertransference feelings about the state of our relationship into it. In my training along more classical lines, I had been taught not to do so, but I have come to wonder about this. I am sure that it takes discrimination on the part of the therapist concerning when and how to do so. For me the value of using something having to do with me increases the impact on the patient and also permits me to be a real person with my patients. Keeping myself and my own feelings hidden most of the time turns me, I have found, into someone who is carrying out a role rather than being a person. To put it another way, it has made me feel as if I am a therapist first and a person coincidentally rather than a person first and a therapist coincidentally. It has also caused me distress as a therapist with the problem of how this role-playing helps patients, since many of the people who come to me for help do so because they are so much caught up in their roles and appearances in life that they have never developed their potential selves to find out who they really are. To be a therapist who invites them to be themselves and attempts to develop a trusting and caring situation in which they can do so cannot be done when I am not being myself with them, but instead have allowed my role as a therapist to imprison me.

For many years Rogers (1958) has emphasized the importance of the therapist's need to be himself as one of the major curative factors in psychotherapy. He has called this factor "congruence" and described it as follows:

> It has been found that personal change is facilitated when the psychotherapist is what he *is*, when in the relationship with his client he is genuine and without "front" or facade, openly being the feelings and attitudes which at that moment are flowing *in* him. We have coined the term "congruence" to try to describe this condition. By this we mean that the feelings the therapist is experiencing are available to him, available to his awareness, and he is able to live these feelings, be them, and able to communicate them if appropriate. No one fully achieves this condition, yet the more the therapist is able to listen acceptantly to what is going on within himself, and the more he is able to be the complexity of his feelings, without fear, the higher the degree of his congruence. (p. 61)

The research findings of not only Rogers and his group (1960) but also of Truax and his co-workers (1966) confirm the importance of realness on the part of the therapist in providing a helpful therapeutic experience.

THE PROCESS OF CHANGE

It seems to me that underlying these contrasting types

of confrontations and the question of how useful the confrontation process is to therapy lies the more fundamental problem of what in therapy helps patients change. When a therapist makes an angry confrontation, he is forcefully pressuring a patient to change. We know that the usefulness of anger is that it often gets people to stop frustrating us and behave in ways that are more acceptable to us. In his unique and fascinating approach to treating children through mutual story-telling, Gardner (1971) has helped to emphasize this aspect of anger. In therapy, however, we are interested not just in the patient's adaptation to his therapist but also in his capacity to change himself for relationships beyond the one he has with his doctor. It is in regard to the process of change that I question the value of the angry confrontation or of any therapeutic intervention that puts pressure on the patient to change. If change occurred in response to such pressure, then it would seem to me that the "nagging superego" would be a much more effective force than it is in producing change. Instead the patient feels in conflict with himself and under pressure to behave in accord with his superego dictates, while knowing at the same time that he is sacrificing another part of himself when he submits to his superego pressures. The angry therapist forces a similar change on the patient through submission and in doing so becomes another voice of the "nagging superego." In the process he loses his alliance with a more reasonable part of the patient, his ego, to arrive at a more sensible way of behaving.

To return for a moment to my work with the engineer, I see myself as having felt under the burden of his kind of demanding superego (because such a superego exists as an aspect of me and because he helped to foster my falling under its sway through behaving toward me as he does toward himself) over meeting his needs in the appointments. My angry confrontation shifted this burden back to him, and he responded by submitting to his own superego pressures to comply. I had fostered his falling under the sway of his harsh superego through my anger. In the work that followed I reestablished my temporarily lost alliance with the more reasonable part of him (ego) to work out the appointments as one reasonable adult with another.

A very different process seems to me to be at work in the empathic confrontation. In this process the therapist works toward understanding, empathizing with and accepting the patient as fully as he can. He becomes alerted to whatever interferes with this process and works on these interferences with the patient both in their relationship and the patient's other relationships. This work consists of trying to understand with the patient how these blocks came about and why they exist. Free from the need to change the patient, as for example, to get rid of or overcome these blocks, the therapist is opened to accepting the patient for what he is, including his blocks or limitations.

This approach is grounded on the observation that when anyone, patient or otherwise, can accept himself for what he is, then he is in a freer position to change and has much better chances to change, which he may then do without even realizing it. On the contrary, if the same individual puts pressure on himself to change, to get rid of those aspects of himself that he does not accept and does not like, perhaps even hates, then he is not free to change. Instead he goes to war with himself over what he is and cannot accept; one part of him demands, "You must change!" and another part replies, "I can't; that's why I am this way." Inevitably he becomes depressed over himself and what he does not like about himself.

It is not that the empathic therapist does not want to help his patient change, but that the change he is working toward is to help his patient accept himself for what he is. Through working toward his own acceptance of the patient, the therapist frees himself from the patient's prejudices about himself and is then able to question why the patient finds it so difficult to accept himself, what it is that he so dislikes or hates about himself that he has to disown, as a consequence of which he becomes divided against himself. The lifting of repression, which Freud (1916) described as "to make the unconscious conscious" and (1932) "to build ego where id used to be," is this very process of coming to accept all aspects of oneself so that no part need be disowned and rejected or kept out of one's awareness.

A therapist who helps the patient work toward greater acceptance of himself for what he is helps to free his patient from this demand to change into a different person and facilitates the patient's becoming more tolerant and understanding of himself. This is what happens in the process of empathy and of an empathic confrontation. On the contrary, a therapist who pressures his patient to change allies himself with the patient's self-critical superego, which is already telling the patient he is no good, inadequate, defective, or worthless for being what he is. In response, the patient becomes more depressed with himself and/or angry with the therapist. This is what happens in the process of the angry confrontation. The therapist may feel successful to see the patient change in response to the anger, yet what he sees is not real change through freedom but submission. He may rejoice that the patient has finally gotten angry with him and expressed it so that now the negative transference can be worked on, but the anger the therapist has helped produce in the patient is not real transference but a response elicited by the demands of a therapist who has allied himself with the patient's critical and condemning superego.

Bibliography

Balint, A. (1937), quoted in J. Fleming, T. Benedek (1966), *Psychoanalytic Supervision.* New York and London: Grune and Stratton.

Brenman, M. (1952), On teasing and being teased; and the problem of "moral masochism." *The Psychoanalytic Study of the Child,* 7: 264–285. New York: International Universities Press.

Freud, S. (1916), Fixation to trauma—the unconscious. Lecture 18. Introductory lectures. *Standard Edition,* 16: 273–285. London: Hogarth Press, 1963.

——— (1932), New introductory lectures. *Standard Edition,* 22: 5–182. London: Hogarth Press, 1964.

Gardner, R. A. (1971), *Therapeutic Communication with Children: The Mutual Storytelling Technique.* New York: Science House.

Hobbs, N. (1961), Sources of gain in psychotherapy. In *Use of Interpretation in Treatment,* ed. E. Hammer. New York: Grune and Stratton, 1968, pp. 13–21.

Loewenstein, R. M. (1957), A contribution to the psychoanalytic theory of masochism. *J. Am. Psychoanal. Assoc.,* 5: 197–234.

Myerson, P. G. (This Volume), The meaning of confrontation.

Rogers, C. R. (1958), The characteristics of a helping relationship. In *On Becoming a Person*. Boston: Houghton Mifflin Co. 1961, pp. 39–58.

―――― (1960), What we know about psychotherapy—objectively and subjectively. In *On Becoming a Person*. Boston: Houghton Mifflin Co., 1961, pp. 59–69.

Truax, C. B., D. G. Wargo, J. D. Frank, *et al.* (1966), Therapist empathy, genuineness, and warmth and patient therapeutic outcome. *J. Consult. Psychol.*, 30: 395–401.

The Technique of Confrontation and Social Class Differences

NORMAN E. ZINBERG, M.D.

In this essay I will discuss a wide range of models of intervention usually grouped together in a particular category as psychotherapeutic techniques. By illustrating the ground rules for each and the different factors operating between therapist/leader and patient/member, I will show that the choice of technique, particularly when it involves confrontation, may be influenced by social class factors. The drug addict, because his plight is much in the public eye at the moment, makes a good example of the need to see these techniques as a means to an end. My discussion will use the addict to show how the perception of a technique by both practitioner and subject can be thought of as a value statement and an end in itself.

Since much of the discussion concerns placing the technique of confrontation within a range of more familiar interventions, I will specify what I mean by the word *confrontation*. Almost anything said by a therapist to a patient or by one group member to another can be thought of as a confrontation if the literal dictionary definition is used. *Webster's Third New International Dictionary* (1965) provides (1) to stand facing, to face; (2) to face boldly,

273

defiantly or antagonistically, to oppose; (3) to set face to face, to bring into the presence of; (4) to set together for a comparison. Generally speaking, modern psychoanalytically oriented techniques are thought of as closest to the third definition. Comments of the therapist/leader are intended to be evocative, to clarify, to distinguish relationships among apparently unrelated thoughts and feelings. Only perhaps with interpretation as defined by Edward Bibring (1954) does the boldness of the second definition become predominant. A reading of Freud's early cases suggests that he was not then so circumspect as he later became, and he often used the bold confrontation. At that time he was more interested in making (forcing) the unconscious into consciousness than in studying the repressing forces themselves. Thus, as his goal (ends) changed, so did his technique (means), leading him in his practice to the third definition.

For the purposes of this essay, the definition of confrontation as a technique will be limited to the second sense; and it is to be understood as a technique used between one person and another, as opposed to its use by one person to evoke an intrapsychic confrontation within the second person. Although this definition could and does cover what might happen in a one-to-one situation, I am using it in this essay exclusively in a group context. Encounter groups gather together for the purpose of boldly, defiantly telling each other "how it is." They report directly not only on what each participant feels but also on their direct emotional responses to what another says or is. While *boldness* and *opposition* are both words present in the definition, they are not synonyms. Boldness can be humorous, even gentle, and not antagonistic or forceful, but it is direct and related to affect.

The old saying is, "For example is no proof," but what I want the reader to think of when I use the word *confrontation* is a group situation where one member responds to another's statement of feeling by saying, "Make me believe it! You say it but I don't feel it. Make me feel what you feel."

One-to-one psychotherapy is the usual therapeutic model (Chance, 1971). Doctor and patient roles are clearly defined. Until the recent growth of community psychiatry and case-finding, the patient sought out the doctor, made an appointment, and explicitly agreed that he had an emotional conflict to discuss. Generally this procedure required some similarity of life experience between the patient and the therapist that permitted them to work out a shared level of ego perceptions and verbal representations. Thus, the therapist's expectations—that is, what he wants for the patient and from the patient—can be made fairly explicit.

Even when the therapist ventures into the community as part of a community health or case-finding team, he goes to seek out troubles; and he maintains a clear view of his position of doctor. Who is to be considered "patient" may be less clear, though this must be defined before a therapeutic situation can be officially established. When the therapist takes the initiative for the therapeutic encounter, there may be confusion over what he wants from the patient or for him.

Small therapy groups follow the individual psychotherapy model. The groups are artificial, arising from the shared, stated desire of each member to study himself. While the members test reality against each other as part of an aggregate, the purpose for which the group was created—work with the individual member—is never entirely lost sight of; nor is there any doubt as to who is the patient and who the doctor, though the various wishes and expectations involved in these roles become a lively part of the therapeutic process.

Large groups that are therapeutic in intent represent a different model. The first reporting of this approach by Dr. Pratt at Tufts Medical School in 1902 emphasized the search for an active solution to a problem. Today there are many such groups organized around a variety of diseases, of which the best known is Alcoholics Anonymous. The individual is essentially anonymous. Anyone who has found a way to transcend the problem qualifies as a therapist, though he becomes recognizable as a patient again if his mastery over the problem falters. Hence patient-therapist is a variable division, but there is no ambiguity about what would be "better" for the patient—whether it be to stop drinking, adjust to an ileostomy bag, or think cheerful thoughts rather than succumb to the hopelessness of depression.

So-called dynamic groups also have a more or less therapeutic purpose. Here the "patient" is not the individual himself or the symptom but rather a task; for example, knowing more about oneself in order to be more effective as a teacher, psychiatric resident, group leader, or whatever. Individuals discuss their conflicts and how they see the world but with the focus, explicit or implicit, not on themselves as patient but on their function outside the dynamic group.

The social distance between leader and member in a dynamic group is clearly less than that between doctor and patient in a therapy group. The group leader is a professional colleague who could easily be socially confused with other members of the group but whose differentiated role creates distinct psychological distance between him and the other group members. The group goals are considerably less structured than in the large problem-mastering groups like Alcoholics Anonymous, but more so than in individual or group therapy. While it could certainly be argued that it is no easier to say what makes a better teacher than what makes a better person, there are more specific task designations around even jobs as ambiguous as group leadership or teaching.

When dynamic groups are assembled by drawing from all over persons who do not know each other, they are artificial, created for the purpose of working with individuals, and are then similar to therapy groups. However, when the group is made up of teachers from the same school or residents from the same hospital, the dynamic group comes closer to a natural group. These people are part of a preexisting social network and have relationships with each other that are external to the group. In this situation, the stated goal of working toward greater understanding for the individual becomes less sharp. The group behavior of a participant can have direct consequences for him and for his institution outside of the group meeting. Once the need for attention to and preservation of these extra-group networks is recognized by the group, the priority of working toward individual goals receives greater consideration.

The potential importance of this dual concern for individual and system can be seen when one looks at other therapeutic efforts such as couple therapy, family therapy, and milieu therapy. The therapist frankly no longer works with the individual but with the system. A married couple, a family, or the ward of a mental hospital forms a natural situation, a small social system, that occupies much of the life space of the individuals involved. In therapy, as in the rest of his life, the individual appears as part of his usual social setting. The therapeutic endeavor is to preserve the system and to consider the individual's responses only insofar as his communications, positive or negative, reflect on the system that is threatened.

In the actual clinical situation of "marital counseling," for example, the question of what the therapist has been hired to do may not be perfectly clear. Just as a dynamic group of residents from the same hospital learns that their goal of knowing more about their individual responses as beginning psychiatrists may need to be modified to protect the system of a closely integrated residency training program, so may a couple who want their marriage treated find that the study of each of them as individuals intrudes on that goal. Thus, in contrast to individual or group therapy, where the value of studying the individual case is accepted as worthwhile, in systems therapy the study of the individual case may be recognized as destructive of the system and, hence, of the therapy. There is no doubt as to who is the therapist in systems therapy, but conflict sometimes arises from the need to give priority to the system over the individual.

The therapist, by his willingness to work to preserve the system, shows that he accepts the system as valuable, and by implication perhaps other conventional social institutions as well. This indeed limits the therapeutic relationship. The more traditional the social structures accepted by the therapist, the smaller the area where he and the patient can meet to consider objectively, without defensiveness, the patient's responses to his social setting.

Encounter or marathon groups, which under the rubric of a therapeutic encounter use confrontation as a technique, place their emphasis on highly charged emotional interactions among participants. These interchanges get tensions out into the open and expressed. The resultant behavioral manifestations of this emotional interchange are accepted and valued. Conversely, a reflective study of the individual as a separate entity and of the factors inhibiting his expression of feelings is devalued. In fact, to focus on conflicts within an individual may be conceived of as a derogatory procedure in the encounter situation. All are in the group together and all are there to "give" to others. There is no group "leader," just as there are no patients.

It would not be too farfetched to describe these groups as a systems therapy in which the system to be treated is the larger social setting itself. Instead of exploring the inhibitions and fears that might interfere with an individual's ability to adjust in society, these groups assume that unreasonable social conditions have resulted in his present distress. The (debatable) premise of psychotherapy—that a transfer of learning takes place from therapy to other life situations—is used here to explain how the experiencing of strong emotion in the confrontation situation can make the participant aware of, and free him from, the constricting influence of more usual social settings. One may wonder why a middle-class person, who is socially accepted, possessed of verbal and intellectual skills, whose emotional problems of living stem from a difficulty in using what he has, needs to fear such social influences so greatly. But we shall later consider how this concept may make more sense when applied to a drug user, labeled deviant by society for his drug use *per se*, or to an inarticulate, low-skilled, working-class black.

The position of the therapist in usual individual or group therapy situations has remained essentially as it was defined by Freud (1913). The therapist, in effect, leases time to the patient. Freud analogized with a music teacher who brought his skills to the time during which he was hired. This view of the therapeutic situation stresses the total voluntariness of treatment and the resulting equality between teacher and pupil. The patient-pupil decides whether he wants therapy lessons; he can stop at any time, but he is responsible for the time that has been contracted. Thomas Szasz (1968), particularly, has stressed equality through contract. Two equal individuals with similar rights and privileges but not identical tasks or responsibilities work together on a common problem. The therapist will do this work for an agreed fee in agreed upon hours, and he will not save hours that are not paid for but neither will he lease the contracted hours to anyone else.

This clarity about arrangements insures the equality of the participants. For if the therapist were to set aside extra time when a patient is called away or suffers a long illness, out of his humanistic subjective concern for the patient, he would be behaving as though he were a philanthropist—a benevolent spirit who graciously provides for the needy patient. Freud believed that a therapist with such total conviction that what he had to offer was "good" for the patient that he could not in all conscience withhold it raised questions about what he wanted from the patient in return. While the payment of a fee does not *per se* guarantee that some therapists will not want and indeed feel entitled to returns of gratitude, the patient's moral betterment, or simply "improvement," it at least sets the stage for an objective, colleagual relationship.

This objective relationship calls for the therapist's presentation of himself as relatively invulnerable. No matter how personal or how intense the statements and the feelings of the patient, whether affectionate or angry, the therapist treats them as manifestations of transference. His benevolent acceptance of these expressions and his attempts to make sense of them are part of the skill for which he is paid. The therapeutic contract protects the therapist's objectivity and offers the patient the freedom to express his emotions without fear. Many people find it harder than one would imagine to differentiate between act and thought, endowing the latter with magical properties. If a patient misses hours because of emotional turmoil or a vacation and desires to continue the therapy, he must pay for those hours. Should he remain silent out of a wish to punish the therapist, he soon realizes that it is his therapy that suffers. The situation is designed to make clear that it is the pupil's desire to learn music that provides the impetus for the lessons, not the teacher's wish that he do so.

While this invulnerability supports the crucial therapeutic neutrality, it also becomes one of the most delicate therapeutic problems. Anyone who can accept without flinching feelings as powerful as the patient regards his own deeper responses must be either callous and uncaring or enormously powerful, with the capacity to succor, to retaliate, or to judge. The therapeutic neutrality can be experienced by the patient as degrading or dehumanizing: "You are too weak and unimportant to have an effect on me," the therapist seems to say. The therapist of course knows all too well that he is not so totally strong, objective, or invulnerable but rather that these properties derive from the situation and his skill at his job. But his ability to show the patient that reactions to the therapist's objectivity are part of the work—perhaps the most difficult though potentially the most fruitful part—depends upon the invulnerable position of the therapist.

In the one-to-one situation, then, the therapist is objective, committed to the study of the individual case, and invulnerable. He values the shared work of the situation and, without disregarding the importance of nonverbal messages, relies heavily on verbal communication and, eventually rationality. His generally neat appearance and carefully selected surroundings announce at least some interest in material comfort and the avoidance of any deviant or disruptive social atmosphere. As the overwhelming majority of his patients share the values implicit in these nonverbal announcements, they contain no mysteries or hidden potential. The questioning of the therapist's value neutrality occurs over issues on which the patient anticipates conflict or disagreement. This anticipation arises when the patient experiences as coming from the therapist some less conscious aspect of his own conflict. Moreover, such projection is usually sanctioned by old parental attitudes, ideological or religious convictions, or official cultural positions. They range from "Stand up straight" and "Thou shalt not even wish to kill" to embarrassed confessions of cheating at cards or an illicit sexual act accompanied by the conviction of the therapist's moral outrage.

Of course therapists are attacked by their patients for their speech, appearance, and surroundings; but they are usually attacked, not questioned, because in almost every case their patients are people who have shared similar life styles and are expressing their own demonstrable personal conflicts. The therapist's own analysis prepares him with an awareness in depth of his own position on such issues. The nearness of the patient's preoccupation to the therapist's own life does not interfere with the therapeutic position of appropriate psychological distance. Thus, by restricting his offering to a discussion of the patient's conflict rather than the manifest reason for the attack, the therapist does not strive for agreement, closeness, or the avoidance of criticism.

By not taking the patient's criticism personally the therapist makes it clear that he does not want anything beyond the contract for or from the patient. This sharp break with the niceties of conventional social interaction is meaningful because both parties acknowledge it as a break. Thus, the working model of two relative equals—one of whose input supplies the subjectivity, the other the objectivity—operates smoothly because both know and accept the same social values.

In the traditional therapeutic groups the positions of therapist and patient follow the same principles save one. As in the one-to-one relationship, the "patient" supplies the individual cases to be studied. The "patient" group hires a group leader of similar social class to bring his objectivity and skills to bear on the problems, with an awareness of the broad outlines of how he might proceed and an acceptance of their interest in his actions as part of the process. All of these factors, including the leader's psychological distance and relative invulnerability, follow the original working model of equality and difference. But in the one-to-one relationship if either party is physically absent no actual therapeutic session can occur. The patient, albeit at a cost, can halt the proceeding, just as the therapist can. In a group, an individual patient loses that equality with the therapist. Group sessions can proceed without any one individual, as long as the leader is there.

One would then expect such groups to be extremely concerned with the issues of authority and dominance as they relate to the leader and to the issue of closeness among members. When the life of the group depends essentially on the existence in that time space of that one person, while others are expendable, he automatically becomes endowed with great power. (Leaderless group meetings occur, but unless the group is greatly experienced, such meetings are idiosyncratic and desultory.) So much power, in fact, does the leader have, that at some conscious or unconscious level almost any group discussion needs to take him into account.

One should never underestimate the force of the transference reaction in the one-to-one relationship, but there are times when the interaction with the therapist is submerged. Individual patients do become involved in their interpersonal conflicts with others outside the therapeutic situation, and they do review everyday decisions they must make with little regard in their associations for the immediate transference implications. Members of a group, on the other hand, find it extremely difficult to minimize in their discussions the constant ongoing emotional relationships to other group members, particularly to the leader; and when they *seem* to, it is usually a transparent defense against a previous or forthcoming group issue.

Dynamic groups, in contrast to therapy groups, are for something other than the study of the individual case. Whether they are assembled to learn about groups or because of the members' desire to function more coherently as teachers, social workers, or psychiatrists, as a result of the knowledge gained from the group experience, they have a stated goal related to an accepted social institution and not just to the individual member. This specific inclusion of the social institution in the relationship between group leader and group member shifts the patient-therapist position as outlined in the one-to-one situation. This acceptance in dynamic groups of a social goal other than the study of the individual case suggests value positions in the leader that raise the question of what he might want personally for the group members and from them. By joining them in an effort to be better social workers or more learned about groups, he indicates that he knows what a good social worker or group leader is, something about the proper way to become one, and suggests that to be one is a "good" thing.

The members, for their part, by their very presence in the group, show confidence in their ability to attain a group goal. The leader may have something special to teach them, which exalts him; but they can legitimately regard themselves as students with a potential social use for what they learn. The role of student differs sharply from that of patient in our society. "Patient" is a deviant role implying sickness or weakness, while "student" promises achievement and the possibility of surpassing the teacher. In fact, to maintain "student" as a viable social role requires hope and activity, as contrasted to "patient" with its accompanying feelings of passivity and helplessness.

In therapy groups it is a long time before a patient can accept the possibility that what another patient has to say may mean nearly as much to him as any comment from the leader (Zinberg, 1964). He longs for curative interpretation from an omnipotent leader. In dynamic groups, anyone who enters as a neophyte social worker, psychiatrist, or group leader—no matter how ill-at-ease or uninformed he feels—wants to be seen as a potential contributor. To gain such regard he must give it. Often the regard is given and accepted grudgingly. But no matter how undeserving he may feel, the group member understands that he must solicit the regard of his fellows. Members, by this giving and accepting, confer status on each other and thus restore a differential equality to their position vis-à-vis the leader.

It is difficult enough in a one-to-one therapeutic situation for a leader to say undeviatingly to a patient: "Yes, I will help you study yourself, and doing so is often an illuminating procedure that will lead you to a greater awareness of choices and inhibitions. But what choices you make, what being 'better' means to you, is your business and not mine." In a dynamic group, once the leader announces (by his presence alone) that he wants the group to achieve a specific state of "betterness" and is willing to work with them to that end, he will find it much harder to deal with the question: "What should we be doing?" His position as dominant in a magical sense has been eased by the group's specific goal and the status that this gives to members, but the idea that there is a "place" for the group to "get" makes the leader more of a grading teacher and less a neutral therapist.

That the dynamic group leader can legitimately be

considered to have a value position about where the group should go does not increase the *social* distance between him and the group members; rather the opposite. His age, social circumstance, general demeanor are all similar to theirs; and there is agreement that the group has a purpose or goal more specifically related to a social value system than the study of an individual case or the process of therapy. Hence, the *psychological* distance evidenced by the different functioning of the group leader becomes both more necessary and more irksome to the group members—more necessary if the group members are to learn what they want to learn by observing their difficulties in dealing with each other, particularly with that differentiated other, the leader (of this they are largely unaware throughout much of the life of the group); more irksome, because once having agreed upon a goal relating to a third party (pupils, clients), it seems only the peculiar stubbornness of the group leader that prevents them from achieving it. If he would stop his habit of commenting on what is happening in the group—or worse remaining silent— and give them straight answers, they might get somewhere. As the group progresses and members become more aware of the hopes implicit in their annoyance with the leader, they tend to shift their attention toward analyzing these hopes and away from the expectation that they be fulfilled. This shift represents an acceptance of the therapist's psychological distance. In the dynamic group the leader's position demands this distance not only because of the social closeness to members but because he trades a degree of objectivity— wanting something for them—for their strengthened identity as goal-oriented professionals.

One would thus imagine that in a dynamic group much of the group work would center on persuading the group leader to join them, to be more like them in function. One would expect it to be harder to get group members to recognize that the study of the group process and their part in it is an end in itself, which each must apply in his own way to his function as teacher or social worker. The group leader's behavior might be seen as less omnipotent than in a therapy group, but equally incomprehensible. Hence he remains clearly differentiated.

The systems therapies (family, marital, milieu) not only find the study of the individual case troublesome, but even more than dynamic groups they struggle with the value positions implicit in the therapeutic goals. Conducting marital therapy commits the therapist to the value of marriage as an institution, though the therapist may maintain his neutrality about the value of the particular marriage he is treating. Once he is committed to that much of current social convention, is it not fair to wonder what other cultural values he holds as "good"? If he has clearly defined positions on what these good behavior patterns are, will he not judge deviations?

The situation is clearest in mental hospital milieu therapy (Zinberg and Glotfelty, 1968). There the therapist is not paid by the patient, but by the hospital. The "patient," is effect, is the hospital ward itself, which exists to establish a milieu that is "better" for all. The hospital also operates on the belief that learning is transferable and that for a person to achieve improved functioning in a hospital ward should enable him to function better in society. The therapist's job has far less to do with individual idiosyncratic responses than with the general demands of establishing a coherent milieu. And that milieu must be coherent within a framework of rules, regulations, mores, values, and principles acceptable to his employer, the hospital. The patient too is limited in his expressions because in ward meetings, no matter how free in intent, he does not leave his usual social setting. Despite verbal agreements about objectivity, the participant's responses can have real-life consequences for him. He can please or offend other participants, including the authorities running the meetings, with whom he must contend after the meeting. Hence in the ward group, as in family, couple, or other institutional groups, it is possible to study the workings of a system, how it uses or rejects parts of persons, what are the open or closed avenues of communication and the sources of power within it, but at the cost of basic restrictions on the freedom of members to study themselves. There are similar restrictions on the leader's flexibility as he becomes the proponent of "reasonable" behavior. The therapist as an individual dealing with a system is clearly differentiated socially and psychologically from individuals who are members of the system, and no effort is made to close that gap. Doubts as to who the therapist is "for" in systems therapy and the extent to which he indeed wants, because of the demands of his job, social conformity from the participants indicate a doctor-patient model quite different from the traditional one-to-one with an objective therapist and a defined patient.

The traditional model contrasts even more sharply with the "patient"-"therapist" relationship in the encounter or confrontation situation. In such groups the concept of leader is resisted. Once the person who calls the group together has performed that function, he makes little effort to differentiate himself from other participants. He talks freely about his own feelings and reactions, and bases his relationship with other group members on these highly charged, emotional interactions, just as they do with each other. The impact develops as a result of these direct expressions of feeling.

Once the "leader" participates directly and indicates that he has feelings that can be aroused or hurt, that he will defend or attack just like anyone else, he relinquishes his invulnerability. This does not prevent group members from having all those transference concerns about authority and dominance discussed earlier. Further, if there is a putative "leader," it is he who is the most natural repository for such feelings despite his renouncing the role. The other group members, paradoxically, find themselves in a position where the free expression that is so valued may have to be curtailed. If a member wishes to please or to attack the putative group leader, he runs the risk of rejection, retaliation, or feeling guilty. He finds this situation very close to an ordinary interactional social situation in spite of the group's emphasis on expression of feeling. For although the decisions about what to express may be different in a confrontation situation— hence loud, angry feelings may please rather than offend— the essential decision is the degree of control or lack of it that one exercises, as opposed to the study of what may or may not originally have inhibited feeling. Little attention is given to understanding past conflicts and inhibitions. Hence, members' reactions to a leader, who takes the privileges of a participant, relinquishes control over his own responses, and thus declares his vulnerability, are experienced as active, rational, and in the present.

This therapeutic method tries to reduce the psychological distance between leader and participants to zero and frankly wants this for participants. It is considered *per se* "better" for people to face each other freely and without shame. The groups are supposed to be democratic and to have the idealistic goal of helping group members to cleanse themselves of hidden poisonous feelings so that they can care for and about each other. Here a means-end conflict develops. Is this reduction of psychological distance a means to an end or the end itself? What are the participants in these groups searching for?

Some encounter group participants, particularly those from the middle class, hope that the experience will teach them, force them to "feel." They express little curiosity as to what may have *stopped* them from feeling, which, after all, is as much part of the human birthright as breathing. If, in their struggle to experience, this comes up at all, it is given a social rather than a psychological explanation. Confrontation groups assume anthropomorphically that our increasingly mechanized society victimizes individuals by recreating them in its own depersonalized image.

In their case the means, reducing psychological distance, seems to become an end. It is not that participants literally do not feel but rather that they do not like what they feel any better than they like internal restrictions against some feelings. They want both the process of feeling and the feelings themselves to be "better." They long to be cleansed not only of hate and anxiety but also of greed, lust, cruelty, sorrow, and especially envy, leaving only love and caring for one's fellow man. An ideal human interaction that eliminates dominance or submission requires more than freedom from conflict: there must also be freedom from difference. The differential equality, described earlier, is not enough, because where there is difference there can always be jealousy, desire, and disagreement. Should such feelings exist, there is no hope for noetic fulfillment, oceanic gratification, or a mystic oneness with each other.

Certainly dynamic groups of all sorts desire to close the division between group and leader and, by reducing that distance, to achieve a unity that would permit them to relate to an outside, third entity (Boris et al., 1972). They cannot be better teachers or group leaders, they believe, until they can decide together what "better" is. Thus they are intolerant of the leader's insistence that they study their differences and divisions. Unrealistically, the group believes that by confronting each other with their "real" feelings, they can eliminate social and psychological differences. Members hope to eliminate narcissistic barriers. In answer to the question "Is each man an island?" they want to be able to shout a "no" so resounding that for an instant each could believe that he might truly and totally share another's feelings.

To the extent, then, that confrontation techniques become an ideologically endowed end for those trying to escape internal and external conflicts and inhibitions, the method appears a gimmick or a fad. In groups so motivated, it is no paradox that the "leader" can become a tape-recorded instruction. What is wanted from the leader is impossible, and hence it matters little what or who he is. Michael Oakeshott (1968) once said, "To try to do something

which is inherently impossible is always a corrupting enter-
prise." Once the aim of these confrontation groups is to exalt
humanity to a totally loving state, the result is the denial of
the dignity of the human struggle.

However, this is a *misuse* of the confrontation techniques and a misunderstanding not only of people but also
of the therapeutic process as a process not an end or an
ideology. The relationship between leader and group,
therapist and patient, teacher and student each has elements
that allow an interaction to proceed. This essay details how
some of them—transference, vulnerability, value positions,
and the like—operate differently when relationships among
participants differ or when social or institutional variables
intervene. The technique is but a means whose elements
may be analyzed in terms of who are the participants and
what are their potential social and psychological relationships
to an ongoing therapeutic operation.

Some groups—drug addicts, for example—also expect
little from leaders. Their monumental apathy in the face of
efforts to show them their self-destructiveness is striking but
perhaps not surprising. One realizes, however, that many
"therapeutic" efforts have had little to do with the addicts'
plight and much more to do with a desire that they be
improved for the benefit of a society from whose paths they
have deviated. Often this greater interest in the society than
in the patient may be conveyed by demanding that he use
the "accepted" means of a traditional technique. When that
occurs the traditional therapist unwittingly may be misusing
a technique as an end rather than a means in a fashion
similar to the faddish middle-class confrontation groups.

It is my contention that the position of a deviant,
particularly for those members of an underclass who have
chosen deviancy, imposes a barrier to communication that
must be overcome before any meaningful work on interpersonal conflict can occur (Zinberg, 1972). To be a deviant
means *per se* to be socially distant from one who is not. Most
drug addicts are virtually lifelong deviants. Middle-class

addicts (the word *addict*, representing as it does a stereotype, is purposely chosen in order to distinguish the group from the new large group of social drug users) are almost invariably people with a long history of psychological disturbance. Fearful childhoods lead them to a search for an escape from sorrow or anxiety that may begin with sniffing airplane glue and end with any one of a number of substances. Generally, in this country it is heroin; but the drug itself makes little difference, for the addiction lies in the total commitment to its use; and it can be anything called psychoactive whose effect is psychopacifying.

Addicts from low-skilled, working-class backgrounds show an astonishingly consistent characteristic profile. Their personal histories have been to follow a distinct pattern: cigarettes at age six or seven, liquor or sex by thirteen, marihuana soon after. Promiscuity and petty thievery merge almost automatically, in late adolescence, into prostitution and organized crime. Drug abusers of this type show a definitely ascending use of drugs, typically moving toward the one with the big kick, H (Chein, 1964). But other things we know about this type are puzzling—in particular, the ways in which their pattern differs from that of the non-addicted delinquent. To begin with, Billy E. Jones (1960) finds that Lexington, Kentucky, drug users are surprisingly intelligent—their average verbal IQ is 105. Contrast this with Sheldon and Eleanor Glueck's (1940) study of penitentiary prisoners. There, sixty-seven percent have a verbal IQ of less than 90. Nor are the family histories of criminals and addicts closely similar. Fifty-two percent of addicts come from homes broken by death before age sixteen. (Indeed, twenty-eight percent of these occurred before age six.) These figures do not refer simply to the loss of fathers, so common to the lower socio-economic class strata; more than twenty percent lost their mothers very early. But non-addicted delinquents are even more deprived of a stable family situation, with seventy-one percent of homes broken by various means, and twenty-eight percent having lost their mothers by age six. So while broken families seem to have something to do with addiction, it is not clear how much they have to do with it.

It also is true that drug takers are only children or youngest children to a statistically significant degree. Yet birth order has never been proven to be a significant factor among delinquents, alcoholics, or the mentally ill.

The most striking single correlation to have been established between parental history and drug dependency is parent-child cultural disparity (Vaillant, 1966). Among Negroes, for example, Northern-born drug takers had Southern-born parents twice as often as would be expected from the census figures. This statistical incidence is shown to the same degree by children of immigrant parents. By contrast, the incidence of drug dependency in a Northern urban sample who were themselves immigrants or Southern-born Negroes was only twelve percent, which is less than half of the percentage an average projection from census figures would lead one to expect.

Most surprising of all, however, is the fact that seventy-two percent of the patients studied by George Vaillant (1966) still lived with their mothers at age twenty-two; indeed, after age thirty, forty-seven percent continued to live with a female relative. Approximately seventy percent were either married or maintained a relatively stable, common-law relationship. These marriages tended to continue in spite of hospitalization. This holding on to relationships is striking, and markedly greater than similar studies show for alcoholics or other delinquent groups. The Gluecks' study of criminal delinquents, for instance, shows only twenty-two percent continuing to live with their family of origin after thirty, while about the same proportion maintained some form of married life.

An incidental finding of the Gluecks' study supports the contention that the drug taker strives for closeness with a maternal figure. When hospitalized or imprisoned, drug takers, like other institutionalized persons, frequently engage in homosexual activity. But in only three percent of the cases studied by Vaillant (1966) do the patients report that homosexual activity is a source of significant gratification to them in their outside adult life. This is a surprisingly low figure, particularly in view of the popular notion that drug addiction and homosexuality go together.

Addicts choose drugs to show their contempt for society and to gain status and companionship. If they happen to destroy themselves to this grim quest, little matter to them or, they believe, to others. Their broken homes, poverty, and closeness to immigrant status are *de facto* deviance from the larger social norm before they turn to drugs. Hence, for those whose personality dictated the addict's path, little change in perceived social state is involved.

Society, including middle-class "helping" professionals and members of their own class who become socially mobile by making a living or giving up drugs, seems only to desire for them that they become like everyone else. As Harold Boris has said (1971)

> It is not seen that this group has other ways of doing things, another culture and social organization, another form of personality patterning; rather it is seen that this group, lacking our own folk-ways and mores, is considered deprived or, more sociocentrically still, disadvantaged; and so we want things for them. Sometimes it is clear—almost —that we want things from them: to get off the streets and stop making trouble, or off the relief rolls and stop costing us our hard-earned money or to stop their profligate impulse-serving behavior so that we can stop contending with our unconscious envy. (pp. 161–162)

These desires of society regarding the underclass that Boris so cogently describes increase geometrically when drug abuse is the issue. We want to confine addicts so as to get them off our consciences and avoid contagion. The social distance between someone in this outcast status and anyone not defined as deviant is virtually unbridgeable. How can anyone not a deviant in a communication situation (a term chosen advisedly over therapeutic situation) show that he can step back from the general social attitude toward the addict and want to know how he chose this path and how it served him, instead of trying to get him off it? Traditional therapeutic techniques, which depend on psychological distance between leader and group, communicator and constituency, therapist and patient, leave few bridges.

In situations where the social distance is great, the reduction of psychological distance is necessary. This is true for professionals working with addicts and with troubled, low-skilled, working-class patients; also in educational projects (Boris *et al.*, 1972) where teachers are supposed to abandon their traditional roles and to act more or less as group leaders with adolescents who want to talk about sex, prejudice, and drugs. The social distance between teacher and pupil is so great that if the self-study group leader maintained the usual psychological distance, there could be few bridges of communication. The leader can readily relax the psychological distance by personal remarks without fear of loss of position, so completely sustaining are the differences in social roles. Surely something of the same sort is involved in child therapy techniques where therapist and patient play games together.

The confrontation technique allows the therapist-leader to express his personal feelings directly and unequivocally. With addict groups, where so much language is not held in common, feelings serve as a *lingua franca*. Here there need be little concern about the fantasies of interchangeability of one member for another, or a desire to reduce ego boundaries and thus threaten the dignity of separate identities, described earlier. The social distance assures separateness and a sense of human individuality between leader-member, communicator-constituent. In their ability to feel similar things and to "make me know it," they establish their common humanity and their potential ability to understand each other.

Here confrontation is a technique—a means, not a gimmick, fad, or end. Answering a question with a question, the establishment of a single pattern in a series of apparently unconnected associations, are techniques just as is a statement from a leader such as, "The way you dribble at the mouth and the way you smell make me feel queasy in this tiny room." They are all ways of establishing communication. There is nothing inherently "better" in puzzling out the meaning of a question or discerning the submerged current of thought in a river of content than in relying on the authenticity of one's own emotions. All such human interactions depend upon the capacity of therapist and patient, leader and group, to achieve an empathic understanding of each other's efforts and of the processes that interfere with these efforts. Techniques may differ; one may spell out the procedures in more conceptual terms than another, but each is a way to begin communication and should not be a goal in itself.

Choosing the right technique to use with different groups is a complex matter; one cannot simply adopt as a rule of thumb that when there is great social distance one should choose a technique that minimizes psychological distance, and vice versa. With groups who have somehow fallen into social crevices, we find some of the same problems as those encountered in systems therapy. Society defines an addict as deviant; not surprisingly, he organizes a relatively coherent identity around what such social institutions as the law, the school, the church, and conventional public opinion think of him. Erik Erikson (1959) describes this as a negative identity. The acceptance of himself as an embodiment of bad characteristics protects the addict from internal conflict but as part of the same dynamic process insures him continued conflict with society. He is seen and sees himself as part of a delinquent social subsystem.

When the leader/therapist does something similar and organizes *his* identity around acts that are really only part of a technique but that he begins to see not as means but ends, then individual interactive elements get lost; and it is system versus system. Traditional therapeutic techniques require the psychiatrist to individualize his patients, to listen carefully and gently and objectively to indicate how he has understood what he has heard. Such techniques are benign and reasonable, hard to fault. However, this behavior leaves the therapist an inviolable, invulnerable, distant being. Furthermore, at this point in history, these techniques must be viewed not just as they are meant by the technician but as they are perceived by the recipient. For such techniques are now well known and can represent stereotypes as readily as do the acts of the drug addict. The stereotypical view associates this sort of approach with the social desire that the addict get "better." Even when "better" means such neutral states as greater ego activity or autonomy for the addict, more choices, and the like, the addict perceives only a representative of the reforming social system—the very social system whose repudiation provides him with a *raison d'être*.

Is the addict justified in his suspicions of a therapist who automatically uses a traditional technical approach? I think so. Insofar as the leader/therapist holds to his traditional techniques, he insists that the addict's conflict is an intrapersonal one and not one between the addict and society. The origin of the conflict that led him to choose deviancy may indeed have been intrapersonal; but once deviancy is defined and accepted, the locus of the conflict shifts. In clinging to a specific technical approach, the therapist does indeed seem to say not only that he wants the addict to get better but that he knows what better is; and we are back to Boris's observation about what practitioners want for and from their constituents. The practitioner's effort to maintain his objectivity, even his gentleness and concern for individual difference within the intrapersonal conflict, which is intended to be extremely relativistic, becomes an absolute value-laden view. His technique has become an end rather than a means, and he and the addict engage in a conflict between different social subsystems rather than in human interpersonal interaction.

The middle-class therapist/leader has often been called upon to empathize with someone with whom he could not share specific subjective experiences: males with pregnant women, females with premature ejaculators, tall persons with short ones, and so on. Hence, his assumption that his invulnerable, relative objectivity permits communication that surpasses difference is rooted in his experience. But what he fails to see is that his experience, as pointed out earlier, is usually with people who have sought him out, who see the problem as an intrapsychic one, and who share a large number of perceptions, assumptions, and values, chief among them their varying degree of relatedness to the social system. Thus the specific subjective experiences that are not shared are surrounded by myriads of shared understandings that slowly overcome mistrust. When a junkie or a migrant worker expresses mistrust of people who haven't experienced what they have experienced, it is hard for the middle-class therapist to separate it from similar statements about differences among people who may be members of his own social class. He fails to see that he and the junkie represent two different social subsystems with little shared social experience that might open avenues of communication and begin a working relationship.

The ex-addicts who try to tell their addict clients that they have indeed shared their experience and can show them the way out often fare scarcely better. In one-to-one situations where the ex-addict, like the member of Alcoholics Anonymous, can frankly fight his own addicted *doppelganger* in the person of his client—where the client knows what the ex-addict wants from him—an understanding can be reached. But when the ex-addict has to join the social system and cleanse *it* of drugs in order to save himself, when his struggle is not personal but moral (members of Alcoholics Anonymous do not say that alcohol is bad, just that they can't handle it), when he is sure he knows what "better" is, the ex-addict represents the same social sub-system, the same absolute value view, and the same substitution of ends for means as the middle-class professional.

Confrontation techniques become one means for a therapist/leader to indicate that he is not a representative of a system. He confronts his constituent and so becomes a vulnerable practitioner who, despite his social distance, manifestly feels, responds.

Though the therapist may present himself as an individual who feels, this does not negate his awareness that he does not share the powerful impulses that have seemed undeniable to the addict and led him to drugs. The use of the confrontation technique with addicts merely recognizes that fat people may have self-destructive impulses, but they are not specifically victimized by our social institutions. One tries with the addict to base the working alliance on a mutual recognition of each participant as an individual and not as a member of a system that needs change or reform by repre-sentatives of another, reforming system. Once an alliance is established much more will be needed, perhaps including the more traditional analysis of why the practitioner's humanity was doubted in the first place. But without an alliance, little or nothing can be done.

Today, people from all social classes think they know a great deal about psychiatrists, social workers, and all potential therapist/leaders. As in so many areas of sudden high visibility, much of what is presumed to be known is myth and distortion. However, these myths, once formed, have the power to enable people to construct stereotypes whose existence affects and changes the subject of the original distortion. Sometimes, if great care is not taken, the subject can become surprisingly like the stereotype. Dr. Grete L. Bibring (1965) once described Freud by saying, "He was many things, but never banal." She meant that he approached each issue freshly, with enthusiasm, even force, and so could not easily be trapped into a litany that spelled agreement with a stereotyped image. Social class differences have been long neglected by most students of therapeutic techniques. This neglect has nurtured an image of rigidity and middle-class specificity for the whole art. This need not be true, and it need not be believed to be true. However, for it to be neither true nor believed to be true, therapists must take questions concerning social distance and system representation into account when they select a technique. For a technique is merely a means that can be as useful at one time with one group as it can be foolish at another time in another group. And it is not to be confused with ends.

Bibliography

Bibring, E. (1954), Psychoanalysis and the dynamic psycho-
therapies. In *Psychiatry and Medical Practice in a General
Hospital*, ed. N. E. Zinberg. New York: International
Universities Press, 1964, pp. 51–71.

Bibring, G. L. (1965), Personal communication.

Boris, H. N. (1971), The Seelsorger in rural Vermont. *Int. J.
Grp. Psychother.*, 21: 159–173.

————, Zinberg, N. E., and M. Boris (1972), The pull of
the status quo. Unpublished manuscript.

Chance, E. (1971), Varieties of treatment contracts. *Int. J.
Grp. Psychother.*, 21: 91–94.

Chein, I. *et al.* (1964), *The Road to H: Narcotics,
Delinquency and Social Policy*. New York: Basic Books.

Erikson, E. H. (1959), *Identity and the Life Cycle (Psychological Issues*, Monogr. 1). New York: International
Universities Press.

Freud, S. (1913), On beginning the treatment (further
recommendations on the technique of psycho-analysis I).
Standard Edition, 12: 123–144. London: Hogarth Press,
1958.

Glueck, S. and E. (1940), *Juvenile Delinquents Grown Up*.
New York: Commonwealth Fund.

Jones, B. E. (1960), Quoted in G. Vaillant (1966), Drug dependence and alcohol problems: 12-year follow-up of New York narcotic addicts. *Am. J. Psychiat.*, 122: 573–584.

Oakeshott, M. (1968), Lecture, London School of Economics.

Szasz, T. G. (1968), Psychoanalysis and the rule of law. *Psychoanal. Rev.*, 55: 248–258.

Vaillant, G. (1966), Drug dependence and alcohol problems: 12-year follow-up of New York narcotic addicts. *Am. J. Psychiat.* 122: 573–584.

Webster's Third New International Dictionary (1965). Springfield, Mass.: G. and C. Merriam.

Zinberg, N. E. (1964), The psychiatrist as group observer: notes on training procedure in individual and group psychotherapy. In *Psychiatry and Medical Practice in a General Hospital*, ed. N. E. Zinberg. New York: International Universities Press, pp. 322–336.

——— (1972), *Untight: The Public's Response to Drugs.* New York: Simon and Shuster. In press.

——— and J. Glotfelty (1968), The power of the peer group. *Int. J. Grp. Psychother.*, 18: 155–164.

Confrontation as a Demand for Change

SIDNEY LEVIN, M.D.

The use of the term *confrontation* is relatively recent in the field of psychiatry; and, like many of the terms in frequent usage, a clear definition has been difficult to reach. Since, however, it is a most meaningful concept, it is important that we make some attempt to explain it.

The process of confrontation is essentially communicative. A therapist might point out to a patient something he does not know about himself, something he knows only vaguely, or something he knows but thinks others don't know. He might also point out aspects of reality that are being denied, or he might extrapolate from present reality in order to help the patient use his foresight more effectively. But when we refer to these communications as confrontations, we not only imply that the patient is being made aware of certain aspects of his neurosis that require exploration and analysis; we also imply that pressure is being exerted on the patient to give up certain neurotic patterns of behavior.

Since neurotic patterns of behavior can take many forms, the opportunities for using confrontation are innumerable and the basis for such use will vary from case to case. In this chapter only a few general issues concerning the role of confrontation will be discussed.

Many neurotic patterns of behavior are derived from attitudes of excessive entitlement. When a therapist confronts his patients with these patterns of behavior, he must also point out the underlying attitudes of entitlement in order to foster further analysis. For example, one patient who was a businessman commented *en passant* to the effect that he expected a high degree of loyalty from his employees, as anybody would. Since this comment was made in a manner that communicated an attitude of excessive entitlement, I tried to explore what the patient meant by "loyalty." He went on to express indignation toward some former employees whom he had taught the business and who had deserted him to take positions elsewhere. As the material unfolded, it became apparent that for this patient loyalty meant that no one to whom he had become attached had a right to leave him. When this implication was pointed out, he became angry; but he immediately realized that it was correct. In subsequent hours he revived memories of severe reactions to brief separations from his parents during childhood and of his extreme reluctance to accept the fact that such separations were necessary. After working through this material, there was considerable mitigation of his pathological attitudes of entitlement.

This confrontation helped the patient not only to gain insight into his excessive entitlement but also to give up his neurotic overpossessiveness in regard to his employees. It was as though he received and accepted the following mandate for change: "You really do not have a right to enslave your employees and to restrict their opportunities for growth and advancement. This type of behavior is selfish, childish, and unfair. It is therefore necessary for you to analyze the childhood basis for this behavior so that you can give it up and eventually have more mature relationships with your associates."

It is not uncommon for a patient to express his excessive entitlement through provocative behavior during therapy. In fact, a patient may be dedicated to making the therapist angry and may also be quite talented in doing so. Under such circumstances, it may be necessary not only to point out the attitudes of excessive entitlement but also to inform the patient that he has succeeded in evoking the therapist's anger. Following such a confrontation, the patient may complain that the therapist has no right to be angry at him; but he then has to be made aware of the fact that this attitude, too, is a form of excessive entitlement. In other words, the patient's self-defined "rights" must be repeatedly questioned since they not only negate the rights of others but also complicate his relationships.

When a patient reacts to these confrontations by controlling his provocative behavior, it may appear that he is merely responding to the threat that therapy will be terminated if he does not change. One might, therefore, be tempted to conclude that the only effect of the confrontations is to motivate the patient to check the acting out and that this motivation hinges primarily upon his libidinal attachment to the doctor and his fear of abandonment. I believe, however, that these confrontations often lead to additional therapeutic effects; namely, to major insights as well as to further exploration and analysis. And the further exploration is usually directed toward determining how this patient reached adult life with the attitude that he was entitled to have so many of his demands met by others.

Although confrontations concerning excessive entitlement can often be made with the therapist presenting a relatively neutral affect, they are often more effective if his anger is not totally suppressed, since an important aspect of the insight being sought is the patient's awareness that the expression of his infantile entitlement *does* evoke hostility in others and *has* evoked hostility in the therapist. Furthermore, whether or not the therapist makes his confrontations with anger, one would expect the patient to respond with anger, since the exposure of his excessive entitlement typically produces a narcissistic injury. The resulting hostility of the patient can then be gradually resolved as he works through the narcissistic injury and advances to a higher level of maturity. It is therefore apparent that a competent therapist has to be prepared to face his patient's hostility in order to make effective confrontations. The therapist who has poor tolerance for hostility may adopt the defensive posture of waiting for the patient to bring forth additional material, in the hope that new insights will arise spontaneously; and he may rationalize this defensive posture by claiming that he is using it "voluntarily" in order to foster the analytic process.

Although many patients have attitudes of excessive entitlement, there are others who have attitudes of restricted entitlement, which may lead to severe inhibitions. In a recent paper (Levin, 1970), I noted that the patient who has attitudes of restricted entitlement may repeatedly defer to others and may even allow others to steal many of the rewards that rightfully belong to him. This type of patient has to be confronted with the fact that he is not standing up for his rights. Such a confrontation also elicits hostility, since the patient tends to feel that he is being called a "weakling." But after assimilating the confrontation and resolving the narcissistic injury resulting from it, the patient usually moves ahead in treatment and explores the excessive childhood fears that have prevented him from asserting himself. Furthermore, he usually begins to face these fears and to master them.

These kinds of confrontations represent the exerting of pressure in a particular direction. When an attitude of excessive entitlement is present, the therapist pushes back the patient's hostility, indignation, and over-assertion and forces him to rework his expectations so that he can arrive at a more mature level of "normal entitlement." When an attitude of restricted entitlement is present, pressure is exerted in the opposite direction. The patient is helped to recognize that, since many of his expectations are restricted, he has to rework them so that he can arrive at a more mature level of "normal entitlement." He is also helped to realize that in order to translate this reworking process into action he has to dare to be more assertive and to master some of his fears (Levin, 1962).

When combined treatment of a husband and wife is undertaken, confrontations represent an important component of the therapeutic armamentarium (Levin, 1969a, 1969b); and it is often necessary for the therapist to use confrontations in the early phases of treatment. For example, in treating one couple I noted that every time the wife began to talk about the husband, he turned the spotlight away from himself and started to cross-examine her. If she mentioned that he showed some hostility toward her friends, he would make a defensive remark, such as, "When was that?" If she then told him a specific occasion, he might answer, "Are you sure that's what I said?" and so forth. I pointed out to him that he was behaving like a cross-examining attorney and that he really did not discuss what his wife had said. He was startled by this comment but replied with surprise, "Yes, you're right." It was then possible to help him understand the basis for this type of response; namely that he became self-conscious and embarrassed whenever the spotlight was turned onto his own behavior. Following this phase of treatment he was freer to look at himself. In a later interview I confronted him with the fact that whenever his wife discussed her unhappiness, he reacted sensitively, as though he felt attacked by her. I pointed this out after his wife had made a neutral comment. I stated that his wife's remark did not sound the least bit critical, yet he was reacting as though it were. He seemed surprised, but it was then possible for him to say that he was beginning to realize how sensitive he was. Subsequently the quality of the interviews showed a pronounced change as his defensive, attacking posture was replaced by a subjective, self-examining posture.

In another married couple whom I saw in treatment, the husband's domination was pronounced. As soon as the wife would make a brief comment, she would be quickly and subtly squelched by the husband, who would then monopolize the interview. I confronted him with his tendency to "jam" her communications and his inclination to intimidate her with his self-righteous attitudes. He was initially surprised, since he could not believe that his wife was afraid of him. But he soon realized the accuracy of my remarks and began to exert control over his dominating behavior. It was not long before the character of the interviews changed and the wife began to communicate more freely.

The use of confrontations should serve the purpose of facilitating the therapeutic process and should not serve as a vehicle merely to effect a change in behavior accompanied by closure concerning the dynamic issues involved. For example, if a patient brings gifts to his therapist and is told only that he is behaving inappropriately, this confrontation can act as a simple prohibition. However, if the confrontation is worded in such a way as to help the patient explore his need to bring gifts, not only will his behavior change, but the process of self-examination and the gaining of insight will be facilitated.

It is worth noting that confrontations which are incomplete may at times be anti-therapeutic. In a previous article (Levin, In Press a), I reported a case in which the analyst pointed out the patient's strong dependency needs but neglected to point out his excessive shame concerning these needs, a shame that resulted in his making strong efforts to hide his dependency from others. Due to the analyst's omission, the patient's shame was reinforced, and he reacted by trying even harder to hide his dependency. It was only later, when the patient's shame was clarified, that it lessened. As a consequence, the patient became more tolerant of his dependency needs and was then able to subject them to careful analytic scrutiny.

Since confrontations tend to produce narcissistic injuries, the therapist usually tries to present them in doses that are tolerable, gradually increasing the dose as he judges it to be appropriate. One might, therefore, think of the therapeutic process as a form of desensitization. Even one's terminology may change as one prepares a patient for a confrontation or builds up to a more complete one. Early in therapy one might indicate to a patient that he has a fear of missing something, later that he feels deprived, and finally that he is greedy or selfish. Or initially one might tell a patient that he appears annoyed, later that he shows resentment, and finally that when he becomes angry, he tends to withdraw into a stubborn form of sulkiness.

Correct timing is obviously of considerable significance, because the therapist has to be reasonably sure that the patient is ready to give up some of his defenses, especially that of justification. If the patient is not ready, he usually responds with a hostile rejection of the confrontation rather than with the more common reaction, hostile acceptance of it.

Although it is usually necessary for the therapist to be tactful, he can easily fall into the trap of being too tactful and thereby deprive a confrontation of its therapeutic impact. In fact, a therapist may use tact defensively in order to avoid struggling with the patient.

Sometimes a therapist has to rely on speculative confrontations. For example, if a patient wants to cancel an hour and gives somewhat vague reasons for making the request, the quality of the patient's responses (suggesting that something is being acted out) may evoke an uncomfortable reaction in the therapist. A therapist's statement that he feels material is being suppressed, even though he does not know what it is, may be the type of confrontation that can lead the patient to bring forth additional data. This content may then substantiate the therapist's speculations concerning "acting out" and lead the patient to consider options other than cancellation. It is, therefore, necessary for a therapist to take his countertransference responses seriously at all times and not be afraid to express his reservations about the patient's stated reasons for his behavior. A therapist must be an explorer, and he is often in the position of Columbus, who dared to sail out across the ocean not knowing where he was going but knowing that he was going to find something new.

But there are also times when confrontations must be

carefully avoided. For example, when reality is being grossly distorted, a premature attempt to confront the patient with this fact might lead to a flight from treament. In a recent paper on the depressive core in schizophrenia (Levin, In Press b), I discussed the therapy of a schizophrenic patient who had a delusion of having a penis growing inside her vagina. This delusion was essential to the patient's psychic equilibrium and had to be respected. I therefore totally by-passed the delusion and focused on the underlying depressive currents. It was only after the psychosis had cleared that I analyzed the basis for her delusion.

Many therapeutic confrontations include a clarification of intense shame reactions, their connection with childhood experience, and the numerous projections to which these reactions give rise. These projections take the form of expecting and often experiencing criticism, ridicule, scorn, rejection, etc., from others, including the analyst. Before the patient's excessive shame can be analyzed genetically, he has to be confronted repeatedly with these projections. It is apparent that one of the basic questions that eventually has to be answered through analysis is "How did the patient become so ashamed of himself?"

It has been my experience that careful explorations of shame are necessary in order for many patients to move ahead in their development. Since shame acts as a barrier to the libido (Levin, 1967), one often has to help the patient make new efforts to overcome this barrier. These efforts tend to arise after the patient realizes that, due to shame, he often does not dare to feel his love for others and often does not dare to express this love. Once this daring process is initiated and mastery of the underlying shame occurs, the ability to love is liberated and many derivative forms of loving are then possible. I believe that this is what Freud meant by reaching the genital level of development. Clinical experience indicates that the inhibitions our patients manifest often arise from excessive shame over sexual thoughts, feelings, and impulses and that, in order for these inhibitions to be successfully removed, the excessive shame must be pointed out and eventually mastered.

The degree of understanding and technical ability that an analyst must have in order to use confrontations effectively can be illustrated by the type of decisions he must make in analyzing shame. In a previous publication (Levin, 1967), I used the term "secondary shame" to refer to instances in which a person feels ashamed of reacting with excessive shame. In a later article (Levin, In Press a), I noted that, when a patient's intense primary shame results in severe blocking, he usually experiences intense secondary shame over the blocking itself and may therefore make strong efforts to override his blocks. But if this effort leads him to bring forth content that mobilizes intense primary shame, he may suffer excessively. In such instances the analyst can usually relieve the patient's suffering by mitigating the secondary shame. This effect is achieved by confronting the patient with his excessive shame concerning silence and by clarifying the projections resulting from this shame; namely the unrealistic expectations of being severely criticized for his silence by the analyst. This confrontation usually leads the patient to relax his efforts to overcome his blocks. On some occasions, however, the patient may relax his efforts too much. It may then be necessary for the analyst to confront the patient with the fact that *now* he is not trying hard enough to express his thoughts. This type of confrontation reactivates the patient's secondary shame and usually leads him to try a little harder to communicate. The analyst may also reinforce the secondary shame by waiting longer before interrupting the patient's silences. However, if too much pressure is exerted in this way, excessive secondary shame may be produced, leading to anger and often depression. In fact, the patient may even become highly resistant and terminate the analysis.

In order to avoid excessive shame, therefore, the analyst often has to make confrontations with the following aims in mind: (1) to exert some pressure upon the patient to reveal his thoughts so that he does not remain silent and therefore experience intense secondary shame; and (2) not to exert too much pressure upon the patient to verbalize, because he may then experience intense primary shame. Furthermore, since the patient will react to each confrontation as a criticism, it is necessary for the analyst to evaluate the patient's sensitivity carefully, since such evaluation enables him to decide how much pressure to exert at any particular time without evoking a severe narcissistic injury. If confrontations are properly dosed, the patient will not experience either excessive primary shame or excessive secondary shame; and he will be appreciative of the fact that, although he is being pressured to communicate, he is also being protected against overexposure.

In order for a person to become a competent therapist, considerable mastery of his own fear as well as considerable resolution of his own shame reactions is necessary. He will then be able to confront his patients appropriately, with confidence that the hostility he evokes in them can be worked through successfully.

It is worth noting that the impetus for making a confrontation often arises from the fact that the therapist has responded with hostility to the patient. The hostility may be mobilized not only by the frustration that the therapist experiences in trying to overcome the patient's resistances. A competent therapist will monitor his own hostility and use it primarily as a barometer so that he can analyze his patient's provocative tendencies, but sometimes he has to express his hostility along with his confrontations. When he does express his hostility, he will try to do so creatively rather than in the interest of exploiting the therapeutic situation for purposes of his own abreaction. Furthermore, the confrontations that he employs will usually carry with them an expression of some positive feeling and a desire to be helpful. The therapist's ability to understand what is going on enables him to continue to feel some affection for his patients even when they are being provocative. However, affection should not be forced.

The therapist who believes that he *must* feel positively at all times may actually manifest a complicating type of counter-transference in which the predominant feature is a reaction-formation of excessive tolerance with a pathological denial of his own hostility.

In some respects, a therapist's role is akin to a parent's, for each must exert appropriate quantities of pressure at appropriate times in order to facilitate developmental steps. This requirement puts the therapist in the position of having to make difficult decisions. Freud (1926) pointed out the problems that parents face in deciding how to deal with the child's sexual behavior and the ways that they can show either too much or too little permissiveness. Parents are often in the position of searching for a "golden mean" in applying psychological stress to the child. The same can be said concerning a therapist in regard to the use of confrontations. He, too, is constantly searching for a "golden mean" in applying psychological stress to the patient.

Each therapist undoubtedly has his own ideas about how he should behave toward his patients. These ideas are acquired primarily during training, mainly through supervisory experiences, and include ideas about the degree of activity advisable. But there is another factor that influences the degree of activity; namely his own personality structure. If a therapist has strong fears of spontaneity, he may be *too passive;* if he is impatient or impulsive, he may be *too active.* If he is too active, he may not permit the patient to struggle through his blocks and to bring forth certain memories and fantasies. If he is too passive, the patient may knock himself out trying to get a response and may become more and more depressed when there is none. If the patient perceives his therapist's silence as disapproval and this feeling is not explored, the patient can thrash around trying to please and can make little progress. Even though the patient's associations might include significant memories, such as times when his mother showed her disapproval through silence, this type of material may not be effectively used until the therapist clarifies the concomitant transference responses.

It is generally accepted that a therapist must not only be free to be spontaneous; he must also be able to exert self-control. There are those who are too active because they are emotionally and verbally incontinent. There are also those who are too active because they have an excessive need to be liked by the patient, and they may therefore deal with the patient's productions in such a way as to reinforce his suppression of hostility. Furthermore, in order to minimize the patient's hostility toward them, they may be too ready to introduce parameters that reduce frustration unnecessarily or avoid essential narcissistic injuries.

It is well recognized that in psychoanalytically oriented psychotherapy, one usually waits for the patient to build up a solid libidinal tie to the therapist before major confrontations are offered. It is this tie that gives the therapist his leverage so that he can make comments to which the patient can respond with anger without fleeing treatment. Although we realize the importance of this libidinal tie, we also realize that people are not cured by their love for us or by our love for them. It is essentially through the acquisition of insight and the consequent building up of new ego structure that the patient eventually moves ahead to higher levels of maturity. And it is essentially with these goals in mind that the therapist introduces his confrontations as major steps in the therapeutic process.

Bibliography

Bibring, E. (1954), Psychoanalysis and the dynamic psycho-therapies. *J. Am. Psychoanal. Assoc.*, 2: 745–770.

Freud, S. (1926), The question of lay analysis. *Standard Edition*, 20: 179–258. London: Hogarth Press, 1959.

Levin, S. (1962), Mastery of fear in psychoanalysis. *Psychoanal. Quart.*, 33: 375–387.

——— (1965), Some suggestions for treating the depressed patient. *Psychoanal. Quart.*, 34: 37–65.

——— (1967), Some metapsychological considerations on the differentiation between shame and guilt. *Int. J. Psycho-Anal.*, 48: 267–276.

——— (1969a), A common type of marital incompatibility. *J. Am. Psychoanal. Assoc.*, 17: 421–436.

——— (1969b), Further comments on a common type of marital incompatability. *J. Am. Psychoanal. Assoc.*, 17: 1097–1113.

——— (1970), On the psychoanalysis of attitudes of entitlement. *Bull. Phila. Assoc. Psychoanal.*, 20: 1–10.

——— (In Press a), The psychoanalysis of shame. *Int. J. Psychoanal.*

——— (In Press b), The depressive core in schizophrenia. *Bull. Phila. Assoc. Psychoanal.*

Confrontation in Psychotherapy: Considerations Arising from the Psychoanalytic Treatment of a Child

MYRON STOCKING, M.D.

A boy of eleven is to have a swimming lesson. The boy has had other lessons, some too early, others too late. He still does not know how to swim. Now he approaches the pool to meet his new instructor for the first time. The teacher is a solid man, observant, well muscled, and sure. The first words between the two are friendly, but the boy seems guarded. While he moves gracefully and appears to be well coordinated, he views himself as a "swimming retard."

After their introduction the teacher invites the youngster to dive into water that is over his head, so they may "see what he can do." Now the encounter shifts. The boy's eyes drop, and he looks sullen. He refuses to enter the pool. The teacher asks the boy again to enter the water, his tone shifting from that of instruction to one of command. The boy is silent and does not move. The teacher steps forward forcefully, and the child edges away. Now the teacher lunges quickly, and the boy darts onto the diving board in retreat. The teacher jumps after him, wrestles with him for only a moment, and throws the boy, squirming crablike, into the

321

water. As he sputters to the surface, the boy looks surprised, even a little confused; but after a moment a smile spreads across his face. His gross dog paddle, accomplished with his head held high out of the water and at ninety degrees to the surface, proves adequate to sustain him until he reaches the edge of the pool.

We cannot pursue in detail here the evolving relationship between the teacher and his pupil or the course of the instruction. Briefly, in only a few lessons the boy was able to change his awkward paddling into a well-coordinated Australian crawl. The teacher was struck by the child's progress. In his opinion the boy could learn "to be a fine competitive swimmer."

Contrast the experience described with that of a four-year-old girl with the same teacher. This child comes to her first lesson with a sister two years older. The two girls are latecomers to a class of seven children that has already met three times. The sisters' entry is dramatic. They are dragged to the pool, screaming and crying, by their mother, who looks harried and embarrassed by their behavior. The mother leaves them quickly. Both children continue crying noisily despite the teacher's first awkward efforts at comforting them. Unsuccessful, he turns his attention to the other children. From time to time he approaches the girls again but is not able to comfort them. While the older child gradually becomes less afraid and is able to control her crying, the younger child remains frightened and continues a morose whimpering and crying throughout each of her lessons. In her fourth lesson, the teacher firmly picks her up and holds her in his arms as he slips into the water. The child panics, and her wild crying leads her near to hysteria. Neither the outburst nor the feelings subside as the teacher tries to show her that she is safe, that he will hold her, and that there is nothing to fear.

In the weeks that followed the child would attend lessons only when forced. Thereafter she would not enter the water on her own, either at the lesson or in other circumstances, although before these lessons she had done so without fear.

The teacher approached each of the two children we have described in a similar way. At a critical point he forced each child to suspend his own judgment of the safety of his situation and to relinquish his own initiative. The teacher expected that his own judgment and determination would enable the child to face an anxiety-provoking situation that he would not otherwise have faced. The critical element in this approach was the instructor's intuitive use of his own person to create a situation in which a child might confront an irrational fear. The two children's stage of development, inherent abilities, and previous life experiences varied. In one instance the approach seemed unusually constructive. In the second situation the same approach was at least temporarily unsuccessful and may actually have been traumatic for the child.

There is in the realm of psychotherapy a technical modality analogous to the approach employed by the swimming instructor in the realm of his instruction. I refer to the therapeutic modality of *confrontation*. While psychotherapists frequently employ this technical tool intuitively, there has been little formal consideration of confrontation as a legitimate technical procedure in psychotherapy. The dramatic therapeutic return it sometimes produces, the frequency with which therapists employ it uncritically, and the potential danger of its inappropriate application converge to create a need for a detailed consideration of confrontation as a tool of therapy.

Confrontation in psychotherapy is the process by which a therapist brings a patient face to face with what he takes to be either a reality, or realities, of the patient's psychological function. The patient may or may not be conscious of the reality considered. In either case, the patient does not see the relevance of the reality to the therapeutic process. He accepts it without examination, apparently unaware of its potential importance for therapy. While his unawareness may appear casual, it expresses a resistance currently effective against the therapeutic work.

In the process of confrontation the therapist assumes the therapeutic initiative. By his activity he creates a therapeutic situation in which it is difficult for the patient to avoid the reality considered or to deal with it on the basis of automatic or unconscious modes of response that he had employed in the past. When successful, confrontation facilitates a new psychological equilibrium based on the patient's integration of the reality confronted.

For the moment I will focus on those instances when confrontation is employed in approaching a reality of which the patient is unconscious. Freud (1914) described a form of behavior that serves as an alternative to remembering, with which some people express the residue of experiences forgotten through repression. In such behavior the patient acts out an experience, reproducing it "not as a memory but as an action; he *repeats* it, without, of course, knowing that he is repeating it" (p. 150). Freud regarded this repeating in action as the expression of what he called the "compulsion to repeat" (p. 150) and stated, "As long as the patient is in the treatment he cannot escape from this compulsion to repeat; and in the end we understand that this is his way of remembering" (p. 150). In Freud's view the transference itself is a special instance of this kind of repetition—a portion of the forgotten past brought "not only on to the doctor but also on to all the other aspects of the current situation" (p. 151). He related transference and the compulsion to repeat to the concept of resistance in this way: under the influence of resistance unconscious experience is deflected from the transference experience into the arena of the patient's life through behavior and action. "The greater the resistance, the more extensively will acting out (repetition) replace remembering" (p. 151).

Confrontation when directed at experience that is now unconscious is a therapeutic activity aimed at translating the patient's behavior into therapeutic communication. If successful the confrontation results in the patient's bringing in themes, issues, or experiences previously discharged in action more directly into the therapeutic situation for conscious scrutiny and consideration. One avenue for this more direct expression of unconscious experience within the therapeutic situation is within the transference. Expressed within the transference, previously unconscious experiences may become accessible to interpretation, a therapeutic modality related to confrontation, but distinct from it.

Interpretation, as defined by Edward Bibring (1954), is a therapeutic technique with insight as its goal. It is a process directed at making unconscious mental phenomena conscious and

. . . refers exclusively to unconscious material: to the unconscious defensive operations (motives and mechanisms of defense), to the unconscious, warded-off instinctual tendencies, to the hidden meanings of the patient's behavior patterns, to their unconscious interconnections, etc. In other words, in contrast to clarification, interpretation by its very nature transgresses the clinical data, the phenomenological-descriptive level. On the basis of their derivatives, the analyst tries to "guess" and to communicate (to explain) to the patient in form of (hypothetical) constructions and reconstructions those unconscious processes which are assumed to determine his manifest behavior. In general, interpretation consists not in a single act but in a prolonged process. A period of "preparation" (e.g., in form of clarification) precedes it. Every interpretation, whether accepted by the patient or not, is considered at first as a working hypothesis which requires verification. This is done in the process of "working through," which thus has two functions. It serves as an empirical test in that it consists in the repeated application of the hypothetical interpretation to old and new material by the therapist as well as by the patient, inside and outside of the analytic session. By the same token it enables the patient (if the interpretation is correct) to assimilate it and thus to acquire full insight. (pp. 757-8)

Confrontation similarly may have insight as its goal. It may also be directed at unconscious process. It differs from interpretation in three essential ways:

(1) In the therapist's attitude towards the understanding he attempts to convey. The therapist who interprets shares a hypothesis with his patient. While he will almost certainly regard his interpretation as a potentially useful construct, he brings it being aware that, no matter how fruitful potentially, a hypothesis requires further validation.

The therapist who confronts brings the patient face to face with "a reality." He presents a view he accepts as real or factual. His construction is not offered as a hypothesis about the patient's world, but rather as what the therapist takes to be either the direct observation of it or a successful reconstruction of it.

(2) The second major difference between confrontation and interpretation lies in the balance of activity between patient and therapist during each process. Interpretation is based on a body of associations or evidence arising from the patient's activity and initiative at times when he has been successful, either alone or with his therapist, in overcoming his inner resistances. Interpretations are rendered at times when it is assumed that the therapeutic alliance is functioning effectively and when it seems likely that the patient will be able to actively integrate the interpretation on the basis of his own initiative or motivation.

Confrontation, by contrast, is used when the therapist and patient have not succeeded in diminishing the patient's resistance, at a time when the therapeutic alliance is ineffective. The therapist assumes the therapeutic initiative and bypasses the patient's inner resistances to bring him in touch with an underlying reality of his functioning. The therapeutic aim is that the truth thus rendered may subsequently be assimilated by the patient. The assumption of the initiative by the therapist is only momentary, and the success or failure of confrontation will be measured by the patient's success in making the reality confronted his own.

(3)   The fruits of the therapeutic techniques of interpretation and confrontation are integrated by differing and distinct processes. As we have stressed, the therapist who interprets presents the patient with a hypothesis. The validation of the hypothesis is obtained through continuing joint work by therapist and patient, which is based on the patient's activity in the ongoing process of free association. Validation arises from the efforts of therapist and patient jointly testing the understanding proposed against new data arising from the associative process. It is by the active process of continuing validation that the patient will make an interpretation his own.

In confrontation, on the contrary, the therapist presents a view of the patient's world or function for which he feels he already has sufficient validation. At the point when a confrontation is initiated, validation of the reality considered will seem unilateral, the therapist's alone. The patient's role in the process of validation has been limited to his participation in the action and behavior that led to the confrontation. For the patient, validation by conscious scrutiny occurs only as a result of the process of confrontation.

Further, the process by which the understanding that results from a confrontation is assimilated is often sudden, not gradual. Awareness of the reality confronted, but until now denied, provides the patient with a new building block with which to construct a view of his psychological world or function. Consider the different modes of problem-solving employed by an adult and a child working together with a construction set. If the grown-up were to help the child, who now had all the needed parts available, by turning one part around and juxtaposing it to others with which it might connect to produce a desired result, this help to the child would be analogous to the process of assimilation that follows successful interpretation. The child would, by his own scrutiny, see if the parts indeed fit and join them together to build the structure envisaged.

Compare this process to another analogous to the process of integration following confrontation. A child struggles to complete a structure, but a necessary part or parts have been left in the toy box or slipped under the rug. The grown-up, either by deduction or observation, has discovered the missing parts. He presents them to the child and now the necessary building blocks are available to complete the structure. Until this point the needed parts have not been available. The new parts are joined in a way that is clearly apparent by their "fit." The "correctness" or the "fit" of the solution is such that there can be little doubt of its effectiveness.

CLINICAL DATA FROM THE PSYCHOANALYSIS OF A CHILD

One morning Robby, a six-year-old then in the third month of psychoanalysis, entered my office. He took a colored marking pen from his pocket and handed it to me. It was identical to others I keep available in my playroom. Two weeks earlier Robby had asked me if he could have one of the pens from the playroom, and I had refused him. I had thought that he had accepted my refusal.

In the early weeks of treatment Robby had occasionally asked for small things from the playroom. His requests had been modest, and I granted them. Once he asked to keep a string of paper clips he had clipped together. Another time I let him take some extra sheets of drawing paper of a kind he had enjoyed using during the hour.

Meeting Robby's request for the pen seemed to me more complicated than fulfilling his earlier wishes. He asked for the pen at a time in the treatment when his relationship to me was shifting. From the first Robby had been lively and active in our sessions. Initially he invested most of his energy and attention in the toys. Only recently he had shown more interest in me, and I thought I saw signs that he was beginning to care for me. During this period his play had gradually been becoming more expressive. Shortly before Robby asked for the pen, he had begun to use it in sequences of fantasy in play that expressed an assertive and intrusive masculinity he had not previously revealed.

It seemed to me that the time was now right to begin responding differently to the impulses that were now emerging in the treatment situation in his asking for things. I thought Robby and I could deepen our understanding of his experience if, instead of quietly gratifying his wishes, I tried to explore them with him in words, with the goal of understanding the organizing experiences that underlay current wishes and demands. For this reason I had refused the pen.

I asked Robby if he had taken the pen from the office, and he denied it. "This is another pen; it belongs to me and my Daddy." Robby went back to the shelf where the pens lay, and he compared the one he had shown me to one on the shelf. He traced off the brand name, first of one and then the other. They were the same. (The pens were of a type not widely available in Boston. I had ordered them by mail.) It seemed to me that in his action Robby was grappling with acknowledging a theft that with his words he had just denied. I told him I could understand it if he had taken the pen. Since I had let him take some things home before, it may have been harder for him to take my "no" on the pen. I wondered if he had decided to take it for himself and now had decided to bring it back. Robby again denied it. His denial put us on delicate ground. I am reluctant to burden a child new to therapy with demands for honesty that he is not ready to meet. I did not want to put Robby in the position of repeating his denials if they were not true. On the other hand, there were further reasons why I felt it important that Robby and I understand more explicitly what had happened.

Only recently Robby had introduced the issue of his own "trickiness" into the treatment. He had told me how sometimes he was able to trick his mother. His attitude, as he described instances when he had succeeded in misleading her, appeared mixed. He seemed to feel proud, strong, and excited; yet at the same time he looked apprehensive.

He had amplified his concerns in play that grew from fantasy. He played with a toy soldier he called Sarge. Sarge was mercilessly bossed by his general. When the general left Sarge for even a moment, he left a watchdog to "keep an eye on him." Even the watchdog ordered Sarge around. Sarge was able to trick both the general and the dog in a variety of ways. Later Sarge was apprehended, and he was nearly killed as a punishment. The general pushed him off a cliff to smash on the rocks below. As he was about to be crushed, the general rescued him, saying that the punishment had only been a trick.

Shortly before Robby began treatment his parents had separated. They had decided to divorce after Robby's mother had deduced that her husband was having an affair, which until then he had succeeded in hiding. The father's deception had not been easy to maintain. A shrewd, capable and attractive man, Robby's father often lied. At times he had lied to Robby. Some of these times Robby had realized that his father was lying to him.

During the period in treatment I have been describing, Robby was actively struggling to cope with the recent loss of his father. His father no longer lived at home and visited the children only one day a week. Robby tried to cope with his loss in a variety of ways. For one, he tried to make himself like the father now gone. Now he was beginning to use his relationship with me to substitute for that with his father.

I felt progress in the analysis of these issues would be at least temporarily blocked if I proceeded on the basis of assessing wrongly whether or not Robby had taken the pen. I believed the act of taking the pen at that point was the most tangible expression of a central and immediate inner conflict. If I had ignored what Robby experienced as a theft and was tricked by it, I thought it would undermine our alliance. His actual experience with me would converge with a repetition in the transference of experiences in which he had deceived his mother and others. He would have felt less respect for me if he tricked me, and he would feel guilty and in danger of punishment if he were detected.

As I considered Robby's persistent denials, he sat down and began drawing with the pen. Quickly he became disgruntled, apparently with the pen and began to throw it against the wall again and again. I said, "I think you did take the pen, and now you feel bad. I think you feel scared and angry now and want to destroy the pen for making you feel bad." I told Robby that I thought he had been trying for some time to figure out what I was good for and what good seeing me could do. I thought he wished I could take his Daddy's place in giving him some of the things he wanted. I told him, "I can't really help in that way. If we both tried hard I might help another way. It might really help if you can learn to see things as they are, without feeling so unhappy and scared by them. If I am to help we must both try to learn just what really happens between us. This is why I care so much about knowing what really happened to the pen."

Robby did not reply with words but quietly placed the pen in my drawer and left it there. I wondered if Robby by giving the pen back to me now was tacitly acknowledging he had taken it. I thought so, but it was hard to be certain since he had not told either what had happened earlier or what he now felt. We had only begun the process of confronting his behavior. As yet Robby and I had not agreed on the reality of his behavior and had not made explicit what unconscious impulses were expressed in his action. Yet, we had at least begun the therapeutic task of confrontation.

When confrontation is experienced positively the process supports the expression of fantasy and facilitates the emergence of the unconscious more directly within the treatment situation itself. As treatment now unfolded, there was evidence that Robby was responding to my intervention in a positive way. In the remainder of this session and in several sessions that followed, Robby's play developed a greater continuity and served for the increasingly clear expression of themes that had to this point been kept hidden.

It was during this period that he began to mix water and paint together to create a substance he called "formula." Formula was in some ways like the milk that his friend Beth's mother made for Beth's baby sister. There was a difference. Formula, Robby's own creation, was more powerful.

He illustrated in his play what formula could do. He had me pretend to be a baby. Robby was a grown-up who left me. He told me to say when he left, "That's what you do that scares me." Then he had me pretend that I am alone, small and helpless. A monster comes to get me. Robby is the monster. He tells me that I can trick the monster with formula. If I drink some and put some on the monster's head, the formula will make me strong and the monster weak. Now he switches the play. He says, "I tricked you. The formula really protects me and punishes you." Then he has me as the infant being "tricky" with formula. He pretends he catches me breaking a promise. He has a TV camera, and he can tell when I do something wrong. He says he knows so many things because of his immunizer shots—formula injected by a pen. To demonstrate he uses one of the marking pens so like the one he had brought in earlier.

In subsequent hours Robby continued to make formula and to explore its properties in his play. While it can make you strong, formula is also dangerous. If you drank two buckets of it, it would kill you. Again he pretends to leave me and returns now as a monster who puts formula on me, which kills me. "It makes you dead, like sleeping gas."

Now Robby resurrects me and asks that I make formula and feed it to him. He is too wise to take it; but he says, "Try and trick me, act nice and tell me how good it will be for me." He now has me coax him into taking the formula. If it weren't for his magical defensive devices, which give him immunity, the formula would kill him.

Shortly, he breaks off this play and decides that he

must make his mother a gift for Mother's Day. He does so and insists he must really take the gift and give it to her. In fact this hour was our last meeting before Mother's Day. This is Robby's first attempt to take anything from the office since he returned the pen a week previously. I tell him it is fine for him to look at the part of what he feels towards his mother that makes him want to give her a present, but I think it would be wiser if he did not really use this as a real present to give her but instead kept it in the playroom. He ignores what I say as he continues to work on his gift. When the hour is over he tries to leave with it. If he is not to leave with it, I must take it from him. I do, by force, and put it in his work drawer. He yells at me, "My mother brings me here for you to help. This would help me." He leaves furious.

I took Robby's present from him because I thought it represented more than just a boy's expression of love for his mother on her day. While that strand of feeling was undoubtedly conscious to Robby, he was also aware that he was now hunting an ironclad justification for taking "a little something" from the office. The action represented his yearning for and his determination to give himself, within the transference, a small token of my love. He could not believe that the love he missed could be given freely to the child of his self-image. He felt entitled to take by stealth what he assumed no grown-up would ever choose to give. In this action he responded at one time to old and unconscious images of his mother as well as to a current conscious idea of me as a real person. I thought it essential to confront his hunger and frustration as well as the emerging personality traits that were derived from them, even if shortly it would be Mother's Day.

In the next hour Robby remained angry and resentful. His play, however, was not blocked by these feelings; instead it served for expressing them. First, he makes more formula. Then he decides I must have an operation. He gives me sleeping gas by putting a glass tube in my mouth. He puts his own mouth on the other end of the tube, near my own lips, and breathes out. Then he takes an imaginary needle and pricks first my ear, and then my ankle. Next he picks up a small metal ball from a miniature croquet set and puts it near my crotch and pretends to cut it from my body with a metal wicket.

Now his play has become too explicit. Robby is clearly anxious and stops playing. He asks if his friend Beth, who actually is awaiting him outside, may come in the office. He denies he is afraid of how I will respond to his "operation," saying only, "Beth's dog swallowed a bone, and I was afraid it would hurt him. That's why I want Beth." He accepts it when I suggest he let Beth wait outside.

He resumes his play making formula; and as he does so, his eyes catch a game that includes some marbles. He takes the marbles from the game board and says he is going to take them home. He needs them. I tell him, "You can get marbles at the five-and-ten-cent store. Toys for home are for a Mommy or Daddy to get a boy. If you took the marbles, what would you or other children do some other time if you wanted to use the marble game?"

He tells me he will replace the marbles with some toy wooden acorns that he took from his kindergarten. While his mood has been playful and light, when I ask if he feels badly when he takes things from school, he becomes serious and looks sad. He says without conviction, "The teacher gave them to me." Then he interrupts himself to acknowledge that he took them and says, still looking sad and troubled, "The other children don't sneak things." I say, "I think I know how sad it makes you when you feel sneaky." He puts the marbles back.

Now I recall with Robby the day he brought in the pen. I say, "I believe you took the pen and then felt sad and brought it back." While earlier Robby had appeared by his actions to acknowledge taking the pen, he now continues his verbal denial. My question has gone too far. Robby says again, "I didn't take the pen." I tell him, "It is too important that we know what really happened to pretend or trick me.

May I ask Elaine (the babysitter who brings him to his session) whether there are pens like that at your home and if your father really gave the pen to you?" He replies, "Sure," somewhat listlessly.

We go out together and I ask Elaine. She is unsure. At first she seems doubtful, but then she says she believes she does recall that the father gave such a pen to Robby. It is hard to tell if she is simply reconstructing the facts or rallying to what she sees as Robby's defense. Whichever the case, as they leave together Robby turns to her and comments acidly, "My good friend, Dr. Stocking, he thought I stole it."

In the next period of treatment Robby's feeling ran deep. He expressed his experience in the transference in play shaped by fantasy. Simultaneously he used his real relationship with me as a battleground for struggling with current issues overlapping those activated in the transference by my confrontation.

Robby was high as a kite in the hour after I checked with Elaine to find out if the pen was his. He waged his battle over two issues. First, he insisted he would take the Mother's Day present he had made and with it he demanded a supply of "goodies" he felt he needed. Second he insisted his mother join him in the hour. I permitted neither. Robby responded at first by fighting to leave the room. When thwarted, he attacked me directly. He was excited and in a mood of giddy naughtiness. He climbed on my desk and stood on it. He threw books off the desk, rang an intercom button wildly, and then destroyed some toys.

Robby's excitement was complex. In the transference he felt caught in a struggle with a mother representative that he experienced not just as withholding nourishment, but as bone dry. He saw me as unloving and threatening retaliation for a fury which he felt I had provoked. In his relationship to me as a real and current figure Robby had at first felt afraid I would detect his theft and punish him. Later, after Elaine had supplied him with a convincing cover story that he had hardly hoped for and certainly had not expected,

Robby could see I felt puzzled and uncertain. He wondered if he had tricked me and now felt a mixture of exhilaration and power intermixed with apprehensive uncertainty that he might yet get caught. While deceiving me would fulfill the powerfully gratifying fantasy that he could meet his own needs by his trickery, in the real world a successful deception would have left him bereft. He would still not have his father, and he would lose as well whatever possibilities were offered by the treatment and the relationship with me. Robby had only just been beginning to see that, in some way he could not yet verbalize, the treatment situation and his experience with me in it offered some new alternatives in his life. Though still ill-defined these alternatives were beginning to seem real.

During the hour I have described I tried to interpret Robby's experience to him. It was hard for me to be sure to what degree I was successful. At the end of the hour he was fighting to stay as vigorously as earlier he had been fighting to leave. I carried him out, despite his wild struggles, to his mother.

Robby's anguish coupled with my own uncertainty of the facts about the pen led me to push still further to try and resolve a confusing treatment situation. As it happened, the next day his father brought him to his hour. I asked his father if the pen came from home. His father responded very much as Elaine had earlier. At first he seemed uncertain. Then he said he was pretty sure the pen did not come from home. Only a moment later he changed his mind. Still later that afternoon he called back to tell me that he had checked with his wife and together they decided that there probably had indeed been some marking pens of the type I had described around the house and Robby must have brought in one of these. In the session after I questioned his father Robby remained hyperactive and giddy. A number of times he attacked me physically.

The capacity of each child therapist to confront consistently a child's untransmuted aggression when it is directed at him and to respond with genuine compassion and empathy must vary greatly. The limits of my own empathy and compassion were being strained in the treatment situation I describe here. Robby and I were in danger of a deteriorating treatment climate that might not be subsequently repaired.

For therapist and patient alike there is an inner aspect to confrontation just as there is an outer one. I can only speculate on Robby's inner experience during this period; I have potentially more direct access to my own. I will not trace the central strands of the inner experience that shaped my behavior during this period of treatment in detail here. Let me say only that essential elements in my own reaction were determined by my own early experience as a very small child and experiences later when I was almost Robby's age. Then I had experienced separations that I was too young to comprehend. I had known the loneliness and the despair that a young child may feel when his mother or father is not there. While I had not then been able to fully master the feelings aroused at that time, neither had the experience stopped me from growing. I had a basis for feeling hopeful that Robby might learn to use positively experiences that were now so threatening to him. While I felt sorry for Robby, I did not feel too sorry. There was an inner discipline to my own response that I felt could be very helpful to Robby if he could make it his own.

When I next met with Robby I was determined that together we identify what he was going through. He entered that hour in a defiant mood. He felt irritated that some toy furniture that he had placed on a shelf had been moved, although he was aware the toys on that shelf are for the use of all the children who come to my office. He said sternly, "How did that happen—hey, what's going on here?" I replied, "I think you still feel very angry with me. I think I may know why. If I were in your place I might feel like you do. I think you are very angry that I asked Elaine and

your father about the pen. I think you were not sure that I
am really on your side. You probably feel towards me like
Sarge did towards the general."

I told him I thought that something else bothered him
even more. I thought he felt bad because he had taken the
pen, because he had lied about the pen, because he had
tricked Elaine and his parents, and was afraid he might trick
me too. I said, "I don't care about the pen, it is not important.
It is very important that you and I learn to see things as they
are, that is the real way I could help you, to see things how
they are and not just how you want them to be." As I spoke
Robby was listening. His manner shifted. He seemed thoughtful and sad. He said, "I think you are right. My father not
being with me is a big problem, but it's not my biggest.
My biggest problem is he has gotten me a Great Dane puppy.
The puppy will grow bigger and bigger, he'll be bigger than
me, and there is no place to hide him.

At that moment I had no idea what Robby was telling
me. I knew he wanted a dog. However, his mother had told
him he could not have a dog because there was not enough
room in the apartment. I had not been aware that his father,
who was openly critical of his wife's decision against the dog,
had gone ahead and gotten Robby a Great Dane puppy.
More important still, from Robby's point of view, was the
fact that his father kept the dog at Miriam's apartment.
Miriam was the girl for whom Robby's father had decided
to divorce his wife. Father was taking Robby there on his
visiting days despite the fact that father and Robby both
knew his mother would feel hurt and angry if she had been
aware of these visits. Father and Robby went anyway, and
father had sworn Robby to keep the arrangement secret.
Robby told me he felt sad to have been keeping such a secret
from his mother and from me. He went on to tell me that he
thought he had been wrong and bad often, but he felt that I
myself had been wrong on one thing. He thought he should
have been able to take the Mother's Day present. I said,
"Maybe you are right. That might have been a time when it

was too hard for you to see what I was talking about. Maybe I should have let you."

Robby sat down and began to make a paper mask, using staples. As he worked he asked me if I knew how he had taken the pen without my knowing it. I said I did not. He showed me exactly how he had sneaked it from the shelf, recalling how he had distracted my attention by assigning me a task on the other side of the room.

Following the period of treatment I have described, there was a dramatic shift in Robby's relationship to me, which was enduring. He never again made a demand on me that was unrealistic, nor did he ever again try to hurt me. He became open in talking with me. He expressed his feelings with candor, but now was able to modulate the intensity of his feelings. He was often forceful, but never again cruel. More often he was gentle. At times he was sad; but now frequently he saw the humor in a situation, even if it were not a happy one.

Outside the treatment situation there was a change manifested in shifts in his behavior and activity that may or may not prove lasting and the significance of which is hard to assess. Several key adults in contact with Robby during this period commented on the shift in his behavior.

His nursery school teacher, whose earlier complaints of unmanageable behavior had provided a strong impetus towards treatment, commented that his behavior was no longer posing a problem in the class. He was better able to sustain himself without the teacher's continuous attention, and he began to develop activities on his own in which he enlisted the participation of other children in the class.

His mother was struck by signs of change that were a relief to her. The climate between mother and child shifted. Robby was no longer always fighting her efforts. He began to dress himself in the morning instead of demanding her help and then struggling against it.

Robby's father noticed a change too. Only a couple of months later, when the divorce settlement was formalized, he referred to Robby's recent improvement in behavior as a reason for refusing to support the treatment further. Fortunately at that time his mother understood his need for more treatment and arranged to pay for continued psychotherapy sessions. In the period of the following six months, now meeting only two times a week, Robby and I focused primarily on a new and impending loss—that of the treatment and therapist. I was surprised by the amount we were able to accomplish in this period, under circumstances that I would have regarded as adverse for continued work.

We do not have the opportunity here to document in detail the work of these final months of psychotherapy. I will only mention here one of the ways Robby used to adapt to the current loss as we worked on the issue of separation. Quite explicitly and consciously he invested new energy in school. He told me in six-year-old language and in repetitive play in which he was pupil and I the teacher that he saw school as presenting the one possible sphere of action and relationships with which to replace his treatment.

Robby's mother communicated with me from time to time over the two-and-a-half years after the termination of his treatment. During that period Robby continued to get along more smoothly interpersonally. He had no recurrence of the anxiety symptoms that had been prominent before his treatment, and he performed quite well in a private school that places high demands on its students for academic performance.

DISCUSSION

Any body of clinical process described in detail will inevitably encompass human behavior and interaction that is too complicated to illustrate neatly any except the most limited kind of theoretical inferences. Because the relationship between the clinical data I have presented and the inferences I have drawn from them may not be perfectly clear, I would like to underline certain points of relationship between theory and the case material.

Earlier we defined confrontation as the process by which a therapist brings a patient face to face with what he takes to be either a reality or realities of the patient's psychological function. What were the reality or realities confronted by Robby and his therapist? They faced together a spectrum of realities within the process of confrontation described. First was the reality of Robby's taking the pen. For Robby this act was simply a fact, a fact of which he was never unconscious. The small theft, revealed only in the process of reparation, was trivial if viewed out of the context of treatment. Yet even this simple act, concrete and tangible, gave expression to the most complex facts of Robby's personality.

Next, Robby and his doctor faced a range of more complicated experiences, such as Robby's visits with his father to his father's fiancée and his owning the dog. These realities too were essentially facts of Robby's life.

The term, reality, as used earlier was used broadly to allude to a range of diverse phenomena of differing degrees of abstractness. Within this broader usage, Robby's personality itself is a reality, and each of its components, and all the modes by which it functions are realities as well. The most elusive sense in which I have used the term *reality*, and the hardest to elucidate, is the one in which I have used it to refer to Robby's unconscious life, both as it had shaped his behavior and as it was revealed by it. Robby's emerging character traits of secrecy and dishonesty, viewed in this way, were realities confronted in the therapy. The analysis of Robby's unconscious experience as it was revealed in his fantasies and play or as expressed in his character could not have been successfully undertaken until the process of confrontation I have described was well under way.

Earlier I stressed three aspects of confrontation that differentiate it from the technical tool interpretation. First, the difference in the therapist's attitude toward the reality with which he is working in interpretation and confrontation was stressed. The therapist who confronts directs himself to what he takes to constitute a reality of the patient's functioning or experience. The clinical instance I have described does not demonstrate this generalization unequivocally. In the early stages of the confrontation I described the work was hampered because I was not sure Robby had taken the pen. At some times I thought he had; at others I was not sure. It was only at the point when I felt sure myself that Robby had actually taken the pen that I was able to respond in a way that supported Robby in acknowledging the act and subsequently in coming to terms with the implications of it.

The second point stressed earlier was that the therapist inevitably assumes the initiative in the early stages of confrontation. At the start Robby's initiative in the process of confrontation was limited to his stealing and returning the pen. Left on his own he would have settled for returning the pen without getting into the deeper issues that taking it had reflected. The assumption of initiative by the therapist, while essential, was only temporary. Later, Robby himself actively brought the relevant data of his own experience. Without this active participation he could not have made the process of confrontation his own.

The third point stressed earlier was the abruptness of the process by which the patient may integrate the therapeutic work encompassed by the process of confrontation. The suddenness of change in Robby's relationship to me and in his behavior outside of the sessions seemed to me to reflect a personal reintegration growing out of the therapeutic process. This inner reorientation did not appear to depend on the ongoing and piece-by-piece working through described by Bibring (1954) as inherent to the process of interpretation.

No discussion of confrontation can be regarded as balanced unless there is some consideration of the risks that are inherent in the process as well as the possible returns from it. Our swimming instructor had the pleasure of a dramatic success, but also the disheartening experience of a sad failure. While confrontation in psychotherapy may yield an unusually dramatic therapeutic return when it is successful, confrontation is a therapeutic tool that involves greater risk than any other.

The element of risk in confrontation arises from several factors. Confrontation requires that the therapist substitute his own assessment of a reality for the patient's. The power of confrontation has its root in the authority of the therapist (whether this arises from love, respect, or fear) and the power inherent in an accurate construction of a tellingly relevant reality. At the moment initiated, confrontation inevitably derives its motive power from the first factor, the authority or the force of the therapist, to gain the patient's serious consideration of a painful reality. It is only subsequently that the patient may have available those returns that can be derived from the accurate reconstruction of "a tellingly relevant reality." The patient must fly blind transiently and only as the reality has been confronted may the accuracy of its delineation, its truth, and its relevance be available to the patient and play their role in helping him establish a new integration. At least temporarily the therapist has substituted his authority for the patient's willingness and ability to judge a reality for himself. The power and gratification the therapist may find in wielding authority, coupled with the gratification some patients find in submitting to it, converge to make confrontation a particularly risky therapeutic tool. Confrontation is a technique that may misfire, limiting the patient's autonomy in the guise of strengthening it.

Confrontation rests on the therapist's conviction that he has identified a reality that, recognized and integrated by the patient, will permit him a more satisfactory adaptation. Yet reality remains hard for humans to identify and to make their own. Which therapist can always be sure of his own construction of it? In the clinical situation I described with Robby, my certainty that he had taken the pen only grew gradually. I acted on the premise he had taken it, but only later did I feel really sure. If I had been wrong I doubt that

Robby could have been able to get over the hurt of the unjust accusation and go on to do real therapeutic work, no matter how I might subsequently try to repair or manage such a mis-assessment of the real situation.

There is nothing inherent in confrontation that insures its success. On the contrary, confrontation is often under-taken in a difficult therapeutic climate when resistance is high and little understood by the patient. Not infrequently confrontation will be undertaken as a heroic measure in the hope that a faltering therapy may be set on a more solid footing.

What when confrontation fails? Often there can be no moving back. The method of confrontation often involves the therapist's revealing himself, putting himself on the line with openness. If the person thus revealed lacks the humor, the integrity, the strength, the warmth, or whatever human quality the patient may require in order to use the therapist to promote his own growth, it is unlikely that subsequently any genuine therapeutic possibilities would exist.

Bibliography

Bibring, E. (1954), Psychoanalysis and the dynamic psychotherapies. *J. Amer. Psychoanal. Assn.*, 2: 745–770.

Freud, S. (1914), Remembering, repeating and working-
through (further recommendations on the technique of
psycho-analysis II). *Standard Edition*, 12: 147–156. London: Hogarth Press, 1958.

Confrontation in the Psychotherapy of Adolescent Patients

HENRY FRIEDMAN, M.D.

The purpose of this chapter is to deal with issues of values, limit-setting, and confrontation as central aspects of psychotherapy with certain adolescent patients. Several authors (Symonds, 1963; Josselyn, 1968; Knobel, 1966; Godenne, 1965; Easson, 1966), in the course of reviewing the general concepts of psychotherapy with adolescents, make some mention of the need for limit-setting. Schonfeld (1968), for instance, lists "willingness to play . . . a parent surrogate role" (p. 471) as one of several qualities required of therapists who work with adolescents. However, he seems to be restricting this to instances where an adolescent is behaving in ways that are dangerous to himself or to the community. This approach is somewhat narrow, in my estimation, as it limits the therapist's intervention to those situations where a physically dangerous action is taken by an adolescent patient. Furthermore, the emphasis in the literature (Brandes, 1968; Spiegal, 1958; Geleerd, 1961, 1964; Rubins, 1968) remains on the need to preserve the autonomy of adolescent patients.

New value systems combined with changing authority patterns within the family may be responsible for the differing requirements of therapy for a growing group of adolescent patients. In the past the need for recognition of the adolescent's right to develop his or her own ways seemed paramount. The therapist often had to refer parents to a social worker or talk directly to them about the need to tolerate the development of the adolescent as an individual. Hence, the task for the parent of the adolescent patient was often viewed as acknowledging his need to take increasing responsibility for his own controls in social and personal spheres of life. The type of neurotic interaction in which the parents attempt to overcontrol and not permit the adolescent to develop independently is still a pattern encountered in psychiatric practice. However, this paper concerns itself with a different type of neurotic family interaction in which the problems faced by the adolescent are complicated by parental figures who have abandoned their position of authority and have even, on occasion, openly advocated their adolescent's indulgence in rebellious and self-destructive behavior or failed entirely to recognize the need to encourage an adolescent's positive adult strivings by setting limits in a variety of settings.

The material for this report is derived from psychotherapy of adolescent patients. It focuses upon the need for the psychotherapist to compensate for parental deficiencies in setting limits with these patients. While the parents in these cases might have been seen concomitantly and urged to resume their parental function, the actual cases involved situations where parental resistance to seeking therapy was formidable. In addition, in all of these cases the patient, though adolescent, showed surprising degrees of maturity when confronted with a new value system. The parents' capacity to question their own value systems was judged to be considerably more impaired than that of the patients. Not only was it necessary for the therapist to take a stand on an issue of values, but it was often necessary to do so firmly while withstanding the angry protestations of the adolescent, which were often supported directly by his parents. This chapter will explore the clinical phenomena while placing basic emphasis upon the therapist's need to function as a firm, limit-setting, parental figure at crucial times in the treatment of these adolescent patients. The hypothesis is that, if a therapist fails to fulfill this role and remains, instead, detached and nonintervening, in the service of promoting so-called autonomy, the therapy may be preserved but the adolescent patient lost in the sense of his failing to refrain from acting-out behavior that would have permanent and damaging effects on his future. Furthermore, in each of these cases the limit-setting, value-promoting, confronting position of the therapist became a crucial part of the work done in the psychotherapy. It served as a fulcrum for moving the patient in the direction of healthy activity while serving as the basis for a therapeutic relationship in which other life problems could be explored. The style of intervention in all these cases definitely had elements of confrontation when this is defined as taking a position that is actively opposed by the patient's neurotic needs and persisting in this position in face of that opposition.

Three cases will be described in detail. Emphasis will be placed on aspects of the parental failure, including, when possible, the basis of parental encouragement of destructive acting out in their adolescent offspring. The nature of the therapist's intervention will be carefully examined in light of the adolescent's basic strengths and weaknesses as well as the clinical indications for parental limit-setting positions.

CASE EXAMPLES

Case One

Richard was sixteen years of age when he first sought treatment with complaints of intolerable feelings of hopelessness and depression. He was referred by a psychiatrist who had treated his older brother. His initial position was to project all his depression and unhappiness onto school, which he found intolerable. He complained bitterly of the excessive work demands of school and insisted that this caused his nervousness. He indirectly and then directly asked that I give him permission to retreat from these excessive school requirements, as his parents frequently did when they reassured him that he should not work so hard because "work led to breakdowns." The patient's problems were clearly not limited to school work. He related serious problems with alcohol; he had been drinking heavily and almost on a daily basis for a year prior to entering therapy. In fact, his desire for treatment was, in part, precipitated by an episode of drinking so severe that he lost consciousness for an undetermined period of time. This frightened him and gave him the added impetus to seek psychotherapy.

The patient's parents were both troubled, despite a veneer of normalcy. Disorders in parental functioning soon became apparent. Father, a man in his mid-fifties, had at least one episode of psychosis several years prior to the patient's therapy. He was treated by E.S.T. and had rationalized his illness in terms of working too hard with little reward from his employer. There apparently was an earlier history of psychiatric disorder, which necessitated separation from the armed services on psychiatric grounds with a permanent disability. Mother, who was more central to the running of the family, had a neurasthenic disposition. She had been a nurse in World War II but also was separated from the service with a psychiatric disability. Neither parent was willing to talk of past psychiatric difficulties but always insisted to the patient that they had worked too hard and gotten ill as a result of this work. There were four children in the family, including the patient, a brother one year older, a brother two years younger, and a sister eight years younger. All four children showed some signs of maladjustment; the patient appeared, in many respects, to be the most reasonable of the four children. This was manifest by his greater cooperativeness and understanding of his parents. The patient, however, was consciously unaware that the parents turned to him to do all the chores around the house rather than confront either of his brothers, who were overtly hostile to the parents and narcissistic in their orientation. What limits the parents bothered to set were only for Richard. This seemed to be related to his ability to comply with sensible limits. When his younger brother brought friends home for bouts of drinking or pot-smoking in the basement, the parents ignored these completely. When the patient informed his parents directly of what was going on, he was told to mind his own business and not tell tales on his brothers. They seemed to set limits in accordance with degree of resistance so that the older brother, who refused responsibility in many areas, was given in to in much greater degree than any of the other children.

Richard's initial motivation involved largely a quest for symptomatic relief and permission from the therapist to view himself as sick. In particular, he wanted the therapist to pronounce him unsuitable for military service and endorse his plan to drop out of school and travel around the country. The parents had agreed to this as a reasonable plan, only modifying it by weakly requesting that he complete high school. Since he was missing classes and doing no homework, a token completion of school was not something that he opposed strongly. I refused to second his plan as reasonable, stating that his obvious good intelligence showed through despite his depression and despair. Since therapy was initiated at the beginnning of his senior year of high school, I pointed out to him that it would be advisable to apply to colleges. This was met with surprise and negativism on his part. I suggested that, since we were embarking on a year's therapy, we would not know how he would feel at the end of that year and that, in my experience, many young patients did confuse the source of their depressed feelings. Richard agreed to this procedure, particularly when it was clarified that applying to college was in no way equated with his having to go unless he felt differently at the time. He had a conviction that, because his grades in high school were so poor, he could not possibly be accepted by any college. This also reflected his intense feelings of worthlessness related at the time to his guilt over drinking.

Work in the therapy depended largely on the patient's encounter with the therapist, who was willing to take stands in opposition to the patient's rationalizations and regressive positions. He was encouraged to express directly his feelings about the inequality of rewards among his siblings. Since his guilt had prevented him from asking his parents to consistently set limits with his brothers, his impressions of the deleterious effects of no limits at home were confirmed by me. Social isolation and retreat from heterosexuality were analyzed.

During a year of psychotherapy on a once-weekly basis, Richard was able to stop drinking and start attending school regularly. When he complained of the sterility of the work at his local high school, he was encouraged to read on his own, which, to his amazement, he found enjoyable and stimulating. A particular area of interest was psychology. He also found some teachers who were willing to be more flexible with him than he had anticipated possible. He was accepted at college in April, reporting at the same time his pleasure at the acceptance and his growing conviction that he could manage college in a reasonable way. He continued in treatment through September when he left for college. Although he had done a considerable amount of work, he felt it would be useful to continue to consult periodically, which the location of his college permitted on about a once-monthly basis. Despite the fact that he had chosen a rather strict school, he managed to adjust to difficult, stressful situations. His view of himself was much more as an individual who could cope with unpleasant situations in life. He still had fantasies of impulsively dropping out and going on the road for a life of wandering with no obligations. His attitudes, however, changed somewhat when his work at school was rewarded with excellent grades. On last follow-up, Richard had completed his junior year, was doing excellent work, and had plans for graduate school that seemed realistic. He consulted me after the break-up of an intense, yet not totally satisfying, relationship with a young woman. The break-up of this relationship had resulted in some symptoms of anxiety and depression again. We decided that a brief period of treatment at his college would be most helpful.

Richard's parents' reaction to his changes was of great interest. They were markedly disappointed in his decision to go to college but focused on the financial aspect of this and indicated to him directly that it would be better for them economically if he did not go to college. This did not reflect an actual economic necessity for them since he did attend a tuition-free college, and their circumstances were not marginal. They were increasingly dismayed by his ability to function and his requests that the home function less chaotically. They never responded to suggestions, which were made early in the treatment, that they might benefit from consultation themselves. The degree to which their much more narcissistic elder son was preferred was striking and never changed during the course of the treatment.

Case Two

Ann sought psychiatric consultation on her own at age sixteen. Her chief complaints were depression and a crippling inarticulateness that made her feel completely out of place at her exclusive private school where outspokenness, drug usage, and sexual freedom were highly regarded by her peer group. She regarded her suffering from two contradictory points of view. On the one hand, she felt that school made her depressed and that the solution lay in changing her environment by dropping out and traveling around the country much in the same fashion that an older brother had done. On the other hand, she seemed to recognize that there were many pressures that influenced her adversely.

Her family history was complicated. Her parents had been divorced when she was eight. Despite the divorce and her father's subsequent remarriage, the family pattern remained basically unchanged. Her father still regarded himself as master of both households and put this into action by continuing to insist on his role as father and husband in his first household. Her parents continued to have strong disagreements about standards for the children. Mother openly embraced the values of the "counter-culture," feeling that drugs, sexual freedom, and goalless living in general represented the wave of the future. Father, as if by creation of some novelist's imagination, embraced the antithetical position of each of her mother's stands. Hence, he was highly moralistic, insistent on formality in human relations, and appalled by even casual drug usage. Both parents continually presented their standards as absolutely correct without any regard for their children's particular personalities or life situations. The patient's mother encouraged her to attend the same exclusive private school from which her brother had dropped out to become a migratory drug-user. Father openly denounced the school as too permissive and responsible for his son's downfall but continued to finance the patient's education at this institution.

The patient initially felt that her depression made it impossible for her to work, and it was pointed out to her that her depression and guilt might be related to some of her sexual promiscuity and drug-taking. She responded with some disbelief that these things could be detrimental to her sense of well-being without being judged from a moralistic point of view. She was surprised to find the therapist willing to take a stand between her mother's fervent endorsement of her peer group's standards and her father's moralistic denunciation. She acknowledged that her own inclination was to feel comfortable with a more conservative approach to life, but she had found no one else who supported such a position. Although she felt some symptomatic improvement on controlling her acting-out behavior, she was still left feeling unable to have any interest in learning. On close examination it appeared that she had been thoroughly conditioned with the idea that learning could occur only if one enjoyed every moment of the learning process. The idea of work as requiring energy, even against wishes for more passive pleasure, was a foreign one to her. The idea of learning as a pure pleasure was markedly enforced by her school and mother. The antithetical notions presented by her father were so rigid as to merely reinforce her acceptance of this idea. Furthermore, her school work was so unstructured and her teachers placed such heavy emphasis on freedom and so thoroughly denounced conformity and actual work that she felt quite justified in doing almost nothing.

In regard to this problem, the therapist actively presented to her the notion that work was not always pleasurable but often required an input of energy. When Ann insisted that she could find no areas of interest in her work, she was encouraged to pursue areas outside of her school's curriculum. Since she was in her senior year of high school, the issue of college became a prominent one. Both her parents failed to encourage her serious consideration of a college education. Her mother's failure seemed to be related to a sincere belief that all such education was no longer helpful to the individual. Her father's position was largely one of indifference toward specifics of what his children undertook in life. Surprisingly, her private high school also encouraged many students not to continue their education but to take time out to "develop themselves." The patient was surprised when I stressed the need to think of college and to make plans, again as a way of feeling better and leading a more productive life. Through direct encouragement, she had pursued a tutoring program for underprivileged children and found, to her surprise, that professional workers approved of her work. Despite her reluctance to see college as a useful endeavor, she agreed that it made sense to apply to colleges in case she felt well enough to attend one after her senior year. However, she insisted on restricting her applications and applied to only one school, which represented an educational philosophy and type of student radically different from her high school.

During the first year of treatment, the therapy con-
centrated on the patient's understanding of herself in relationship to her family. She was able to recognize the neurotic
quality of her parents' continual bickering. Awareness of her
father as a narcissistic man enabled her to lessen her pains
from his persistent tendency to ignore her real needs and
wishes. For instance, despite the obvious improvement in her
depression in the first year of treatment, he continued to
maintain that therapy was worthless and that she should stop
it as soon as possible. He would complain to her bitterly
about the expense of therapy, although the cost of once-a-
week psychotherapy was meaningless to the family. The
rigidity of her father's narcissism emerged during the course
of the treatment. Sharing with her the recognition of these
qualities in him was considerably important and enabled her
to understand overt slights and peculiar actions on her
father's part. With understanding, her usual reaction of
depression turned into one of recognizing the problems of
dealing with a difficult parent. Mother's heavy use of alcohol
was also recognized as a problem; during such periods she
would make grandiose and confusing statements that could
be taken less seriously. She also saw that both of her parents
denied that her brother's way of life was severely disturbed.

After eight months of treatment the patient went on a
prolonged summer vacation and joined a group dedicated to
the rediscovery of outdoor living. Characteristically, when
this group suggested to her that she drop out of school the
next year and live in the out-of-doors for the next winter,
both of her parents easily gave their consent with ample
indication that they did not see it as important that her school
plans not be interrupted. Although the patient presented
herself as determined to act on these plans with her parents'
consent, she seemed relieved when the therapist questioned
the wisdom of such a move and indicated that he shared none
of her confusion as to which would be a more constructive
activity. With this supportive definition of limits, she proceeded to attend college. Despite many complaints about the

dullness and lack of relevancy of her work, she did face squarely that sometimes one had to work despite lack of enjoyment. At mid-semester she informed the therapist of having received straight A's in her course work. She also came to the conclusion on her own that a more challenging academic situation would be better for her. She proceeded to apply to several more challenging colleges and had by this time evolved an identity of her own that involved plans for the future, including work with children, probably in the area of child development. Despite the dramatic changes in this patient's life, father still continued to wonder why she was in psychotherapy and what use it could possibly be. When he complained of this to the therapist, the patient remarked that at least he was beginning to complain to the right party rather than making her justify the reasons for her treatment.

A third case is presented in brief to illustrate the fact that failure of a therapeutic intervention to deal with issues of values and set limits can have long-standing effects on the patient's life that still may be modified by a later therapeutic intervention that does not neglect these issues.

Case Three

This twenty-three-year-old patient, who was chronologically beyond adolescence, sought treatment on her own initiative. She had just returned from a five-year sojourn on the West Coast. In that time she had lived a life marked by gross disorganization, communal living, and physical neglect. She revealed that she had been an extremely bright student through her freshman year in college when, despite excellent achievement, she decided to leave school for economic reasons. She was convinced that formal education was not important and that, furthermore, her parents could really not afford to continue to support her education. On the West Coast she lived a chaotic life, in spite of her being in psychotherapy. Her parents, who were professional people, visited her and, despite their seeing first-hand the state in which she lived, in no way questioned its appropriateness for someone of her background. An immediate characteristic that became clear to the therapist was her exquisite sensitivity to rejection and intense need for approval. She responded precipitously and strongly to signs of disapproval from those surrounding her. Many of her friends and her parents had values that made success, in terms of achievement, quite unacceptable to her. She had difficulty accepting that the therapist felt she had misused her talents and was indeed "letting herself go." She could state directly her belief that to be successful and middle-class was unacceptable. With support and clarification of her right to success, she embarked upon an ambitious academic program that enabled her to complete college within two years and gain entry into a first-rate medical school. Her depression and destructive acting out disappeared within the first year of treatment. She was able to articulate the fact that encountering a value system that permitted work and success enabled her to express her talents in a positive fashion.

DISCUSSION

While Gitelson (1948) stressed the role of the therapist in promoting character synthesis in the adolescent patient, there is little in the literature that deals extensively with such factors as group pressures on the adolescent patient, parental failure to provide reasonable standards or set limits, and the therapist's need to fill the gap and present to his patient a viable code of standards. There are indeed strong opinions expressed against the approach presented here. The presentation of a value system to the adolescent patient has been viewed as a countertransference problem. To quote Spiegal (1958),

Countertransference problems may interfere significantly

with the analysis of adolescents, particularly certain expectations of the analyst . . . . In a society which stresses conformity the pressure within the analyst towards having his adolescent patient adjust and succeed is probably very strong and it may be more difficult for him to refrain from imposing his philosophy and hopes on his adolescent patients than on his adult ones. (p. 300)

To view the role of the therapist in these three cases (and many others with similar characteristics) in proper perspective it is necessary to consider certain changes in cultural forces brought to bear on modern adolescents. The adolescent today is subjected to forces from outside that differ radically from those of past decades. While the tasks of adolescence may have remained unchanged, whether these be viewed from a biological-analytic point of view or from a sociological-identity formation point of view, the external forces impinging on the adolescent have changed. For the sophisticated adolescent, the "counterculture" standards are a reality. Drug-taking, sexual promiscuity, and dropping out are there not only as fantasy temptations but as concrete examples in friends and close acquaintances. Not only are these values prevalent at the high school level, but they are also presented with great skill and force by popular authors, such as Paul Goodman, R. D. Laing, and Charles Reich. The views of these individuals have been widely disseminated and indeed have affected values of parents and adolescents alike. Laing's image of society as a destructive force, causing the elaboration of false selves, calls for a revolt against the essence of this society; namely, concentration on achievement and expression of self through work. Although the parents of a particular adolescent, as in the first case, might never have heard of, much less read, any of these authors' ideologies, they may either be psychologically tuned in to these aspects of revolt or disarmed by these arguments when they are presented by their more interested adolescent offspring. When an adolescent patient begins to rationalize his lack of effort in scholastic areas by pointing out our society's participation in a corrupt war, then it is necessary for the therapist to point out that the extension from our participation in a corrupt war to the total corruption of society is not a proven fact and that it is being used to rationalize. In the area of sexual activity the therapist may also take a stand against promiscuity while making it very clear that he views sexual activity as a natural and healthy part of life. He may have to point out to the adolescent patient the symptomatic un-happiness resulting from casual sexual activity while making it very clear that he is not being puritanical in his standards. The sexual unreadiness of many adolescents that has been found by Dr. Helene Deutsch (1967) can indeed be con-firmed in talking with adolescent patients. The adolescent, in his natural need to detach from the family, may fall prey to group standards that are incompatible with achievement and responsibility. The so-called permissiveness of the new free-dom may involve actions that, although attractive and instinctually gratifying, may be at variance with the consciences of numerous adolescent patients.

Parents may abdicate their role as providers of reason-able standards for adolescents for a number of reasons. First, as indicated above, they are subject themselves to changing standards. Second, the widespread dissemination of so-called analytic ideas about adolescence has led many parents to take an anything-goes approach to their adolescent offspring. Since the word on adolescence is that it is a period of in-tensely disturbed behavior for most adolescents, the parents may misinterpret this as meaning, more or less, that anything goes. Third, parents may be so overwhelmed by personal problems, either acute or chronic, that they are unavailable to expend energy on their adolescent children. In the detailed cases presented earlier, parents condoned acting-out behavior on their children's part that was close to areas in their own lives where actions and fantasies had actually occurred. In the case of Richard both of his parents resented work as an activity in their lives and both yearned for excessive passivity.

In Ann's case, the father's large inherited wealth enabled him to indulge in certain narcissistic positions that would have been impossible under other economic circumstances. He had indeed never depended upon his work for earning a living and may well have been encouraging in his children a similar position because, in fact, inheritance would make work unnecessary for them in later life.

In each of the case examples there were indications that the patients would be able to use a tactful confrontation from the therapist. They had been extremely active, for adolescents, in seeking psychotherapy almost on their own. None of them was sent by irate or worried parents. A tendency to view the therapist in a realistic fashion as a helpful physician with special knowledge was marked. Although there was a confrontation over values as expressed in action, this was not done in an angry or dictatorial fashion. Care was taken to remind the patients that they were free to reject my different interpretations of their actions but that I would not agree with them to avoid conflict.

None of these patients was absolute in a commitment to a regressed mode of living, as is often the case in adolescents who have been acting out extensively by dropping out of constructive activities, taking large amounts of drugs, and living in casual, shifting, and gratifying sexual relationships. They often are sent to a psychiatrist by their parents or school authority. In my experience they are often resistant to any constructive goals in psychotherapy and find my mention of values repellent. In these instances the style of approach described in this paper is not applicable. Here a therapist may need to accept that the main goal of treatment is to keep the patient coming, in hope that the manifest regression is related to some hidden stress or conflict in the patient's life.

CONCLUSION

The perils of adolescence as a developmental stage have been increased during the past decade. The adolescent is faced with the task of being active in working out a future that includes satisfying human relationships and work activities. Since it is a time of uncertainty and biological stress, regression becomes a possible solution. The seductiveness of ideas concocted by adults (and perhaps representing the product of their repressed and suppressed passive yearnings) is particularly great. Drug usage, sexual freedom, states of intense closeness, and an anti-work ethic have been vigorously promoted by the media. The result is a group of adolescent patients who have not been able to navigate between the Scylla of excessive rigidity and the Charybdis of passive gratification. For them effective psychotherapy requires a therapist who is willing to help them develop skills in navigation by recognizing the dangers from both sides. Currently, for certain adolescents, the pulls of passivity and the pleasure principle create the most danger. When parents are unable or unwilling to challenge extreme, irrational values, it becomes, in my opinion, essential that the psychiatrist be willing to step in and fill the gap. Taking such a position may seem anti-analytic and a bit mundane. Furthermore, many therapists may feel uncomfortable with interacting in such a direct way with adolescent patients. Josselyn (1957), who has written extensively about private outpatient psychotherapy of adolescents, calls attention to this problem:

Probably one reason there is so little in the current literature in regard to general concepts of therapy with adolescents is because of the self-consciousness of the therapist . . . . So often the most successful therapeutic results with this age group either are attained inexplicably by seemingly unorthodox therapy, or by means scarcely justifying the dignity inherent in the concept of psychotherapeutic methods. At other times they have been accomplished too easily to warrant credit to the therapist. In contrast, so often nothing has been achieved in those cases in which the therapist was most convinced that he understood the case and was using the right therapeutic approach. In the author's experience, practically every successfully treated case of an adolescent warrants the criticism from colleagues either that the case was not "analyzed," an attack against which a psychoanalyst has no answer, or that the so-called treatment was just an example of common sense or relationship therapy, an attack against which no psychiatrist has a defense. (p. 28)

Indebted as any psychiatrist need be to psychoanalytic concepts, there are times when certain so-called psycho-analytic techniques have been misinterpreted and/or mis-applied to psychotherapy. The idea of analytic neutrality and regard for the autonomy and independence of the patient is a case in point. While crude directives are certainly to be avoided in the treatment of adolescents, there is no doubt that patients are subjected to such authoritative directives from other sources in their lives. The therapist may have to stand firm against such influence with adolescent patients. He may have to do so with vigor and force when the adolescent's inner life is enforced by authority figures who define autonomy in passive regressive fashions, and he must do so despite accusations from within and without of being old-fashioned and rigid.

Bibliography

Brandes, N. (1968), The disturbed adolescent: discussion of an outpatient psychotherapeutic approach. *Ohio Med. J.*, 64: 1272–1274.

Deutsch, H. (1967), *Selected Problems of Adolescence*. New York: International Universities Press.

Easson, W. (1966), The ego-ideal in the treatment of children and adolescents. *Arch. Gen. Psychiat.*, 15: 288–292.

Geleerd, E. (1961), Some aspects of ego vicissitudes in adolescence. *J. Amer. Psychoanal. Assn.*, 9: 394–405.

——— (1964), Adolescence and adaptive regression. *Bull. Menninger Clin.*, 28: 302–308.

Gitelson, M. (1948), Character synthesis: the psychotherapeutic problems of adolescence. *Am. J. Orthopsychiat.*, 18: 422–431.

Godenne, G. (1965), A psychiatrist's techniques in treating adolescents. *Children*, 12: 136–139.

Josselyn, I. (1957), Psychotherapy of adolescents at the level of private practice. In *Psychotherapy of the Adolescent*, ed. B. Balser. New York: International Universities Press, pp. 13–38.

——— (1968), Adolescents: everyone's special concern. *Int. J. Psychiat.*, 5: 478–483.

Knobel, M. (1966), On psychotherapy of adolescence. *Acta Paedopsychiat.*, 33: 168–175.

Rubins, J. (1968), The problems of the acute identity crisis in adolescence. *Am. J. Psychoanal.*, 28: 37–47.

Schonfeld, W. (1968), The adolescent in contemporary American psychiatry. *Int. J. Psychiat.*, 5: 470–478.

Spiegal, L. A. (1958), Comments on the psychoanalytic psychology of adolescence. *The Psychoanalytic Study of the Child*, 13: 296–308.

Symonds, A. (1963), Special problems in the treatment of adolescents. *Am. J. Psychother.*, 17: 596–605.

Confrontation in Short-Term, Anxiety-Provoking Psychotherapy

PETER E. SIFNEOS, M.D.

Confrontation is a therapeutic technique that is widely used in various kinds of psychiatric treatment. During desensitization therapy, for example, the therapist confronts the phobic patient repeatedly with the object which he fears. In snake phobia, first a snake is shown to the patient on film or video tape. This fear-provoking confrontation is repeated until the patient is ready for the next step, which involves the introduction of a toy snake. A child playing with a live snake (nonpoisonous, of course) is then presented to the patient. When he is able to deal with a fear-producing situation adequately, a more anxiety-provoking task is presented to him until he, finally, is able to handle the snake all by himself. This progressively painful confrontation helps desensitize the patient. Great success has been claimed by this technique for these kinds of monosymptomatic phobias (Bandura, 1968).

In hypnosis, the therapist confronts the patient who seeks to stop smoking with the harmful effects of tobacco on his health, while he is under a trance, and suggests to him ways by which he can overcome this self-destructive habit.

In this chapter I shall discuss confrontation as it is

used in a kind of dynamic psychotherapy of short duration that is called "anxiety-provoking." During this treatment the therapist uses anxiety-provoking confrontation early in order to stimulate the patient to deal with the emotional conflicts in an effort to help him solve his emotional problem. If the therapist makes a decision to act forcibly and present to the patient certain aspects of his behavior that he is ignoring and that make him anxious, he must be convinced that such a technique will achieve better results than a less forceful and more gentle approach. Although there may be counter-transference reasons that play a role in the therapist's choice to use confrontation, for all intents and purposes, the achievement of the therapeutic goals will be considered to be his main motivating force for the use of confrontation here. (Sifneos, 1969)

It must be fairly obvious that the therapist's goals must be more or less in tune with what the patient wants to achieve, but this may not always be the case. The patient who is ordered by a judge to seek psychiatric treatment or face a jail sentence because of her periodic sexual offenses has no clear cut goals. The patient who has unrealistic expectations of the results of psychotherapy and who is unwilling to accept more modest and realistic goals creates a situation that sooner or later will end in an impasse. Finally, there is the patient who wants "to place himself" in the hands of his therapist and whose passive attitude projects the therapist into a role of the omnipotent healer who is expected to perform a miraculous cure. Such an attitude is reinforced by the familiar pattern of the doctor-patient relationship that is usually encountered in medical practice and that, at the same time, relieves the patient from taking any action and responsibility for his own treatment. Mutual agreement, then, about the therapeutic goals has a great deal to do with getting the treatment job done well.

The selection of appropriate patients who are able to arrive at a decision with their therapists about the goals to be achieved by psychotherapy is, in my opinion, of crucial importance for future success. In addition, after the completion of the psychiatric evaluation, based on his observations of the patient's capabilities, the therapist must be in a position to know what kinds of technical tools to utilize in order to achieve these specified goals.

In short-term, anxiety-provoking psychotherapy, we use five criteria as guidelines for the selection of appropriate candidates to receive this kind of treatment. These criteria attempt to evaluate the patient's psychological strengths. Every effort is made to define clearly the emotional problem that brings the patient to the therapist and that he had been unable to solve by himself. One of the reasons for this failure has to do with the patient's reluctance to experience the painful emotions that are associated with his emotional conflicts. Furthermore, some kinds of agreement must be reached on the area of emotional conflicts that the therapy should concentrate on in order to solve the patient's emotional difficulties.

Short-term, anxiety-provoking psychotherapy is based on psychoanalytic theoretical concepts. Technically there are some differences. Anxiety is generated rather than suppressed during the interviews and is used as a signal to alert the patient of dangers and to motivate him to continue his efforts to solve his emotional problem. Throughout this type of psychotherapy the therapist communicates to the patient that he has confidence in him to be able to face and to experience unpleasant emotions in order to understand his conflicts, but this is not based on blind faith.

In contrast to gentle persuasion, confrontation creates pain. The therapist who plans to use it must be fairly certain that it will help set in motion a process of self-understanding that eventually will be beneficial to the patient. He must also be convinced that the patient is able to withstand considerable strain. It is because of this latter consideration that a great deal of time must be spent during the psychiatric

374 CONFRONTATION IN PSYCHOTHERAPY

evaluation on the assessment of the patient's strengths of character and on his ability to face the vicissitudes of this kind of psychotherapy.

As has already been mentioned, confrontation then is the key technical tool. By virtue of the fact that anxiety-provoking psychotherapy is going to be of brief duration, it compels the therapist to perform his work as quickly as possible before complications set in that will make this therapeutic task impossible. In my opinion, this occurs invariably whenever the transference neurosis is allowed to develop, and it always happens when psychotherapy continues over a long period of time. Because the therapist does not have access to all the patient's fantasies as the analyst has when he uses free association and because he is limited by the face-to-face interaction as well as by the lack of frequency of the interview, the psychotherapist is unable to analyze the transference neurosis as the analyst must do in order to bring the psychoanalysis to a successful end. It is for this reason that dynamic psychotherapy of long duration ends so often in an impasse.

One must consider the possibility that confrontation is sometimes used as a result of the therapist's annoyance at some behavior pattern of the patient that he considers to be anti-therapeutic. In short-term, anxiety-provoking psychotherapy the therapist, instead of being taken by surprise by some destructive action on the part of the patient, is, on the contrary, well prepared for whatever may happen. When he confronts the patient with the reality of an unpleasant or ambivalent aspect of his relationship with some member of his family, he anticipates that sooner or later the same unpleasant features will be repeated in his transference relation with him.

As an example of confrontation used during the early part of short-term, anxiety-provoking psychotherapy, let us consider a thirty-five-year-old man who complained of angry outbursts at work and of a rapidly deteriorating relationship with his wife, despite his love for her, and had mentioned that these difficulties in some vague way stemmed from his relationship with his parents. From the information that he gave during psychiatric evaluation, it seemed indeed likely that his present difficulties with his wife were connected with his unresolved and ambivalent feelings for his mother.

During the third hour the therapist had observed a fleeting but ecstatic smile on the patient's face when he described picking wild flowers while he was walking in the woods with his mother at an early age. This seemed to be unusual to the therapist because he had observed that during the two previous interviews, the patient's facial expressions had been distorted with rage when he had talked about his mother's preference for his younger brother, who was three years his junior. With this discrepancy in mind the therapist decided to confront the patient as follows, "You have repeatedly emphasized how angry you were at your mother and enumerated episodes when you have felt discriminated against by her. Your facial expressions spoke eloquently of your anger during these occasions." The patient nodded in agreement and the therapist went on, "On one occasion you clenched your fist when you spoke about the time when your mother had taken your brother shopping with her; and although you had cried and had begged her to take you along, she had refused and had sent you to practice the violin. It seems that you are making an effort to tell yourself and convince me that you hated your mother." The patient again nodded approvingly. The therapist continued, "This seems paradoxical, however, because a few minutes ago when you described to me the episode when you were picking wild flowers in the woods while in your mother's company, an angelic smile came on your face." The patient looked completely surprised, was silent for a while, and soon tears came to his eyes. He spent the rest of that interview reminiscing of the good times with his mother *before* his brother had been born.

The therapist's confrontation produced an emotional response that helped clarify an area in the patient's early life and that, by virtue of its being partly suppressed, had been unavailable to him up to that time. His awareness that it was his love for his mother that was responsible for his jealousy and rage at her and his ability to see that the same feelings were repeated toward his wife whom he loved, helped him to keep her out of this emotional conflict of his early childhood and lead to a rapid improvement in their relationship.

The therapist was neither angry nor annoyed at his patient; but rather he saw himself clearly in the advantageous position of an outside observer who, by virtue of his not being involved with the patient's emotional difficulties, was best suited to confront him with paradoxical situations and to stimulate him to face the unpleasant emotions involved. It is, of course, possible in longer term psychotherapy after the transference neurosis has set in—which is actively avoided in this kind of treatment as it has already been mentioned—that the patient's persistent resistances and endlessly repetitive behavior patterns are more trying for the therapist and may lead him at times to make an angrier confrontation than he would ordinarily have liked to do.

There is no doubt, however, that confrontation indeed does involve a certain degree of harshness on the therapist's part. In this sense, it could be compared to a surgical intervention. The surgeon, however, before deciding to operate, must first of all assess whether his patient's organism has the strength physiologically to withstand this painful procedure. In a similar way the therapist creates a kind of emotional crisis knowingly because he is confident of the patient's capacity to withstand his unpleasant feelings and his motivation to understand himself.

I am convinced then that for short-term psychotherapy, confrontation is a key technical procedure. One may think, however, that I am not being permissive enough or that I am trying to defend the use of this technique too vehemently. This is not the case. In my opinion there is a certain degree of passivity in the therapist who uses gentle persuasion exclusively. If one has to be unusually gentle, persuasive, and permissive, he must view the patient as being too weak to endure the therapist's powerful force. Since this superior power should not be inflicted on another human being, the conclusion is reached that the patient must be dealt with very gently and he must be pampered and protected. Such an attitude on the part of the therapist may emanate from his own ideas of omnipotence and exaggerated superiority over the patient. In this way, an excessively gentle persuasion does not seem to give the patient the benefit of the doubt. I have purposefully exaggerated this point in order to make the simple observation that gentle persuasion exclusively is neither gentle nor persuasive. As Myerson states (Chapter One), we cannot be absolutely certain whether confrontation will be effective or not, but I do think that we should make an attempt to answer this question.

At the Ciba Foundation Symposium on the "role of learning in psychotherapy" held in London (Porter, 1968), experimental psychologists, psychoanalysts, psychiatrists, ethologists, and educators attempted to delineate certain aspects of learning theory and its impact on the effectiveness of various kinds of psychotherapy. The stimulus-response concept, which has been used to explain how psychotherapy works, can be incorporated partially within the context of learning theory; but in this case the word *learning* must not be used in its strict cognitive (neocortical) sense, but rather in a combination of both cognitive and emotional (limbic autonomic nervous system) factors.

We have been interested in this type of learning because the patients who were seen in follow-up interviews after they had received short-term, anxiety-provoking psychotherapy emphasized that as a result of this treatment, they had "learned a new way to solve their emotional difficulties."

These follow-up findings encouraged us to set up a controlled study to evaluate the outcome of short-term, anxiety-provoking psychotherapy. The results of this study have been published elsewhere (Sifneos, 1968). Suffice it to say that, having learned to solve his emotional problem, the patient feels better about himself; this change in his self-esteem helps improve his interpersonal relations. Although the symptoms sometimes persist, their painful impact is greatly diminished so that they do not seem to interfere with the patient's overall performance. One aspect of this improvement, in my opinion, has to do with the patient's identification with his therapist both during and after the end of the treatment. This identification implies an ability on the part of the patient to learn and to utilize the techniques that the therapist has used during psychotherapy. Since confrontation is a *sine qua non* of this kind of therapy and has been used extensively by the therapist, it is this same kind of technique that the patient uses on himself. He does this to look for cues, to explore possibilities, and to raise questions, as he has learned to do during his psychotherapy, that will lead eventually to the solution of his emotional problem.

The best way to demonstrate this kind of confrontation is to quote from one of our patients who was seen in follow-up two years after the end of his therapy. "There I was, trying to find an answer to my new dilemma. I didn't know what to do until I started remembering what my doctor used to do, and all of a sudden I found myself trying to jolt myself in the same way that he was jolting me. It was like trying to jar something loose in my brain in order to get myself going. I said to myself, 'You are pampering yourself, Mr. W,' in the same way as Dr. R used to say during my treatment."

A case example at this point may be in order. A twenty-three-year-old female graduate student was seen in anxiety-provoking psychotherapy over a period of four months. Anxiety was the symptom that brought her to the clinic. It usually became intense whenever any one of her numerous boyfriends would try to change their platonic friendship into a sexual affair. During such time she would always break up the relationship. The oldest of three sisters, she was an attractive young woman, who thought of herself as being unattractive and felt jealous of her sister who was four years younger. She had been very close to both her mother, whom she described as being somewhat passive, and to her youngest sister, who was eleven years her junior. She claimed that she had always been proud of having helped her mother to bring up her sister. During the evaluation interview, it became apparent that her anxiety alerted her to avoid getting intimate with her boyfriends and soon motivated her to reject them. It was also thought that her ambivalent feelings for her father were being reexperienced with her boyfriends and shaped the pattern of her behavior with them. It was decided that this should be the area to concentrate on during the short-term psychotherapy.

In the early phase of the treatment, the patient made several attempts to understand the reason for her anger at her father and claimed that she had experienced similar feelings for her last boyfriend, whom she had stopped seeing recently. On one occasion she made a slip of the tongue and had referred to her father as her "mate." The therapist wanted to collect all the facts, and on that occasion he decided not to make a comment about it. Another time she referred to her younger sister as "my baby." Again the therapist did not say anything. On the fifth interview she related a dream. The scene of her rejection of Rod, her last boyfriend, was being reenacted in the dream. She was married to Rod, yet she was unsure of his identity and added that it could be someone else. She was also pregnant. While she was recounting the events, she remembered clearly how she had ordered Rod to get out of their apartment and how very sad she had felt for having done so. In the dream she cried bitter tears, and constantly she kept referring to herself as "poor Mrs. M." The one thing that had impressed her most in the dream was the sorrow that she had felt about her rejection of Rod. This seemed peculiar to her because, in reality, she had not given their separation much thought.

When the therapist asked her what the name "M" reminded her of, she was vague at first; but then she mentioned casually that she remembered that her paternal grandfather had a hyphenated Spanish name. When he had emigrated to the United States, he had dropped one of the two names and that name was "M . . . ." At this point the therapist had all the evidence that he needed to make this confrontation. He proceeded as follows:

Dr. What is your dream trying to tell us?

Pt. Oh well. The usual thing! I always seem to dream about separations. The whole mess with Rod was repeated all over again.

Dr. Was it really the separation from Rod that you dreamed about?

Pt. What do you mean?

Dr. You seemed to dream about *a* separation, but the question is a separation from whom? Putting it in another way, I wonder if Rod represented someone else. Don't forget that you were unsure of his identity and that you emphasized how painful it felt in the dream.

Pt. Yes, it is true, but who else could it be?

Dr. What comes to mind?

Pt. Well . . . Yes, there was something about it in the dream that seemed to come from the past; I don't know exactly. . . . the apartment? . . . There was something old-fashioned about the apartment . . . Yes! It was somewhat like the one we lived in while we were in Memphis. We moved to New York when I was eight years old.

Dr. So?

Pt. Well, maybe it had something to do with my father.

Dr. Not only with your father but also with your husband, Mrs. "M."

The patient was silent. She seemed to be thinking.

Dr. Well, do I have to spell it out?

Pt. I vaguely know what you are talking about, but . . . (becoming teary)

Dr. Let me put it this way. You may remember that you had made a slip of the tongue some time ago and called your "father" your "husband." Today you had the dream when you were Mrs. "M." You used the hyphenated Spanish name of your father's family. It was disguised somewhat but not completely. There was a great deal of pain in your dream, a great deal of sorrow. You were not sure if it was Rod who was your husband. It was someone like him. You were also pregnant. Was this child your baby sister, Mrs. M?

At this point, the patient started to cry; but despite her strong feelings, she was able to reminisce about how close she had been to her father when she was young. He seemed to have changed, however. He had started to drink and had become cold and uninterested in her when she grew up.

I assume that one may consider this confrontation as being possibly somewhat too harsh. In my opinion, this was not the case. The therapist could rely on the facts. This solid evidence was provided to him by the patient during her treatment. The emotional outburst and the ability of the patient to associate to the earlier experiences with her father seemed to confirm that the confrontation was timely. The question is was it therapeutic?

The answer to this question must come only from long-term follow-up of patients who have received this kind of anxiety-provoking psychotherapy of short duration.

From what we learned in our controlled study already mentioned, we are able to answer this question in the affirmative. Our patients not only mentioned that they had learned how to solve their emotional problem during the treatment but also that, as a result of it, they were able to utilize effectively this newly acquired problem-solving ability to solve new problems *after* the treatment had terminated.

In the opinion of two independent evaluators who interviewed these patients, this new attitude was confirmed only when the patients were able to give examples of new problems that they had solved. This they were able to do in the majority of the cases. There was also evidence that a dynamic change had taken place.

In sum then, confrontation, in order to be effective, must be based on the therapist's observations about a series of paradoxical behavioral patterns, contradictory statements, accumulated details; and by arousing the patient's feelings, it must motivate him to look at himself from a different point of view.

If the patient is willing to learn from this experience and tries to apply it in various situations, he may eventually be able to use it to solve new emotional problems that he may encounter in the future.

In short-term, anxiety-provoking psychotherapy, confrontation has both a therapeutic and an educational role. In this latter sense, it may have a great deal to do with learning, which plays a crucial role in making psychotherapy therapeutic.

Bibliography

Bandura, A. (1968), Modelling approaches to the modification of phobic disorders. In *The Role of Learning in Psychotherapy*, ed. R. Porter. London: J & A Churchill, Ltd., pp. 201–217.

Myerson, P. G., (This Volume), The meaning of confrontation.

Porter, R. (1968), *The Role of Learning in Psychiatry*. London: J & A Churchill, Ltd.

Sifneos, P. E. (1968), Learning to solve emotional problems. In *The Role of Learning in Psychotherapy*, ed. R. Porter. London: J & A Churchill, Ltd., pp. 87–97.

——— (1969), Short-term anxiety-provoking psychotherapy. An emotional problem-solving technique. *Seminars in Psychiatry*, 1: 389–399.

Index